Mark,

Thank you once again for your contributions to this project. I look forward to hearing from you in the future.

Sincerely,

Jeff

Palgrave Studies in the History of the Media

Series Editors
Bill Bell
Cardiff University
Cardiff, UK

Chandrika Kaul
University of St Andrews
Fife, UK

Alexander S. Wilkinson
University College Dublin
Dublin, Dublin, Ireland

Palgrave Studies in the History of the Media publishes original, high quality research into the cultures of communication from the middle ages to the present day. The series explores the variety of subjects and disciplinary approaches that characterize this vibrant field of enquiry. The series will help shape current interpretations not only of the media, in all its forms, but also of the powerful relationship between the media and politics, society, and the economy.

Advisory Board: Professor Carlos Barrera (University of Navarra, Spain), Professor Peter Burke (Emmanuel College, Cambridge), Professor Nicholas Cull (Center on Public Diplomacy, University of Southern California), Professor Bridget Griffen-Foley (Macquarie University, Australia), Professor Tom O'Malley (Centre for Media History, University of Wales, Aberystwyth), Professor Chester Pach (Ohio University).

More information about this series at
http://www.palgrave.com/gp/series/14578

Jeffrey P. Stone

British and American News Maps in the Early Cold War Period, 1945–1955

Mapping the "Red Menace"

palgrave
macmillan

Jeffrey P. Stone
Hill College
Fort Worth, TX, USA

Palgrave Studies in the History of the Media
ISBN 978-3-030-15467-7   ISBN 978-3-030-15468-4   (eBook)
https://doi.org/10.1007/978-3-030-15468-4

© The Editor(s) (if applicable) and The Author(s), under exclusive licence to Springer
Nature Switzerland AG 2019
This work is subject to copyright. All rights are solely and exclusively licensed by the
Publisher, whether the whole or part of the material is concerned, specifically the rights of
translation, reprinting, reuse of illustrations, recitation, broadcasting, reproduction on
microfilms or in any other physical way, and transmission or information storage and retrieval,
electronic adaptation, computer software, or by similar or dissimilar methodology now
known or hereafter developed.
The use of general descriptive names, registered names, trademarks, service marks, etc. in this
publication does not imply, even in the absence of a specific statement, that such names are
exempt from the relevant protective laws and regulations and therefore free for general use.
The publisher, the authors and the editors are safe to assume that the advice and information
in this book are believed to be true and accurate at the date of publication. Neither the
publisher nor the authors or the editors give a warranty, express or implied, with respect to
the material contained herein or for any errors or omissions that may have been made. The
publisher remains neutral with regard to jurisdictional claims in published maps and
institutional affiliations.

Cover illustration: ClassicStock / Alamy Stock Photo

This Palgrave Macmillan imprint is published by the registered company Springer Nature
Switzerland AG
The registered company address is: Gewerbestrasse 11, 6330 Cham, Switzerland

FOREWORD

Jeffrey P. Stone first appeared on my radar a decade ago, when I was editor of the twentieth-century volume of the *History of Cartography*, released in 2015. Our publisher was the University of Chicago Press, which required a comprehensive peer review of the 40-page prospectus that apportioned the volume's million-words among more than 500 entries. After Chicago's Board of University Publications greenlighted the project, I was free to recruit contributors, with advice from our 35-member board of internationally prominent scholars, one of whom mentioned that Jeffrey Stone had recently received an outstanding dissertation award from the University of Texas at Arlington. Dr. Stone's dissertation "Mapping the 'Red Menace': British and American News Maps in the Early Cold War Period, 1945 to 1955" made him an ideal contributor for our "Cold War" entry.

Editing a scholarly encyclopedia presents a delightful opportunity to work with scholars committed to factual accuracy, understanding, clarity, and meeting deadlines, but some contributors made the experience as pleasant as cleaning other people's bathrooms. Professor Stone, I am pleased to say, was not only in the former group but also in the top ten percent of our more than 300 contributors and co-contributors.

In saying this, I must disclose a bias toward his choice of topic. News maps—the term encompasses maps in periodicals with a daily, weekly, or monthly news cycle and in the electronic news media as well—have not received attention commensurate with their broad audience and likely impact on the public understanding of geography. Moreover, their effectiveness as a tool of persuasion reflects the journalistic cartographer's eager experimentation with a map's projection, centering, and geographic scope as well as with color and pictorial illustration.

Professor Stone's book is a refinement of his dissertation, which addressed the evolving portrayal of global and regional power relationships in weekly news magazines in Great Britain and the United States. Although the two nations remained committed allies after World War II, their interests changed as the shared threat shifted from Nazi Germany to Soviet Russia. In addition, Britain faced the challenge of a crumbling colonial empire, while America sought to solidify its position as a world power while denying the existence of an American empire—a phrase no American editor or politician was willing to use. The reworking of European boundaries and alliances after 1945 became a major cartographic challenge, willingly accepted by the American press after Winston Churchill embellished a March 1946 speech with the term "Iron Curtain" but downplayed in the British Press, which anticipated a less contentious struggle with our former Russian ally. Contestation shifted from military to economic issues as Britain and the United States developed different designs on Middle Eastern oil.

The focus on weekly news magazines rather than daily newspapers is important and useful. A seven-day news cycle was more conducive to clever cartography than a 24-hour cycle, and both countries had several prominent weeklies. Professor Stone highlights cross-national differences such as the rationing of paper and red ink several years beyond the war's end, which not only limited the size and abundance of British news maps but ceded a significant role to maps in advertisements. No less notable is the British press's reliance on outside mapmakers in contrast to America's weeklies, which had their own map departments as well as maestro mapmakers like Richard Edes Harrison, who drew for *Fortune* and *Life*, and R. M. Chapin, his counterpart at *Time*—Harrison and Chapin are known for engaging maps centered on or near the North Pole that emphasized the proximity to the United States and the USSR. Stone also calls our attention to the comparatively obscure British monthly *Serial Map Service*, which rivaled the cartographic flair of *Fortune* and *Time*.

British and American News Maps in the Early Cold War Period, 1945–1955, offers valuable insights on the influence of technology and work culture on cartographic discourse. Its informative mix of world history and map history will enhance your appreciation of how maps explain and persuade.

Syracuse University, Syracuse, NY, USA   Mark Monmonier

ACKNOWLEDGMENTS

As every published historian knows, no manuscript sees the light of public consumption without the assistance of others. First and foremost I must thank the faculty and staff at the University of Texas at Arlington (UTA; where this study was conceived) who contributed their time, attention, and input to steer this work toward its studied completion, all the while grooming me for the world of academia. My dissertation panel Chair, Richard Francaviglia, proved particularly vital in this regard. Over the years his careful edit notes and encouragement inspired me to seek not only publication of this work but also the publication of many of my research papers in academic journals. Another panelist, Thomas Adam, helped me to frame this work in an international context—which I am convinced—added impetus for its publication. More than this, Dr. Adam has been my most diligent guide into the often prickly arena of publishing. It was he who landed me my first writing contract, my first published works in academic journals, and the successful publication of my contribu- tions to *The History of Cartography* project. Panelist Dennis Reinhartz encouraged me to diversify my interests in Cold War cartographic history, and he introduced me into the academic circles necessary for a historian of, dare I say, our stripe. Finally, panelist David Buisseret who now resides at the Newberry Library lent his considerable academic experience to the betterment of this work.

Both during and after my doctoral studies, the staff at the UTA Libraries have been patiently helpful, attentive, and generous with their time in assist- ing my research. Initially my co-workers while I worked at the library during my doctoral studies, they in time became fierce friends. The library's Special

Collections Cartographic Archivist, Ben Huseman, has afforded me a lasting friendship, which I have repeatedly "exploited" over the years. It was Ben who suggested, and later curated, the first public exhibit of the imagery associated with much of the research presented here. The UTA's Special Collections has grown to become an impressive body of unique and important maps, books, and journals, and continues to be irreplaceable for students of cartographic history.

I remain ever thankful to the UTA History Department for the crucial research grant that allowed me to plunder valuable archives in New York, London, Frankfurt, and other far-flung cities.

In New York, the offices of *Time* magazine generously allowed me an entire day with the head of the graphics department, to question him relentlessly and mine his office's collection of news cartography "nostalgia." This bit of networking eventually put me in contact with Paul Pugliese, *Time's* last Chief Cartographer (now retired), who kindly consented to a fascinating telephone interview. I must also mention the outstanding staff assistance of the New York Public Library, which made four days' research there far more productive and efficient than it otherwise ever could have been.

I most certainly owe a considerable debt to citizens across the Atlantic. In England, staff assistance at the British Library was invaluable, especially given the massive archival relocations that were ongoing at the time. Research assistants at the British Newspaper Archive (then still located at Colindale) were indefatigable in their accommodating my multitude of microform, microfiche, and copying requests. And, in Germany, I was graciously rewarded with the opportunity to present preliminary research at the Institute for Cultural Diplomacy at Goethe-Universität, Frankfurt am Main.

Lastly, on a more personal note, I very much appreciate the efforts of my good friend, Thomas Dieb, whose tireless readings and re-readings of this study and our numerous resulting conversations have been of great personal and professional benefit to me.

CONTENTS

LIST OF FIGURES

CHAPTER 1

Introduction: Cold War–Era News Maps in Historical Context

The onset of the Cold War in 1945 brought significant changes to global geopolitics. Great Britain and the United States felt compelled to reexamine their relationship with their former ally, the Soviet Union, and, by 1949, with newly communist China. The postwar division of Europe, the advent of the Air Age, the decline of the British Empire, and the Containment Doctrine highlighted differences between British and American foreign policies. The future of the famed "special relationship" between England and the United States was uncertain. In this pivotal era, maps appearing in British and American national news journals served as valuable tools to relate "new realities" of the Cold War to millions of readers. This map imagery was often powerful, even more so than the printed word. The news journals in which the maps appeared were extensions of national political parties that promoted specific ideas about the political world with cartographic imagery. But British and American news maps often depicted the early Cold War world in very different ways. A study of these maps reveals differences, both obvious and subtle, in how American and British societies viewed global geopolitics in the early years of the Cold War. Moreover, serial news journal maps provide a sort of chronology of political opinion on enduring Cold War crises. British and American cartographic portrayals of the Cold War world over time can be tracked and compared alongside contemporary texts. And if the axiom about journalism being the "first draft of history" is true for the Cold War era, then news maps provided the first historical map imagery of the period.

© The Author(s) 2019   1
J. P. Stone, *British and American News Maps in the Early Cold War Period, 1945–1955*, Palgrave Studies in the History of the Media,
https://doi.org/10.1007/978-3-030-15468-4_1

The similarities and, more importantly, the differences in the way American and British news maps envisioned the Cold War world offer valuable new insight into how the two nations perceived each other and the communist world. In the introduction of his book, *Great Britain and the United States*, Robert M. Hathaway quoted a leading British statesman who, in 1987, said that Englishmen should not assume that "Americans see their interests and objectives as always identical to ours...We should never take it for granted that Americans see what we see."[1] Hathaway used the quote to argue that the perceived "special relationship" between the two countries has, more often than not, been a strained one despite both nations growing closer in their mutual fight against communism since 1945. The quote bears special relevance to this current study in three important ways. First, in the figurative sense that Hathaway intended, the quote warns of the often dissimilar foreign policies of the two nations despite the idea of a "special relationship." Second, the quote implies that Englishmen and Americans who follow Cold War foreign politics often have very different worldviews—views that may be uniquely and vividly portrayed in maps. Third, and most importantly for this study, the quote can be used to describe the reality that English and American news journals, through articles, photos, ads, *and especially news maps*, usually portrayed Cold War international developments in decidedly different ways. A critical result was that American and English magazine readers, who relied then as now on news journal maps to help shape their perceptions of foreign places and international events, literally saw very different portrayals of the world than their counterparts across the Atlantic Ocean. These differing map portrayals fostered powerful and often conflicting notions of Cold War geopolitics and national security in the minds of American and English citizens even though both nations' governments were strongly unified to thwart communist expansion all over the world.

For example, in October 1949, a political cartoon appeared in the *London Daily Express*, one of the then several Tory-controlled English news journals (see Chap. 4, Fig. 4.8).[2] The cartoon lampooned Tory Lord Beaverbrook's overconfident and simplistic solution to England's declining international status. It depicted Lord Beaverbrook addressing leaders of the English government, who were all clones of himself, before a room-sized map of the world with the caption, "The Shadow Cabinet meets, and solves the crisis in the twinkling of an eye." According to the map, entitled "Map Of The World (Up To Date)," the world consisted only of Great Britain, its colonial holdings, and the United States. Conspicuously absent from the map were all nations that did not have favorable political or economic trade agreements with Great Britain. Most notably absent were the Soviet Union and China—communist nations whose recent post–World War II rise to superpower status threatened British claims to Middle Eastern oil reserves and lucrative Chinese trading port colonies. The Beaverbrook cartoon offered a good example of how Western maps were often employed in the Cold War to devalue and delegitimize areas under communist control or influence. Omitting nations on maps to devalue them is one of the more obvious ways mapmakers have, through the centuries, used maps to alter map readers' perceptions of the world. In the early stages of the Cold War, this practice was taken to a high art in English and American news journal maps.

But the omission of communist nations was not the major point of the Beaverbrook map; this was merely a collateral issue. The main thrust of the map was the United States, a nation whose borders were dotted rather than solid, and whose interior was colored pale white compared to the solid black demarcation of the British Empire. The cartographic point made here was clear: the United States was disappearing from the British Tory worldview. To Tories, and indeed to all major English political parties of the period, the humor of the cartographic cartoon was evident. Given the conflict between postwar British and American foreign policy goals, whereby American ideas of international universalism often ran counter to Britain's plans to preserve her pre-World War II empire, Lord Beaverbrook's humorously simplistic solution was a new English map of the world that no longer included the United States and its troublesome policies.[3]

Three months after the Beaverbrook cartoon was published, an American, and decidedly different, map portrayal of the Cold War world appeared in the American serial *Time* magazine. The *Time* map, labeled "Two Worlds," was a multicolored portrayal of the Containment policy in action.[4] *Time* magazine, then a conservative Republican-leaning journal, used the early 1950 map to describe the perceived bipolar struggle of the Cold War, and in doing so, it placed England as a valuable lynchpin in an effort to surround the dangerous advances of the Soviet Union. The placement of England within the realm of a US-dominated "European Barrier," through suggestive coloring and text labeling, ran counter to Lord Beaverbrook's vision of an English-dominated world with the United States conveniently disappearing. More striking was the American portrayal of the Soviet Union which was the dominant feature of the map, very unlike the Beaverbrook map which omitted all communist nations. The "Two Worlds" map not only sought to highlight the threat of Soviet communism but also portrayed Chinese communism as merely a puppet extension of the Soviet power. But the "Two Worlds" map had its share of omissions too. The "Two Worlds" label, for example, referred to the capitalist nations' (colored blue) and the communist nations' (colored red) struggle for global politics, thereby excluding the majority of non-aligned nations (various colors) that would eventually become known as the "Third World." Also omitted, and hence devalued, were most of the world's nations that lay in the southern hemisphere, nations that, at the time, had no noticeable part to play in the rapidly unfolding Cold War.

Although English and American news journal maps were not always so disparate in their depictions of world politics, this comparison shows how dramatically different the two nation's worldviews often could be in the early stages of the Cold War, despite the "special relationship" harkened to by both nations' foreign policymakers in the fight against communism. This comparison more importantly illustrates several ways Cold War American and English news journal maps dealt with the post–World War II communist threat; the Beaverbrook cartoon omitted all references to communist nations, thereby devaluing them, while the "Two Worlds" map vilified all communist nations by portraying them in wholly negative imagery.

These news journal maps graphically illustrate how national news journals, which usually carry a noticeable political bias, often use maps for political rhetoric. Their comparison also speaks to the ability that maps have to relate complex geopolitical concepts with relatively simple cartographic imagery. This study is chiefly concerned with showing how national news journal maps of the early Cold War period were used to define and promote changing worldviews in America and Great Britain. These journals, as stated earlier, were themselves extensions of national political parties, and the parties' attempts to reach public readers and indoctrinate them as to the dangers of the communist threat.

The examination of news journal maps as sources of Cold War political and cultural rhetoric represents a new direction in scholarship about this era. Until recently, historians of the Cold War have relied almost exclusively on political documents as sources. Official government publications, public and private speeches by government officials, foreign policy documents, and published memoirs were the most commonly researched materials. And the value of these documents is undeniable. They help us understand the motives, fears, hopes, and strategies of the politicians and governments that shaped global geopolitics during the Cold War. Thus, *political* histories of the Cold War by George F. Kennan, John Lewis Gaddis, and Gabriel Kolko, to name a few, and those edited by Michael J. Hogan, Thomas G. Paterson, and others, focused on the workings of the Cold War superpower governments. But while these political histories offer invaluable insights into government policy, they inherently ignore the impact of the Cold War on the general public.[5] These political histories also tend to ignore visual media. And virtually no political histories examine era maps in any regard. Or, as noted cartographic historian J.B. Harley lamented, traditional "historians have tended to relegate maps—along with paintings, photographs, and other nonverbal sources—to a lower division of evidence than the written word."[6]

With the fall of the Soviet Union in the early 1990s and the subsequent opening of many formerly closed archives, a new type of Cold War history began—what has been called Cold War *cultural* history. Authors including Walter Hixson, James Aronson, Alvin A. Snyder, and Jessica Gienow-Hecht have led this field by examining ties between Cold War governments and the mass media. Their studies of national propaganda efforts have largely focused on officially sponsored programs while ignoring more informal interrelationships between national governments and private (but politically biased) news journals. What is also missing from these studies is a discussion of the ability of unofficial propaganda—particularly, news maps—to quickly relate complex and dynamic geopolitical ideas and, hence, to shape public opinion about the dynamic Cold War world.[7] Academic neglect of news maps is all the more confounding when one considers the vast circulation numbers of both British and American news journals during this era.

Most historians of cartography have been equally deficient in discussing Cold War–era maps in general, with only a handful of scholars even recognizing a separate Cold War cartographic trend. Central to this general lack of attention to Cold War map propaganda is probably that the Cold War, as an era, has only recently come to a close. Nevertheless, Mark Monmonier has examined the nature of the news map profession in the twentieth century, with much attention to the Cold War era.[8] Walter Ristow and Susan Schulten have studied the impact of commercial and news maps on the American public.[9] Zbigniew Brzezinski, former National Security Advisor to President Jimmy Carter, revealed the role maps played in promoting Soviet and American views of Cold War geopolitics in the 1970s. More recently, Dagmar Unverhau edited a series of essays examining the extent of Soviet map secrecy in the German Democratic Republic.[10] Still, these studies have only begun to reveal the full importance *news maps* had in shaping public visions of Cold War geopolitical crises.

Noticeable Cold War map themes emerged to redefine and polarize the world along political lines and to label certain geographic regions and peoples as either good or bad. Although this polarization predated the Cold War, it did not gain popularity until after 1945. After World War II, a map iconography specific to the Cold War developed, and its populariza- tion helped transform the mental maps of British and American citizens concerned with geopolitical affairs. This study will compare the Cold War map iconography in England and the United States. As we shall see, there were indeed many important differences, and they reveal much about the American and British worldviews which were often at odds. In this way, this study will follow the recommendations of noted cartographic histori- ans J.B. Harley, David Woodward, Denis Wood, Mark Monmonier, and Denis Cosgrove, who argued that studying a society's maps can offer pow- erful insights about societal culture.[11]

Weekly news journal maps, rather than maps appearing in daily national newspapers, were selected for review for three reasons. First, weekly news journals regularly featured more detailed and colorful maps because the cartographers (and kindred cartoonists who also drew maps) employed by weekly journals had much more time to design, draw, and paint their maps. As a result, weekly news journal maps tend to display more artistic license, which usually correlates to a more heightened political bias in the cartographic imagery. Therefore, these maps display a more versatile pal- ette, both literally and figuratively, by which cartographic propaganda can be recognized and dissected. However, several examples of American and English daily news maps will be used for comparison. Second, weekly national news journals in the 1940s and 1950s almost always had an abun- dance of maps portraying foreign places, as these journals attempted to summarize a week's worth of geopolitically newsworthy items in a rela- tively small amount of space. In this way, weekly news maps tended to be much more discursive, both politically and culturally, playing off of certain national political fears and hopes, especially in times of international crises. Moreover, when daily newspapers used maps, these maps tended to be simple "locator" maps of more regional or local scope to illustrate local daily news articles. And third, only national news journals, not local or regional papers, were unencumbered by local or regional political concerns, focusing instead on national and international political issues most prevalent in early Cold War history.

Five national news journals from England and five from the United States were selected for this study because they present the widest scope of national political views that existed in the ten years after World War II. Conveniently, and for the purposes of this study, the selected publications (see later in the chapter) also represent some of the most widely distributed news journals in both countries. The 1945–1955 time period was chosen because by 1955 the Cold War had reached the end of what many scholars consider to be its first major phase. Charles S. Maier, for example, argued that by 1955 the Cold War had reached its first "thaw" due to a combination of factors. Stalin's death in 1953, coupled with his successors' attempts to reverse many aspects of Stalinization in Eastern Europe, followed by the two monumental Geneva Conferences in 1955 and 1956, all brought the first period of international relaxation.[12] Similarly, D.F. Fleming has written that Western powers were compelled to attend the 1955 Geneva Conference because the Cold War had reached its first stalemate. The United States sought to escape from the Formosa (Taiwan) crisis, while British Conservatives hoped to use the peace conference to win support for their candidate, Winston Churchill. However, both Great Britain and the United States attended the summit conference with the general goals of ending the global fear of atomic war, especially since the international nuclear arms race had, by 1955, also reached its first stalemate.[13]

By 1955 Great Britain and the United States were not as close as they had been at the end of World War II. They had become disillusioned with postwar international cooperation as well as their relationship with the Soviet Union. In other words, they had settled into their relatively stable and respective foreign policies and worldviews, which were, at their heart, anticommunist. Also, in the first ten years after World War II public opinion about world affairs in American and British societies solidified and became static. The Stalinization of Eastern Europe, the Greek Civil War, the Marshall Plan and the Truman Doctrine, the Berlin Blockade, the Soviet invasion of Czechoslovakia, the Containment Doctrine, the development of the nuclear arms race, the "fall" of China, the Korean War, the rise of McCarthyism, and the death of Stalin all caused increased levels of anxiety over the fate of world affairs. The year 1955 is also a logical endpoint for this study because it marks what many historians claim to be the end of the "special relationship" between Great Britain and the United

States. Although major geopolitical differences existed between the two nations throughout the period of this study, it was not until 1956 that the United States publicly distanced itself from Great Britain's foreign policy goals. In that year, the Suez Crisis drew the two nations, and France, into a heated political debate as the United States condemned England's and France's attempts to thwart Egypt's nationalization of the Canal Zone. From 1956 onward, and with the British capitulation to the American position on the Suez Canal, England's ultimate subordination to American foreign policy had been realized. Until that time, British foreign policy-makers' anxiety over becoming a junior partner in the developing perception of an American-Soviet-led settlement of World War II was almost always restricted to official foreign relations documents and was not, by and large, publicly discussed nor a public concern.

The primary American national news journals selected for this study are *Time, Newsweek, Life, Christian Science Monitor, U.S. News and World Report*, and *Look*. Other journals used for comparison include *American Legion, Junior Scholastic, Nation, Saturday Evening Post*, and *Stars and Stripes*, although many other weekly and daily journals were consulted as well. English journals chosen are *Time and Tide, Economist, The Spectator, London Tribune*, and the monthly *Serial Map Service*. Unlike their counterparts in the United States, the English weekly news journals suffered drastically low print runs after World War II, as did English daily newspapers; and relatively few weekly journals existed due to war damage and ongoing paper rationing. Consequently, more daily newspapers are used in the English sampling than in the American case. The *London Daily News* and the *London Herald Tribune*, in particular, are cited frequently for comparison purposes. Where applicable, examples from the Soviet journal *Krokodil*, the German (English language) journal *Facts in Review*, and other foreign periodicals are used for contrast.

As will be demonstrated, national news journal maps reveal much about how England and the United States viewed the world in the formative years of the Cold War. These news maps were the most widely read and reproduced maps in both nations at the time, and the maps' portrayals of the early Cold War period played on preconceived public fears and hopes of the geopolitical world that were particular to each nation. As such, these maps bring to light important similarities and differences between American and British public sentiments concerning the Cold War.

Ultimately, this study is a work in Cold War *cultural* history, a saga revealed through the imagery of news maps in the early Cold War period.

This is not an attempt to examine the methods of news map creation. Other authors including Mark Monmonier and Walter W. Ristow have documented these methods (see earlier in the chapter). Nor will this study seek to "tease out" multiple readings of the imagery it examines. Though it is tempting to attempt such a layered reading, to do so detracts from the intended immediacy of the map imagery. Rather, this study will attempt to examine the maps in the context of their original intent—as periodic and temporary cartographic imagery designed to quickly relate Cold War geopolitical propaganda. It must be remembered that these maps were produced cheaply, in high volumes, read quickly, and discarded with the news journals in which they appeared. With this dynamic in mind, I have attempted to recall the all-but-forgotten phenomenon of Cold War–era news maps and their own compelling brand of messaging for the masses.

Before an analysis of British and American news journal maps can begin, it is necessary to define certain terms. Whenever the terms *postwar* or *postwar era* appear, they refer to the period that began with the end of World War II in mid-1945 and ended in early 1947. During this time, the former World War II allies—Britain, the United States, and the Soviet Union—began to drift apart and into polarized camps of capitalism versus communism that characterized international Cold War relations for the next forty years. Unless otherwise noted, the terms *British press* and *American press* refer to national news services in newspaper, news journal, and popular journal formats. This does not include book publishers, but for the purposes of this study, it does include private map publishers. In ways described later that deal with map production and advertising, American and British national presses had very close ties with private map houses—ties that spanned the postwar Atlantic World. In fact, the term *Atlantic World* has often been controversial because it has no constant definition. The public conception of the Atlantic World changes throughout this study, as do a number of other geopolitical labels. The examination of these changes in public discourse, and especially in maps, is one of the goals of this study.

The act of linking terms, or ideas, to political entities has very often been controversial. However, this is exactly what news mapmakers have always done, and they did it with great enthusiasm in the British and American press during the early Cold War. The labeling of political entities here will follow the labels of the postwar British and American press, although many of them are technically incorrect by modern standards. Even though the United States and Britain were the closest of the Allied nations during World War II, by 1945, they comprised very different political entities with similarly different geopolitical outlooks.

In both the American and British presses, the *United States* and *America* were used interchangeably throughout the Cold War. By 1945, the United States consisted of forty-eight contiguous states, the large territory of Alaska, Puerto Rico, and various Pacific island possessions including Hawaii, Midway, and Guam.[14] Although American territory in the Pacific sometimes did get coverage in American and British national news maps, these maps usually portrayed the United States as the forty-eight states and Alaska, while the inclusion of American lands in the Pacific appeared only occasionally.

Defining the boundaries of Britain by 1945 is a bit more complicated given the history, size, and complexity of the British Empire. The many geopolitical names associated with Britain hint at this complexity. The term *British Isles* generally describes all the islands directly off the north-west coast of Europe. Within this group of islands is a host of political and cultural realms that both connect and delineate the peoples living there and in the British Empire abroad. The largest island of the British Isles is called *Great Britain*, which is dominated by the nation of *England*, and also contains the sovereign nations of *Scotland* and *Wales*. The *United Kingdom* (UK), also called the United Kingdom of Great Britain and Northern Ireland, describes the political union of the Great Britain nations, Northern Ireland, and fourteen overseas island territories comprising the *British Commonwealth*. *Ireland*, fiercely independent from England since 1922, was neutral in World War I and World War II. As will be shown, virtually all postwar American and British news maps portraying the British Isles and the British Empire graphically delineated Ireland from all things British.

Meanwhile, the term *British Empire* encompasses the UK and the British Commonwealth nations including Canada, India, Palestine (later Israel), South Africa, Australia, and the Anglo Egyptian Sudan. But as with the British Isles, the British Empire was a multilayered and complex assembly of political entities by 1945 that were linked by many economic and political treaties. British-made maps of the empire illustrated this complexity with many colors and symbols "arranged in a series, to show gradation of governmental forms [ranging] from direct military administration, through full responsible government by universal suffrage, to complete self-government."[15] A map of the British Empire published in 1946 by the London-based *Serial Map Service* described no fewer than five levels of affiliation between the British Isles nations and the Commonwealth.[16] In one group were the United Kingdom, Ireland, and the "self-governing dominions" of Canada, Australia, South Africa, and New Zealand. A second group consisted of the territories of India and Burma with a "large measure of internal self-governance." A third group contained over twenty "colonies, protectorates, and protected states" scattered worldwide. The fourth group, formalized after 1945, described United Nations-mandated trustee areas mostly found in Africa. The last group composed several Pacific islands under joint administration with other nations.

This study will use the term *British* as a generic cultural label for all imagery and political ideology that emerged from London, which was the capitol city of England, the home of the Fleet Street press, and the control center for the British Empire. Moreover, the Fleet Street national press, the American press, and both national governments usually preferred the term *British* rather than *English, Anglo-Saxon,* or any other hegemonic cultural label. These political labels notwithstanding, the British and American presses differed somewhat in their labeling of British lands. The British press was naturally more conscious of the many political combinations involved in the British Empire, but it relied on a few standbys. Even though the seat of postwar British political and cultural power resided in London, England, the British press most often labeled its cultural and political ties as British rather than English. Similarly, the term *British Empire* was most often used by both presses to describe all British overseas possessions.

NOTES

1. Robert M. Hathaway, *Great Britain and the United States: Special Relations since World War II* (Boston: Twayne Publishers, 1990), xv.
2. *London Daily Express*, n.15,390 (Oct. 12, 1949): 4.
3. Get *Daily Express* citation for this—awaiting interlibrary loan.
4. Map by R.M. Chapin, Jr., *Time* v.60, no.1, 36.
5. George F. Kennan (under the pseudonym "Mr. X"), "The Sources of Soviet Conduct," in *Foreign Affairs* (1947), vol. 25, no.4, 566–582; John Lewis Gaddis, *The United States and the Origins of the Cold War, 1941–1947* (New York and London: Columbia University Press, 1972); Gabriel Kolko, *The Politics of War: The World and the United States Foreign Policy, 1943–1945* (New York: Random House, 1968).
6. J.B. Harley, *The New Nature of Maps: Essays in the History of Cartography* (Baltimore and London: The Johns Hopkins University Press, 2001), 34.

7. Walter Hixson, *Parting the Curtain: Propaganda, Culture, and the Cold War, 1945–1961* (New York: St. Martin's Press, 1997); James Aronson, *The Press and the Cold War* (New York: Monthly Review Press, 1990); Alvin A. Snyder, *Warriors of Disinformation: American Propaganda, Soviet Lies, and the Winning of the Cold War* (New York: Arcade Publishing, 1995); Jessica Gienow-Hecht, *Transmission Impossible: American Journalism as Cultural Diplomacy in Postwar Germany, 1945–1955* (Baton Rouge: Louisiana University Press, 1999).

8. Mark Monmonier, *How to Lie with Maps* (Chicago and London: University of Chicago Press, 1996) and *Maps with the News: The Development of American Journalistic Cartography* (Chicago and London: University of Chicago Press, 1999).

9. Susan Schulten, *The Geographical Imagination in America, 1880–1950* (Chicago and London: University of Chicago Press, 2001).

10. Dagmar Unverhau (ed.), *State Security and Mapping in the German Democratic Republic: Map Falsification as a Consequence of Excessive Secrecy?* (Berlin: Lit Verlag, 2006).

11. J.B. Harley and David Woodward (eds), *The History of Cartography, I* (Chicago and London: University of Chicago Press, 1987), 2–3. Also Denis Cosgrove's "Mapping New Worlds: Culture and Cartography in Sixteenth-Century Venice" in *Imago Mundi*, v. 44 (1992): 65–89.

12. Charles S. Maier, *The Cold War in Europe: Era of a Divided Continent* (Princeton: Marcus Wiener Publishers, 1996), xii.

13. D.F. Fleming, *The Cold War and its Origins, 1917–1960* (Garden City, NY: Doubleday, 1961), 737–740.

14. The oceanic possessions of the United States by 1945 were Hawaii, Wake Island, Puerto Rico, Guam, the Philippines, the Midway Islands, the US Virgin Islands, and American Samoa. The United States also had control over the Panama Canal Zone since 1903.

15. See "A Contrast in Empire Building" in *Serial Map Service*, v.7 n.8 (May 1946): 91.

16. See map 352 and 353 entitled "The British Empire," in *Serial Map Service*, v.7 n.7 (April 1946).

CHAPTER 2

Trends in British and American News Maps by the End of World War II

By the end of World War II, British and American news journals were more different than similar. Nevertheless both nations' major news journals were privately owned by politically active, wealthy entrepreneurs. Both nations' journals were designed chiefly to make a profit while making a political statement, even if that statement was a claim of political nonpartisanship. And both nations' journals operated in a free market economy with generally no overt intervention by their national governments. That, however, is where the similarities end. In terms of volume of publications, use of graphics and maps, distribution and sales levels of journals, and political affiliation, the two presses were very dissimilar. The pace of news was much faster in Britain given the nation's relatively high number of news publications per capita—competition that kept news debates livelier than anything in America except during the McCarthy Era of the early 1950s.[1] But the American press was much more influential, commercially successful, and technologically superior. Although both presses had access to roughly the same printing equipment by 1945, economic conditions favored America and kept British printing a step behind in terms of imagery reproduction and capacity. In fact, by the end of World War II, the greatest difference between the American and British presses was economic in nature. Simply put, the British economy was in ruins, while the American economy soared. The British war effort bankrupted the great

© The Author(s) 2019
J. P. Stone, *British and American News Maps in the Early Cold War Period, 1945–1955*, Palgrave Studies in the History of the Media, https://doi.org/10.1007/978-3-030-15468-4_2

empire, and by 1945, its 2.7 billion pound war debt, largely owed to the United States, forced a sale of almost all its foreign assets, totaling over 1 billion pounds.[2] In that year Britain became the world's largest debtor nation.[3] National rationing of almost all commercial goods during and after the war, especially of newsprint paper, negatively impacted most British news publications.

British newsprint rationing was imposed by the Control of Paper Orders from 1940 to New Year's Day of 1959, a span which amply encompasses the period studied here.[4] The British press had been dependent on imported wood pulp since the 1920s, and by the early postwar period, journalists lamented that "Nowadays we cannot afford adequate supplies of the better Scandinavian wood-pulps and North African esparto grass....Home-produced straw...must suffice."[5] Most daily London newspapers were reduced from an average of twenty pages to ten or twelve pages, as national newsprint consumption was reduced to twenty percent of prewar levels.[6] Weekly news journals such as the Conservative *Spectator*, one of the five British weekly titles examined here, were reduced from around ninety pages to twenty pages. Newsprint rationing was more than a national economic reform to support the war effort, though. It was also a way for the British government to control the press well into the postwar period. Keeping print runs low kept criticism of national foreign policy down. Indeed during the entire rationing period (1940–1958), while national newspapers suffered, British-made newsprint was consistently exported.[7] Both major British national parties were often hostile to the press during and after World War II; *indirect* government censorship was common and will be discussed later in this chapter. Newsprint rationing did not affect all English newspapers equally, however. The larger weekly news journals, also called "the heavies," suffered most as they were forced to reduce their page numbers and shrink ad space in an attempt to maintain circulation levels.[8] Conversely, smaller daily papers, which could never compete with the vast prewar circulation levels of the heavies, actually experienced circulation increases as consumers began buying more than one paper to get more comprehensive news after rationing began.[9] Many smaller circulation left-wing papers consequently generated greater advertising revenue and hence became more competitive. The leftist *Daily Worker*, for example, increased its 1939 circulation of 1.75 million to 3 million by 1946.[10] In general, though, the English war effort was devastating to the press, and it caused shortages of more than paper. By 1944 over a third of British journalists were stationed overseas in the armed forces.[11] Material and labor shortages combined to reduce English journalism to what one 1947 critic called an "air of pre-fabricated impermanence."[12]

World War II–era British paper rationing reduced the frequency of news maps in two important ways. First, the scarcity of newsprint forced all editors to sacrifice graphics space in favor of text space. As British journals have always been more text oriented than image oriented, especially in comparison to American journals, this was not too much of a shock to British news style. This British preference for text over imagery is a very important distinction from the American press and will be a factor in many sections of this study. Second, and more importantly, rationing forced editors to give up precious revenue-generating ad space to accommodate news text. Still, after World War II, British journal *advertisements* often exhibited more maps and cartographic imagery than did proper news articles. These ad maps were almost always tied to contemporary news events, and as such, they offer insights about how British news readers perceived the world cartographically, especially in the postwar era when British news maps became scarce. However, to date no cartographic historians have discussed ad maps in any historical context.

Another liability of the British weekly press, and of news maps, imposed by rationing was the inability to produce color imagery. However, it must be said that historically, the British press has never been as inclined to use color graphics as the American press. In fact, no British news journal regularly used color graphics before World War II. This was, in part, due to the "ingrained tradition, especially among elite newspapers, of verbalizing the news, rather than illustrating it."[13] However, by 1945 the British press was looking ahead and trying to compete with the phenomenal sales of the graphic-rich American journals and lamented its inability to employ colored inks. But the lack of color imagery and maps was not due to inferior British printing techniques. In 1947 British journalist James Shand noted that the British "lack neither competence nor skill in any department of printing technology" and indeed British news graphics, which includes news maps and ad maps, has been on par with American printing since before World War II.[14] Since the 1920s, however, the British press had been dependent on American printing technology to stay modern. As Shand's article observed, "English printing owes much to America....The Linotype and Monotype are *both* American in origin and development....At the other end of the production line most specialized binding machinery in this country...is American in origin."[15] Similarly, American cartographic historian

Mark Monmonier noted the evolutionary links of the British and American presses, acknowledging, however, that "principal recent developments are almost wholly American."[16] But immediately after World War II, the newest American-made high-speed color rotary presses were not yet available in Britain. Nor were they available in 1947, when Shand stated that "in type-setting, colour-photography, process engraving and duplicate rotary plate-making [the Americans] show no standards we cannot match for quality."[17] Shand added that "in these American periodicals rotary letterpress four-colour printing at high speeds…is now commonplace… [but] there is little English letterpress rotary magazine production worthy of comparison."[18] The liability of the British press, then, was not inferior color reproduction techniques but rather a lack of high-speed equipment that could produce considerable volumes of color imagery necessary for national weekly circulation.

The British press was keenly aware of its comparative shortcomings in the field of color printing, and it constantly measured itself by other national presses. By 1945, British dependence on American, and to a lesser extent German, printing technology compelled British editors to con-stantly compare their news coverage with that of their American counter-parts.[19] But despite American dominance in the field, or perhaps because of it, English newsmen did not always look favorably on the new printed media trends being exported by the United States. Although Shand admired the color content of "American mass-produced periodicals," he acknowledged a British press bias against "the contents of American 'glossies' as they are cynically referred to in Fleet Street."[20] Indeed, the British and American presses compared themselves, and each other's respective geopolitics, in their respective news journals quite frequently throughout World War II and the early Cold War, as this study will show. These geopolitical comparisons included the use of maps in news articles, travel ads, and political cartoons as vehicles for rhetoric and imaging the "Special Relationship" partner across the Atlantic Ocean. These topics will be elaborated upon in the following chapters.

Imagery and graphics in the British press were, compared to the American press, noticeably less popular. This applies to news maps and is somewhat of an oddity for an industrialized nation with a long history of mapping its empire. Here the Fleet Street press offers a twist on carto-graphic historian Denis Wood's correlation of map development and soci-etal development. Wood argues that what separates non-mapping societies from mapping societies is the development in the latter of map "labor specialization," including "surveyors, cartographers, map engravers, copy camera operators, plate makers, pressmen, [and] sales representatives for commercial producers of maps."[21] Wood uses the example of the Mexican native group of the Zinacantecan as a non-mapping society due to its lack of such mapmaking labor specialization. However, as noted earlier, British society certainly had all the aforementioned specialization of labor and a tradition of mapmaking dating back hundreds of years. So the relative absence of maps in the British news press does not correlate with the absence of such labor specialization. And the dearth of British news maps was not simply an effect of wartime rationing of mapmaking materials—indeed, British news journals did not favor news maps before the war. Rather, British news culture favored text over imagery which precluded maps as a popular news medium. Fortunately, the relatively few news maps that did appear in weekly journals, the more numerous British advertisements featuring cartographic imagery, and the many maps published by the *Serial Map Service* constitute an adequate collection for this study.

Although the British press may have been a "casualty of the Second World War," the contemporary American press soared to new heights along with the American wartime economy.[22] Even before the United States entered the war in late 1941, the national economy had already rallied for the war effort. Under President Franklin Delano Roosevelt's "arsenal of democracy" program, American exports, chiefly to Britain, rose from 3.2 billion dollars in 1939 to over 14.3 billion dollars by 1944.[23] After 1941 the economy grew at an accelerated pace until 1945. By 1944 real weekly manufacturing wages, for example, had risen over 53 percent from prewar levels.[24] The national mobilization of American industry was coordinated by the creation of the National Defense Mediation Board in 1941, and just as in Britain, rationing was common.[25] But unlike in Britain, American rationing programs (begun in 1942) never had a major impact on the national printed media. The list of rationed items in America was long and included tires, gasoline, shoes, sugar, coffee, and various other consumer goods needed for the war effort.[26] The only item on this list that may have impacted the operation of news agencies was typewriters, but since they are not consumable commodities, and hence do not need constant replacement, their rationing had no major negative consequences in the American press.

On the contrary, the American press benefited tremendously from World War II. Before the advent of television in the 1950s, the only source of timely images and maps of the war effort were issued by newspapers and news journals. The three most popular weekly news journals in this period—*Time* magazine, *Newsweek*, and *U.S. News and World Report*— met the public demand for war imagery and cartography, and they all experienced large circulation increases. From 1940 to 1945, *Time*'s circulation increased from 759,520 to 1.18 million; *Newsweek* increased from 327,838 to 585,897; and *U.S. News and World Report* increased from 86,523 to 207,257.[27] By sheer popularity and prestige, *Time* was America's leading weekly news journal as its yearly circulation was more than that of *Newsweek* and *U.S. News and World Report* combined. Given this metric, *Time* maps will be given special attention in this study as they reached more Americans than any other news maps while also setting the tone for cartographic style in national journalism.

Rationing kept British weekly circulation levels much lower than their American counterparts, but the British national press boasted twice as many major weekly titles. World War II and postwar circulation figures for the six British weekly journals are hard to come by since the British Audit Bureau of Circulations (ABC) records are inconsistent for those periods. Most of the postwar circulation figures quoted here were taken from a summary of a 1947 Royal Commission inquiry into the ownership and political orientation of the British Press. Other circulation statistics, as well as newspaper sponsorship information, were provided by a 1950 study of British news periodicals written by William Ewert Berry Camrose.[28] The *Economist* launched in 1843, and by 1947 it was hailed as being in a "field of its own...read in many countries, particularly in America," with circulation at about 70,000 and actually increasing to over 105,000 by 1955.[29] *New Statesman and Nation* had the largest circulation of all the weeklies, at over 153,000 in 1947; but readership fell to 130,000 by 1955.[30] First published in 1828, *Spectator*'s circulation decreased significantly after the war, from about 100,000 in 1947 to just over 75,000 by 1955.[31] Figures for *Time and Tide* and *London Tribune* are limited to 1947 when both journals sold about 80,000 copies. The final national weekly, *Truth*, was mentioned by Camrose, but no circulation statistics were given, nor did the ABC list such figures. It is likely that *Truth* sold fewer than 80,000 issues per year.

Media historian Bernard C. Cohen has noted that most news agencies assume that their publications will be read by a wide demographic spanning from the common man to national politicians.[32] But only the elite national newspapers and news journals of the era, such as the ones examined in this study, specialized in the news of foreign affairs. Smaller local newspapers, by contrast, did not normally cover international events, and their editors assumed people seeking such coverage would turn to national news publications.[33] By 1945, British and American weekly national news journals targeted largely the same cosmopolitan audience in their respective nations. Whether it was *Time*'s promotion of a "statesman's view of the world"[34] or the *Economist*'s addressing the "concerns of businessmen dealing in commodities, railroads, and other investments,"[35] both nations' journals sold primarily to well-educated white collar, middle- to upper-class white males interested in international affairs.

POLITICAL ORIENTATIONS OF THE BRITISH AND AMERICAN PRESSES BY 1945

The British and American presses are extensions of their respective national political systems and traditions, and these were very different by the end of World War II. British politics has always been more heterogeneous and fractured than American politics, and the British press reflects this diversity. By 1945 the six weekly news journals operating in Britain spanned the national political spectrum. The independent press included the radical *New Statesman and Nation*, the nonpartisan journals *Economist* and *Time and Tide*, and the conservatives *Spectator* and *Truth*.[36] The only official weekly British party paper, or non-independent, was the *Tribune* which billed itself as the "voice of the left."[37] Contrast this diversity with the smaller lineup of postwar American weekly news journals, which was dominated by the Republican-leaning *Time* magazine, the Democratic-leaning *Newsweek*, and the (then) largely independent, but Conservative *U.S. News and World Report*.[38] The comparative diversity of the British press, however, is best seen with the various daily and Sunday edition papers that, in terms of numbers of titles available at any given corner market, dwarfed the American press. Although the American press boasted many more local daily papers by 1945, they usually dominated only the small towns in which they were printed. Hence, for many English press historians looking at American newspapers, "the land of the free [was] also the home of one-newspaper towns."[39]

Another major difference between the two national presses by 1945 was their links to their respective political parties. Without exception, every American national weekly news journal and virtually every American newspaper claimed to be politically independent. The claim is understandable because representing the news without the influence of any political party ideology was considered wholesome in 1945, while the printing of obvious political propaganda was generally seen as a negative activity in the United States. Not so, however, in Britain, where many reputable news journals publicly announced their political orientation on the front page. As mentioned earlier, *Time and Tide* is subtitled "The Voice of the Left." One of the most influential press barons of the postwar period, Lord Beaverbrook, shamelessly announced to a Royal Commission on the Press that his *Daily Express* was chiefly a propaganda journal for the Conservative Party—a proclamation that never would have been made in the United States by such a media mogul.[40]

Rather than discrediting the British press, acknowledged political partisanship has been the basis for political debates in the press that not only sold more papers but also made American news coverage seem bland by comparison. (Interestingly, that blandness may be true in terms of textual dialog but not visual dialog—as we shall see.) However, this study will show, somewhat ironically, that the political leanings of both nations' journals were relatively unimportant in the early Cold War period in terms of foreign policy as all national parties sought largely the same ends overseas—the containment of totalitarian communism.

The British national press may have been more diverse, with more individual publications than its American counterpart by 1945, but it had long been centered in one part of one major city—the Fleet Street district of London. The apparent provinciality of this centrality contrasts sharply with the international flavor of British news journals that had been concerned with the workings of the far-flung empire since well before World War I. The American press, although less diverse but more numerous, had no such news center. Although New York City is the traditional American publishing capital and the location of *Newsweek* corporate headquarters, many influential news journals were located in other urban centers. For example, *U.S. News and World Report* was centered in Washington, D.C. Both *Time* and its counterpart popular photography journal, *Life*, operated out of Chicago. Two of the most popular journals of the era, *Saturday Evening Post* and *Look* were published in Philadelphia and Des Moines, Iowa, respectively. And unlike the British press, the American press has, historically, tended to vacillate, along with public opinion, between international isolationism and interventionism. By 1945, as will be shown, the American press was returning to isolationism, while the British press remained strongly international in flavor and news coverage.

News Maps in Britain and America, 1945–1947

Now that the political, economic, and journalistic factors have been established, a comparison of British and American news maps can commence. It must be noted that the majority of journalistic map trends prevalent in the early Cold War period were variations of map conventions that date back to World War II and even earlier. This is not to say that Cold War–era maps offered nothing new—they absolutely did—but even their more innovative developments have origins in pre–World War II mapping. Predictably, though, British and American news maps transitioned from the World War II era to the Cold War era in different ways that highlighted each nation's particular worldview, geopolitical place, and cartographic style.

The most obvious difference was the high frequency of American cartographic imagery versus a relative dearth of it in British journals by mid-1945. While "more Americans came into contact with maps during the Second World War than in any previous period," British citizens looking for detailed news journal maps of the war were usually out of luck.[41] It was not uncommon for 1945 American weekly journals to publish three or four two-column, multicolored maps of various war fronts, while contemporary British journals such as *Spectator* had no news maps relating to the war whatsoever in 1945 and 1946. Given this difference in map production, it is no surprise that the American press dominated the field of news cartography by 1945. The most important development in American news mapping was brought about by the advent of the Air Age, which began in the 1920s and reached maturity during World War II. The Air Age caused a sort of revolution in news cartography by the end of the war mainly by promoting the use of long forgotten map projections that deviated from convention, allowing a rethinking of spatial orientation and world geopolitics. This "challenge to American cartography" was led by a new generation of news cartographers, such as Richard Edes Harrison, who were trained not as professional cartographers but rather as architects, interior designers, and advertising illustrators who brought graphic innovation to a relatively cloistered news map profession.[42] This revolution, and its proponents, will be discussed in the following chapter. Although the beginnings of this revolution extend back before World War II, its legacy was not fully realized in American news journals until after 1945. What follows, then, is a brief summary of British and American cartographic trends present at the end of World War II that held sway over the majority of news publications before the Air Age revolution fully took hold.

BRITISH AND AMERICAN NEWS CARTOGRAPHERS
AND THEIR METHODS

It must be stated at the outset of this section that to date there have been precious few studies, published or otherwise, discussing news cartographers and the methods they employed during and after World War II. This is largely due to the fact that modern scholarship has only recently begun to realize the importance news maps, and their makers, have had in shaping public opinion. Notwithstanding the few cartographers who achieved some measure of fame during and after World War II in the United States (see Chap. 3), most British and American news mapmakers have gone unacknowledged even by the publications that employed them. Much of the information in this section was taken from a telephone interview with Paul Pugliese conducted by the author in the summer of 2004. Pugliese was a full-time staff cartographer at *Time* magazine in the 1960s and served as the journal's last Chief of Cartography from 1975 to 1990.

As discussed earlier, Mark Monmonier has shown that by World War II, news cartography methodology and technology emanated from the United States over to Britain, although the latter could not capitalize on much of the color printing technology due to war rationing. But many generalizations of news map ordering, design, and construction still apply to both nations' presses. The first is that unlike mapmakers at daily journals, weekly news journal cartographers had more time to design their maps, which were usually ordered at the beginning of the week by managing news editors.[43] As there were obviously no computers used in the designing of these maps, they were all hand-drawn and lettered. News maps were usually ordered to accompany specific articles, but it was up to the mapmaker to decide how relevant the map would be to the accompanying news text.[44] This could lead to some obvious discrepancies between articles and maps, as will be shown in later chapters, but for the most part, news maps in the 1940s and 1950s did not function to literally illustrate news articles, but rather to offer supplementary location and detail information to news text. This gave news cartographers wide latitude for employment of map icons, lettering, projections, and labeling.[45]

American weekly news journals had more departmentalized and professional cartography divisions by 1945 than did British weeklies. *Time*, *Newsweek*, and *U.S. News and World Report* all had separate Departments of News Cartography, largely due to *Time*'s organizational model. These map departments dealt directly with the managing news editor to decide what types of maps should be run, how big they should be, if they should use color, and so on. Only American news journals employed titled Chiefs of Cartography who oversaw their Department of News Cartography. These map chiefs, and many of their underlings, often did contract and consulting map work for private organizations, state and federal governments, and other news publications in addition to their weekly news map projects.[46]

If American news cartographers were underappreciated, their British counterparts were virtually anonymous. This was due to simply more than the British penchant for prioritizing words over imagery in their news publications by 1945. It was largely due to the fact that, given the historically low frequency of maps in British news journals, they could not be produced economically in-house. In Britain, the rapid and tremendous public demand for war maps during World War II forced most journals to outsource their news maps to private mapmakers, thereby crediting each map with a generic corporate title instead of a mapmaker's name. The few weekly news maps that are credited to individuals are sporadic, and they do not offer any real body of reference. This was also true of British daily newspapers, which regularly ran maps in their Sunday editions. The lack of professional staff cartographers at British news journals left news editors with two choices for their news maps. The first, and the most expensive, was to pay for the reproduction of sections taken from privately made atlases for use as locator maps. The second was to have a staff artist, untrained in cartography, draw a simple locator map with pen and ink. What resulted, then, were two very dissimilar categories of British news maps—professional looking reprinted maps versus crudely drawn in-house maps. These dissimilar processes imparted idiosyncratic characteristics to their maps, which will be discussed in the following chapters.

PROJECTIONS USED IN THE NEWS

One of the most prevalent trends on both sides of the Atlantic Ocean was the common use of certain types of map *projections* to relate images of empire.[47] A mapmaker's choice of projection, which is defined as how the spherical globe is transposed onto flat paper, is one of the most deterministic of a map's features. A particular method of projection is responsible for the framework, scope, and distortions inherent in the resulting flat map. Many different map projections have been used since the time of the Greeks, but the American and British professional map orthodoxy of the

1930s was dominated by the Mercator, one of the many variants of flat projection. Named for the famed sixteenth-century Flemish cartographer Gerardus Mercator who invented it, the Mercator projection long dominated the Western cartography.

From the Age of Discovery to World War II, Mercator projection maps were valued as navigational aids because they were most accurate in their representations of land near the equator where major oceanic lanes existed, and because they referenced directions consistently.[48] The "long-standing devotion among the military, naval and teaching professions" to this flat projection was probably due to its preservation of straight lines and compass bearings over great distances, as well as its wide, expansive presentation of the world's continents.[49] Although the popularity of Mercator maps has certainly been threatened by the rise of other projections (to be discussed later), the Mercator projection remains widely used to this day. But the Mercator projection, like all projections, involves inherent distortions. In the Mercator projection, those distortions involve the size of land masses, which are most accurately represented near the equator, but which become exponentially exaggerated toward the higher latitudes near the poles. Many Mercator maps, such as the aforementioned map, contained no depictions of either of the Polar Regions since the resulting exaggerated polar landforms would cover the entire top (northern) and bottom (southern) edges of the map. Even with the Polar Regions omitted, higher latitudinal landform exaggeration is still very evident and will be elaborated upon in subsequent chapters.

Before the Japanese attack on Pearl Harbor in late 1941 "challenged isolationist notions about the impregnability of the Western Hemisphere,"[50] the American Lend-Lease Act (March 1941) "brought out the world maps" in popular news journals to explain national involvement in the war effort.[51] During World War II, the Mercator projection was easily the most popular type used in American news journals because its wide spacing of the continents provided an analytical space to illustrate the outflow of the national war effort to far-flung overseas locations. All American national weekly news journals strongly supported the war effort, so it is no surprise that World War II–era news maps were very nationalistic. And it is well in evidence how frequently, and similarly, news war maps and official government war maps employed the Mercator projection. For example, notice the similarities between the "Forecast: Weather and War" map that appeared in *U.S. News and World Report* in October 1941, and a government map featured in *Life* magazine promoting the Lend-Lease program two years later.[52]

In both examples, the United States was centered on the map, which necessitated placing the bisected halves of the Eurasian continent at opposite ends. The centering of a nation on its own maps is nothing new. It dates back to antiquity with the "omphalos syndrome" of religion-inspired centering of empires on Mesopotamian, Chinese, and Greek maps, for example.[53] During World War II, this centering visually put the United States in the middle of the world *and* the war effort. The wide oceanic gulfs on either side of the American Hemisphere—gulfs that were exaggerated in the higher latitudes by the Mercator projection—were ideal *tabulae rasae* upon which to chart the American war effort on both Atlantic and Pacific fronts. These maps reassured Americans that the war was thousands of miles away, if *potentially* a threat. The exaggeration of the size of Soviet Union, then a valuable ally, was comforting, as American logistical lines of support rendezvoused with the hulking Allied Asiatic landform. The wide oceans yet seemed reliable barriers to direct US involvement in what Americans initially saw as a foreign war. Not surprisingly, these World War II Mercator maps usually omitted the Polar Regions altogether since they were not viable avenues for Allied shipping or military operations. The Mercator projection "Lend-Lease Map," discussed earlier, is also an excellent example of the American press living up to cartographic historian J.B. Harley's observation that "in newspapers [and other media]...military leaders are frequently shown in front of maps to confirm or reassure their viewers about the writ of power over the territory in the map."[54] Certainly American national news journals were replete with such examples throughout World War II. However, such appearances of political and military leaders in association with news maps were virtually absent in the contemporary British press. Moreover, the British press did not rely on multi-continent, small-scale Mercator projection news maps during the war in any event.

It is curious that during the entire World War II period, which for Britain lasted six years (1939–1945), not a single Mercator projection war map of the world is known to have appeared in any British weekly news journal. Neither did such a map appear in the *Sunday Times* for the sampled war years 1939, 1942, or 1945. Moreover, of the six British weeklies surveyed, only *Spectator* produced a map—one non-Mercator map—of the Pacific theater, which appeared in September 1939.[55] This is probably due to the fact that English news readers, unlike those in the United States, were more concerned with the local European fronts than with the *global* war effort, for which the expansive Mercator projection was ideal. Given the close proximity of the British Isles to Germany and their virtual immunity from a direct Japanese attack, it is no wonder that virtually all British weekly war news maps were regional or local in scope rather than global.

The more limited scope and the larger scale of regional British World War II–era news maps classify them more as what cartographic historians call *locator maps*, or maps that serve simply to show somewhat specific locations of news events. Locator maps do not normally exhibit many of the expository contents of global or worldwide *thematic maps* designed to make an argument.[56] Locator maps are, in fact, the most common type of news map because they are easily processed by the map reader, and their generally small size allows them to be inserted almost anywhere on the news page.[57] Although virtually all locator maps are on flat projections, their smaller scope usually negates the distortions evident in similar projections depicting larger regions and great landmasses of the world. While the small dimensions of these maps can severely limit the inclusion of helpful map icons, symbols, and text, locator maps were the preferred vehicle for relaying cartographic information in British news journals and newspapers throughout World War II and the early Cold War period. This was mainly due to the fact that these smaller maps literally fit well into the space-conscious news publications still restricted by national rationing after World War II.

Nevertheless, beautiful, multicolored maps of the world were available to British weekly news readers throughout World War II and the early Cold War through several privately owned, London-based map publishers. In a highly symbiotic relationship, daily and weekly news journals made up for their lack of large, detailed maps by advertising where the cartography-hungry British public could buy detailed map sets. In that way, news journals could claim to focus on analyzing foreign affairs events with text while leaving the global cartographic imagery to privately published map collections such as those for sale from the journal *Serial Map Service*. Or, as a 1941 ad for *Economist* stated in the November issue of *Serial Map Service*, "Just as the Serial Map Service records the physical changes in the international situation, so the Economist provides an analysis and interpretation of current events."[58] Begun in 1939, the monthly *Serial Map Service* was the only regular British cartographic journal available during World War II, and it produced all manner of political, economic, and military maps until its run ended in 1948. Published by the Phoenix Book Company, the *Serial Map Service* was "designed to help the general reader to appreciate the geographical and historical background of the war and international politics."[59] Until 1948 when the journal ended, it produced collections of multicolored maps measuring 11½ inches by 9 inches, designed by Fleet Street cartographic publisher George Philip and Son, Ltd. With each map, it presented commentary on the implications of recent geopolitical events by British military officers, foreign policy experts, staff cartographers, and even diplomatic correspondents from London newspapers. As such, this journal offers critical insight into British cartography and geopolitics in transition during and after World War II.

The lion's share of World War II commercial maps, though, did not come from cartographic journals but from professional map houses such as those operated by J.F. Horrabin and George Philip and Son, Ltd. Also known as "the man who makes maps speak," Horrabin placed ads in *Spectator* throughout the war that offered detailed, colorful maps of recent war developments.[60] Fleet Street's own George Philip and Son was the oldest commercial mapmaker of this group, with publications that date back to the early nineteenth century. Philip's "maps, atlases, globes and books" sold so well in journals such as *New Statesman and Nation* that by 1945 the company was overwhelmed with back orders.[61] Daily newspapers such as the *Daily Telegraph* cashed in more directly on the lucrative war map market by offering its own line of maps, through London-based mapmaker Geographia, which "achieved a phenomenal sale by 1940."[62]

London's private map houses employed many different types of projections as will be illustrated in later chapters, but the Mercator projection was most common. The large, colorful, flat projection maps provided by these private mapmakers were heavily advertised in both daily and weekly news journals. These maps usually highlighted wartime political borders, trade routes, war logistics, and international alliances, as did contemporary American news maps. But unlike the American cartographic practice of placing itself in the center of the map during World War II, British Mercator maps of the world often placed the British Isles to the left and above the center, thus highlighting the importance of the Indian and Pacific regional trade routes linking the British Commonwealth (Fig. 2.1).[63] Curiously, such maps ignored the many British colonies in the Western Hemisphere, and especially the large British Dominion of Canada. In a technical sense, most of these were not actually maps of the world but maps of the *British World*, which very often was depicted as a strictly Eastern Hemispherical domain.

28   J. P. STONE

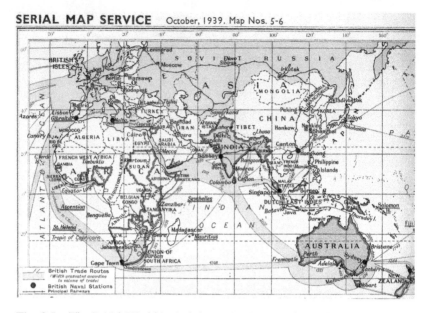

SERIAL MAP SERVICE   October, 1939. Map Nos. 5-6

Fig. 2.1   The British World in *Serial Map Service*, October 1939. British maps of the empire often centered on the Indian Ocean, not on London, and ignored the many British colonies in the Western Hemisphere. But here the importance of the Western colonies was implied by the blue naval trade routes extending off the left side of the map

Immediately after World War II, before the United States became directly involved with containing communism, Americans drifted toward isolationism. Mercator maps that formerly rallied American interventionism during the war were now retooled to convey a sense of geographic isolation from the world's postwar geopolitical hotspots. These maps often did this by placing the Americas on either the left (West) or the right (East) side of the map while locating all the other continental landforms at the opposite end. One such map, entitled "Three Worlds and their problem spots," appeared in *Newsweek* magazine in early February 1946 and conveyed a very different image of America's geopolitical position than was presented in Lend-Lease maps (Fig. 2.2).[64] Although the "Three Worlds" map labeled several hot spots that concerned the United States, the wide Pacific Ocean seemed to safeguard the area of "US Influence" from foreign instability. The exaggerated size of Greenland, Alaska, and

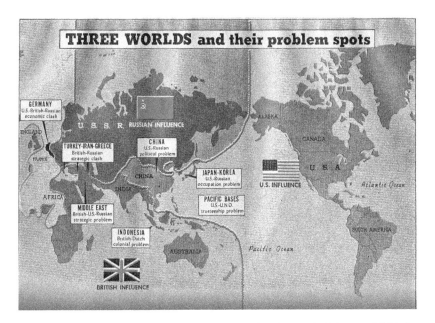

Fig. 2.2 Early Cold War Mercator projection in *Newsweek*, February 1946. In the last month before Winston Churchill's "Iron Curtain" speech, this map made sharp distinctions between areas of "British Influence" and "US Influence." These distinctions began to disappear on maps as Anglo-American anticommunist efforts increased after 1946

Canada bulked up the geostrategic appearance of the American-controlled area denoted with a prominent US flag. The selective use of national flags corresponded to the (then) three recognized "policemen" of the world— the United States, Britain, and the Soviet Union. But the placement of the British and Soviet flags near the hotspots implied that the instability was Russia's and Britain's problem even though the text labeling indicated direct US involvement. It is interesting that although French-controlled lands were denoted, no French flag was shown, delegitimizing French international prestige in an era when her imposed Nazi collaboration had only recently ended. As with the World War II–era Mercator maps, no representations of the Polar Regions were given.

The isolationist symbolism evident in the "Three Worlds" map meshed neatly with overriding contemporary American concerns of being pulled against its will into foreign disputes after World War II. As historian

C.J. Bartlett has pointed out, even before July 1945 when the Potsdam Conference briefings began arriving at the US State Department, President Franklin Delano Roosevelt, Vice President Truman, and Senator James Byrnes had all voiced fears of being drawn into the developing quarrel between Britain and the Soviet Union over the rehabilitation of Europe and the Mediterranean region.[65] And all the attention to the "Special Relationship" notwithstanding, immediately after World War II, most American foreign policy experts were weary of fostering closer Anglo-American ties for many reasons. Of utmost concern was the fear of alienating the Soviet Union and jeopardizing its reluctant, but steady, cooperation in dismantling the German war machine if the United States sided with Britain in disputes over Anglo versus Soviet oil claims in the Middle East.[66] But the United States was also generally suspicious of Britain's new Socialist Labour government that was elected in mid-1945 and its designs of colonialism. There was also a general distrust of London's policies in Palestine.[67] As will be seen in later chapters, however, once the Cold War began heating up, American Mercator news maps were once again retooled to promote interventionism via closer Anglo-American ties to thwart communism.

Zbigniew Brzezinski, former National Security Advisor (1977–1981) to President Jimmy Carter and current Professor of Foreign Policy at Johns Hopkins University, is one of the few politicians to recognize the importance maps like these have had in international relations. Brzezinski showed how maps can "foster a false sense of the true distribution of power by distorting relative size and by creating a misleading sense of geographic centrality" in the minds of civic leaders and citizens.[68] Surely the British and American Mercator news maps presented here do that. On American news maps, the United States was centered during World War II but not during the immediate postwar years, which corresponded to a return toward international isolationism. Such maps recall the earlier pseudo-isolationist Monroe Doctrine maps of the interwar period. The "Three Worlds" map, for example, placed Greenland and Iceland at the right (eastern) extreme of the frame. During World War II, however (see Chap. 3), these great landmasses were conspicuously mapped as part of the Monroe Doctrine area.

British maps, by contrast, kept the same geopolitical center—the diffuse British Empire—throughout World War II and into the postwar years which relegated the empire's power center (England) to the maps' extremities. As such, British maps more closely resembled Soviet government maps, which put Moscow at the center and placed the entire Western

Hemisphere far to the left, than American maps.[69] Both British and Soviet maps placed the Soviet Union at their center. The Soviets did so to center the capital city of Moscow; the British desired to highlight important trade routes in the Pacific Ocean. And both nations' maps split the United States, and indeed the entire Western Hemisphere, into two unequal halves at the maps' periphery. Notice that the British Overseas Air Routes map included an inset map of England centered at the top to remind map readers of the hub of British air traffic and to offset the peripheral placement of the governing region in the main map. It also included a north polar projection map inset in the lower right corner, illustrating the centrality of London in the future of air travel when transpolar flights would be available.

Although Mercator maps were the most common type of projection used in news articles, they were usually not global, but rather regional or local in scale. These larger-scale news maps allowed for a concentration of the map reader's focus on key events and places that shaped the larger context of international relations. During World War II, most American and English news journals used larger-scale Mercator maps to depict the unfolding war effort on a regular basis, which resulted in a staggering number of maps that has not been equaled in any subsequent war period. But given the vastly different national economic conditions of the British and American presses, it is no surprise that even their larger-scale maps were very dissimilar.

WORLD WAR II MAPS IN THE NEWS

World War II–era British news maps were dull and repetitive compared to their American counterparts. Their most obvious deficiency was their absence of color, which American news maps had in abundance. But British news journals compounded their poor cartographic depiction of the war effort by frequently recycling the same map several times—a practice American journals almost never employed. The journal *Spectator* was the greatest perpetrator of the British weeklies. Between July and September 1939, for example, *Spectator* reprinted the same map of Europe four times as a supplement to its war news articles.[70] This map was created by making a black and white detail copy of a section of a larger, full-color map, originally printed by George Philip and Son, showing no map icons or other visual indicators of conflict. One week later an even smaller detail of this already copied map was published as the journal described the front in greater detail—a detail of a detail of a copy. The *Spectator* map seems dull compared to a 1943 map printed in the now defunct American newspaper *PM*.[71]

Many British news maps, though, were hand-drawn by anonymous staff cartographers and lacked the professional polish of American news maps. And even these hand-drawn maps were often reprinted; some with no changes, some with progressive embellishments to illustrate changing war fronts with added details. *Spectator* and *Time and Tide* often recycled in this way, for example, with news maps of European battle fronts between France and Germany throughout World War II.[72] Given the British need for weekly maps of the war effort, coupled with the aforementioned shortages in newsprint and labor during World War II, it is not unexpected that British journals reprinted maps in this fashion. (This practice did not survive the war era, however. By the mid-1940s, with the impetus for war maps subsiding, British news journals renewed their inclination to focus on textual news, and news map usage returned to paltry prewar levels.) The widespread repetition of hand-drawn locator maps during the war aptly illustrates the level to which British news journals were unprepared to handle the huge public demand for war-related maps.

American news maps during World War II differed from their British counterparts in almost every regard. As mentioned, the most striking contrast was the American use of color which gave their news maps vitality not found in Britain. American World War II–era maps were usually broader in scope and included many powerful icons not found in British maps. These distinctions, and others, placed American maps out of the category of simple *locator maps* and into that of *thematic maps*—maps designed to make a point—whether that point is scientific or political.[73] Judith Tyner has argued that thematic maps, or what she refers to as "persuasive cartography," can be distinguished from simpler maps that "may approach total objectivity" using seven guidelines.[74] These criteria include a high degree of generalization, a lack of scale, the absence of projection labeling, simple layout, colors and symbols with high emotional impact, and a minimal use of descriptive text.[75] World War II–era American news maps certainly had all these qualities.

Contrast the appearance of British news maps of the war with two American examples from *Time* and *Newsweek*. A map entitled "Steps to Berlin," published by *Newsweek* on July 17, 1944, made many of the same cartographic statements as the "Cracks In The Fortress" map issued by *Time* one week later, although each map used different iconography and coloring.[76] Both maps described battle areas larger than those found on most British locator maps of the war. Both maps presented Europe as a fractured region but in different ways. The *Newsweek* map did it with stark, jagged red lines of military conflict that progressed from west to east denoting the advancing Russian troops while the *Time* map portrayed the region as a literal, cracked surface with underlying red wounds. Both maps used colorful arrows to denote Allied troop movements with no distinctive negative labeling of communist forces—such distinctions typically appear on later Cold War American maps. Although the *Newsweek* map caption indicated movement of the "Red Army," the advance of the Russian forces was portrayed as a positive, liberating force. Neither map denoted its projection, while both maps used simple layout and labeling. The use of coloring conveyed a strong sense of urgency to the war effort.

The two maps illustrate the colorfully expository nature of the average American news map during World War II—a character which continued into the early Cold War era. The maps' prominent size (on average, at least two columns wide) and their bold, often square form coupled with placement on the same page as the textual coverage of the war drew readers' attention. With their large size, powerful colors, and meaningful icons, American maps were attention getters. British locator maps of the war, by contrast, were less conspicuous, often placed as afterthoughts on the back page of journals and, as such, did not as heavily factor into the news readers' experience.

BRITISH WATERWAYS AND AMERICAN LANDS

Although much has been presented to show that British news maps commanded less interest and attention, they were certainly not inferior in every respect. As compared to American maps by the end of World War II, the British press could claim one distinction of superiority—their cartographic portrayal of the world's waterways. In general, British news cartographers paid more attention to detailing and labeling coastal areas, rivers, lakes, and oceans, than did the Americans. This tradition, no doubt, can be traced back to the maritime tradition of the British Empire, which still dominated English news cartography by the end of World War II despite the onset of the Air Age that had begun in the 1920s. Even when focusing on land-based and politically based issues, British daily and weekly news maps usually depicted waterways in very detailed and rich fashions that gave the otherwise dry, black and white locator maps a considerable measure of artistic quality.

As discussed earlier in this chapter, World War II–era British news maps were usually large-scale, flat projection maps of European, land-based battlefronts. British news cartographers tended to leave mapped lands unshaded and sparsely labeled to give clear, but plain, illustrations of battlefronts and associated place-names (toponyms). The darker, richer areas of these maps were usually depictions of waterways that contrasted greatly with the nearby, relatively empty landforms. Oceans, seas, and lakes were often located on the maps' periphery but were heavily embellished with hatch marking or line shading which gave waterways a more vivid appearance. News maps in the British journal *Spectator* typified this trend throughout the war. The journal's map of the northern Mediterranean coast in April 1939 accompanied an article describing the political situation in the Balkan Peninsula (Fig. 2.3). Though the article described events on land, the map's plain white landforms with sparse labeling paled in comparison to the mapmaker's portrayal of the surrounding waterways.

Fig. 2.3   British news maps usually portrayed waterways with much more artistic flair than they did the landforms. This 1939 *Spectator* map of the northern Mediterranean Sea was meant to illustrate an article on Balkan politics. But it was the mapped waterways that received the greater portion of ink

The dark, line-shaded waters richly framed the relatively banal landforms. Careful labeling of not just the Mediterranean Sea, but also the Adriatic, Black, and Aegean Seas—each label oriented to run the length of the mapped water body—drew the map reader's eye away from the national borders and landforms.[77]

Even *Time and Tide* which, it may be recalled, had some of the simplest hand-drawn locator maps of the war, employed this method on many maps. Its map of Greek Macedonia, which appeared in December 1945, portrayed the Aegean Sea with rich line shading, while the nearby important Greek–Yugoslavian border (the focus of the map) was shown as a relatively unimpressive dotted line.[78] The map was included at the request of one H.S. Paynter in an op-ed response to a previously published letter from the Director of the Greek Government Department of Information. Although Paynter hoped the map would offer a "more accurate picture of Macedonia," most of the ink on the map was dedicated to illustrating the Aegean waters.[79]

Fleet Street's preference for the maritime over the terrestrial naturally downplayed the importance of landforms, and by extension, their importance in recent political events often described in articles that accompanied news maps. The 1939 *Spectator* map's omission of the Danube River—the second longest river in Europe and the largest river in the mapped area—would have been a familiar landmark to any targeted British newsreader. Traditional reliance on the waterway's thalweg as the northern limit of "the Balkans" and the Romania–Bulgaria border merited a cartographic mention, especially since adjoining editorials relied on the same. And although the city of Belgrade was indicated on the map, its noted strategic position astride the Danube had to be imagined. There was no cartographic mention, either, of the stark and fractured mountainous terrain that dominated the topography and which had figured strongly in the nearby geopolitical commentary. Omission of the Caucasus Mountains denied British readers the reminder of that time-honored barrier between Eastern Europe and Asia Minor. Taken together, the numerous significant orthographic regions missing from the map—for example, the French Aps, the Carpathian Mountains, and the Apennines—would have effectively complemented contemporary news commentary more cognizant of the geophysical underpinnings of the geopolitical landscape.

Some British locator maps displayed rich waterway depictions not because they were hand-drawn that way by anonymous staff cartographers, but because they were black and white copies of small sections of full-color maps previously published by private London map houses. When these full-color maps were copied and reproduced in black and white, the original light blue oceans and lakes became dark, textured hatch prints or dot matrices in weekly news publications, giving the water bodies an unusually textured look not found on the original colored atlas maps. This conversion process was neatly illustrated in a black and white ad for the full-color "*Daily Telegraph* War Map No. 5" that appeared in *Spectator* in June 1941 (Fig. 2.4).[80] The originally light blue oceans appeared doubly textured by the resulting black and white dot matrix shading coupled with a wave artifact produced by the conversion process. The formerly multicolored nations, now reduced to white landmasses with black political borders, made the oceans appear more detailed by comparison.

This illustration is a skeleton reproduction. The actual map is fully coloured, referenced, and contains a wealth of detail.

Fig. 2.4   Reproducing full-color atlas maps in black and white British journals made oceans appear unusually dark and textured as in this 1941 *Spectator* ad. Coincidentally, this unintentional texturing effect continued a British cartographic tradition of artistic detailing of oceans and other bodies of water

In contrast, American news maps of war fronts usually textured landforms but not bodies of water. These were rendered very sparsely, as the examples in this chapter illustrate.

The British maritime tradition had other expressions in news maps besides textured oceans by the end of World War II, likely relating to Britain's long and rich tradition of canal and waterway development. Foreign bodies of water, often including large lakes and smaller rivers, were usually labeled prominently in maps even when these bodies were not integral to the map's purpose. This labeling, like the textured oceans, was usually seen on maps that were copied from very detailed atlas maps produced in London. In 1941, for example, a simple *Spectator* locator map, copied from an atlas made by George Philip and Son, portraying the Battle of Leningrad labeled no less than twelve rivers, two canals, and the Russian Lake Ladoga.[81] Smaller-scale maps of larger regions did not diminish this attention to waterways. Another *Spectator* map—this one a copied 1939 map of Asia from George Philip and Son—labeled twenty rivers, six seas, two oceans, one lake, one bay, and one gulf.[82]

Waterways were so integral to the British worldview that bodies of water sometimes dictated map orientations which were often unconventional, at least by American standards—that is, maps not oriented with north at the top. With respect to most European colonial powers, however, this seeming irregularity was a time-honored cartographic practice dating back to the Age of Empires. Many British maps of colonial sea islands, for example, oriented the top of the map to the direction of maritime approach to the colonial ports. In fact, the very first British map to be created on American (New World) soil was a 1677 map of New England which oriented the West at the top of the map to display the north–south running coastline along the horizontal length of the map (Fig. 2.5). J.B. Harley cited this map as an example of an early anti-Indian propaganda map.[83] However, Susan Danforth correctly noted this was also the first British "news map" created in the Americas. Entitled "A Narrative of the Troubles with the Indians of New England," the map sought to inform British news readers of the colonial struggles in the ongoing King Philip's War (1675–1678). The map's unconventional westerly orientation related a maritime approach to Cape Cod and the "Merimack" [sic] River.[84] And as with the previous example, this map portrayed the colonial waterways with rich texture.

The onset of World War II revitalized the importance of waterways on British news maps as viable pathways of warfare. Of course for the British, the English Channel was the most immediately important wartime waterway.

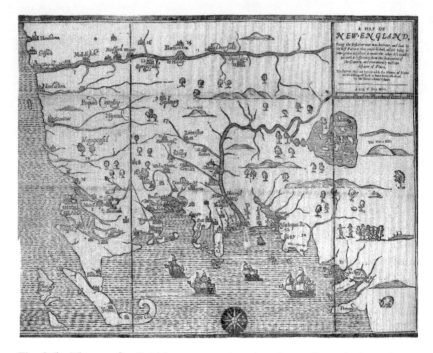

Fig. 2.5 The very first British map created on American soil was, in fact, a "news map" oriented with the West at the top of the map. This 1677 map of New England updated readers on the perils of King Philip's War, and portrayed a mariner's approach to Cape Cod. The map's compass rose at bottom center indicated true north with a fleur-de-lis in the three o'clock position

Several war-era maps of the English Channel region were published, with the length of the channel running horizontally, and north lying on the right side of the map. For example, the *Serial Map Service* printed a war map in October of 1941 entitled "Channel Coast Offensive," which oriented the channel to run the length of the map from left to right, thereby offsetting the normal North Pole orientation by a considerable degree.[85] The resulting map had no indication of true north and made England appear to be directly north of France. Nautical distances from England to all major Western European mainland ports were measured and charted. However, it is interesting to note that the map did not contain any political boundaries. Instead, England and all other depicted Western European nations were inked a homogenous yellow. Where were the Nazis? Where were the land-based battlefronts? No such labels were given. Only the unnamed military resource icons decorating the coastal areas hinted at a Nazi menace. But every major European river was labeled, as were numerous capes, bays, and other coastal geographic features. This had the effect of prioritizing the waterways, not the warring nations and their armies. Though such apolitical maps were in the minority during the war, and nonexistent in the contemporary American press, the appearance of this map speaks to a general British cartographic preference of waterways over political borders. This trend will be discussed in greater detail in the next chapter.

British ads, too, during the war occasionally oriented maps away from true north to favor maritime views. One of the more regular advertisers in this regard was the Canadian Pacific Shipping Lines which ran cartographic ads promoting British travel to Canada and the Great Lakes region before and during the war (Fig. 2.6). The ad maps were oriented with north on the left side of the map, which promoted a mariner's view from the Canadian coast looking outward across the Atlantic Ocean to England. The familiar richly textured ocean surface was dominated by a cruise ship following a dotted line from east to west (i.e., from top to bottom on the map) and approaching the reader. The ad text described the mariner's view from on board the ship as "standing on the deck of a Canadian Pacific liner" and listed the destinations passengers could encounter as they moved from east to west from the Atlantic Ocean, up the St. Lawrence Seaway, and ultimately to the Pacific Coast.[86]

The most obvious peculiarity of this particular cartographic ad campaign is that it abandoned the Age of Exploration "captain's view" directional orientation for what might be called the "destination view," that is, a map oriented with the imagined destination of the voyage situated at the bottom. Readers may have imagined they were "standing on the deck" as they steamed westward, but their glimpse of Canada was from a bird's eye perspective looking eastward across the North Atlantic to a misleadingly proximal British Isles. Such a perspective also departed from a more recent British trend of promoting travel to, and trade with, Commonwealth destinations with cartographic renderings that dwelled on amenities found at destination sites. Instead, it would fall to the imaginations of perspective Canadian Pacific holiday wayfarers to envision the arrival attractions mentioned in the ad text—the grand cities of eastern Canada and northeastern United States, Niagara Falls, the World's Fair, and all points west of the St. Lawrence River Valley.

Fig. 2.6 British ad maps occasionally used projections which favored coastal layouts over northern orientations. Here a 1939 ad for Canadian Pacific Shipping Lines put true north to the left of the map to foster a sense of sea travel to the Canadian coast

. . . standing on the deck of a Canadian Pacific liner, right in the middle of the Atlantic Ocean on the *biggest* holiday of your life ; outward bound for Canada and the United States by the short sea route. Everything's grand about this holiday ; the Atlantic crossing, the cruise up the smooth St. Lawrence Seaway ; Quebec and Ottawa, Niagara Falls, New York and the World's Fair. And if you have time, the Prairies, the Rockies and the Pacific coast.

23 escorted holiday tours to Canada and the United States. From 3 to 7 weeks. All-in fares from £48.

CANADA BY *39% Less Ocean*

Canadian Pacific

Apply your local agent or Canadian Pacific, Trafalgar Square W.C.2 103 Leadenhall Street, E.C.3, and at principal cities

A more subtle peculiarity is the fact that despite the violent outbreak of World War II only a few months after the commencement of the decade-long ad campaign, and despite the long and grueling cataclysm that ensued, Canadian Pacific preferred to recycle its optimistic prewar cartographic vision in ads throughout the war. Ireland's neutrality in the war was never distinguished as the British Isles remained cartographically united. The visible parts—southern England, Wales, and most of Ireland—were always presented as a borderless archipelago cast in Albion white.

The "hand" of Ireland's southwestern coast seemed to be waving at the tourist ship. And offers of agreeable voyages from Southampton, England, to Quebec, Canada (and back again) were immune to the developing realities of the deadly six-year-long Battle of the North Atlantic. No Nazi periscopes or Allied "hunter killer" patrols were ever seen parting the overly textured cartographic seas. Never mind the swaths of sea mines that soon blanketed the North Sea and the English Channel as those inconveniences lay conveniently outside the map's scope. But then again it would not do to alarm potential wartime customers. And as the war raged, Canadian Pacific's now Panglossian offer probably came to complement a growing British (and larger European) desire to escape the hellish conflict albeit not as a contracted "round trip."

NOTES

1. See Louis Heren's essay "The Postwar Press in Britain" in the introduction of Dennis Griffith's (ed) *The Encyclopedia of the British Press, 1422–1992* (New York: St. Martin's Press, 1992), 60.
2. F.S. Northedge and Audrey Wells, *Britain and Soviet Communism: Impact of a Revolution* (London: Macmillan, 1982), 105.
3. G.D.N. Worswik and P.H. Ady, *The British Economy, 1945–1950* (Oxford: Clarendon Press, 1952), 65.
4. Heren, 57, and see Aled Jones' essay "The British Press, 1919–1945," 53; both in Griffith.
5. James Shand, "English Printing—I" in *Time and Tide*, v.28, n.30 (August 9, 1947): 858.
6. Heren, 57.
7. Ibid.
8. Ibid.
9. Ibid.
10. Jones, 55.
11. Ibid., 53.
12. Shand, 858.
13. Mark Monmonier, "The Rise of Map Use by Elite Newspapers in England, Canada, and the United States," in *Imago Mundi*, v. 38 (1986): 56.
14. James Shand, "English Printing – III" in *Time and Tide*, v. 28, n. 32 (August 23, 1947): 906.
15. Ibid.
16. Mark Monmonier, *Maps with the News: The Development of American Journalistic Cartography* (Chicago: University of Chicago Press, 1989), xiii.

17. Shand, brackets added, 906.
18. Ibid., brackets added.
19. Shand, 906. Shand's article noted that "the two principle large circulation illustrated weeklies in this country are both printed indifferently by rotary photogravure, one on presses imported from prewar Germany and the other by a licensed process from America."
20. Ibid.
21. Denis Wood, *The Power of Maps* (New York and London: The Guilford Press, 1992), 39–40.
22. Heren, 56.
23. Gilbert C. Fite and Jim E. Reese, *An Economic History of the United States* (Boston: Houghton Mifflin, 1973), 555.
24. Ibid., 551.
25. Ibid., 550.
26. Ibid., 554–555.
27. All US circulation stats were taken from the respective year volumes of *N.W. Ayer and Son's Directory of Periodicals* annual series printed in Philadelphia.
28. William Ewert Berry Camrose (First Viscount). *British Newspapers and Their Controllers* (London: Cassell Press, 1950), and British Audit Bureau of Circulations (ABC), v.8. Camrose's circulation summaries are assumed to be six-month totals since his stats correspond to six-month totals from corresponding Audit Bureau of Circulation records.
29. Ibid., 145–146.
30. Camrose, 147 and ABC, v.8.
31. Camrose, 148 and ABC, v.8.
32. Bernard C. Cohen, *The Press and Foreign Policy* (Princeton: Princeton University Press, 1963), 108.
33. Louis Liebovich, *The Press and the Origins of the Cold War, 1944–1947* (New York: Praeger, 1988), 4.
34. Matthew Fox, *Religion USA: Religion and Culture by way of Time Magazine* (Dubuque, IA: Listening Press, 1971), 15–17.
35. Monmonier, 63.
36. See David Butler and Gareth Butler's *British Political Facts, 1900–1985* (New York: St. Martin's Press, 1986), 498–499; and Camrose, 145–152.
37. Ibid.
38. Monmonier, 62–63.
39. Heren, 57.
40. Ibid.
41. Susan Schulten, "Richard Edes Harrison and the Challenge to American Cartography," in *Imago Mundi*, v. 50 (1998): 174.
42. Ibid.

43. Walter Ristow, "Journalistic Cartography" in *Surveying and Mapping*, v.17 n.4 (October 1957): 369.
44. Author's interview with Paul Pugliese, August, 2007.
45. Pugliese interview.
46. Pugliese, for example, did contract atlas work for the State of Arizona and Harcourt Brace and World. He noted that his boss at *Time*, Robert Chapin, Jr., contracted with the US Army and many corporations. Richard Edes Harrison, noted mapmaker from *Fortune*, did contract work for the US Army during World War II, and he made numerous private atlases and maps. See Schulten, 174–187.
47. Whenever possible, map examples from World War II and early Cold War news journals will be used even though better quality examples are available in scholarly publications. This is done to illustrate the prevalence of maps in news publications.
48. John Noble Wilford, *The Mapmakers: The Story of the Great Pioneers in Cartography – from Antiquity to the Space Age* (New York: Alfred A. Knopf, 2000), 87–90. The map in Fig. 2.3 was taken from (no author) "History Makes New Maps" in *Life*, v.13, n.5 (Aug. 03, 1942): 61.
49. Quoted from Schulten, 175. See also Wilford, 90.
50. See Alan K. Henrikson's essay entitled "Mental Maps" in *Explaining the History of American Foreign Relations* (Cambridge and New York: Cambridge University Press, 1991), 186.
51. Ross Hoffman, "Europe and the Atlantic Community" in *Thought*, v.20 (1945): 25.
52. See *U.S. News and World Report* v.11 n.17 (Oct. 24, 1941): 12–13 and *Life* v.14 n.13 (Mar. 29, 1943): 13.
53. J.B. Harley, *The New Nature of Maps: Essays in the History of Cartography* (Baltimore and London: The Johns Hopkins Press, 2001), 66.
54. Ibid., 73.
55. See map entitled "Asia" in *Spectator*, v.163, n.5801 (Sept. 9, 1939): 340.
56. Patricia Gilmartin, "The Design of Journalistic Maps/Purposes, Parameters and Prospects" in *Cartographica*, v. 22, n.4 (1985): 1–3.
57. Ibid., 2.
58. See *Economist* ad in *Serial Map Service*, v.3, n.2 (November 1941): 135.
59. See "The Monthly Record," the proceedings of the Royal Geographical Society, in *The Geographic Journal*, v.90, n.4 (April, 1940): 324.
60. See ad for *Horrabin's Atlas History of the Second Great War, Vol. II* in *Spectator*, v.165, n.5858 (Oct. 10, 1940): 343.
61. See ad for George Philip and Son, Ltd. in *New Statesman and Nation*, v.29, n.745 (Jun. 6, 1945): 360.
62. See ad for *Daily Telegraph's* War Map No. 5 in *Spectator*, v.165, n.5 (Aug. 16, 1940): 173.

63. See map entitled "British Trade Routes" in *Serial Map Service*, v.1 n.2 (October 1939): map 5–6.
64. See map entitled "Three Worlds" in *Newsweek*, v.27 n.5 (Feb. 4, 1946): 35.
65. C.J. Bartlett, *British Foreign Policy in the 20th Century* (New York: St. Martin's Press, 1989), 68.
66. Robert M. Hathaway, *Great Britain and the United States: Special Relations Since WWII* (Boston: Twayne Publishers, 1990), 12–13.
67. Ibid.
68. Zbigniew Brzezinski, *Game Plan: A Geostrategic Framework for the Conduct of the U.S.-Soviet Contest* (Boston: Atlantic Monthly Press, 1986), 6.
69. The "Global View from Moscow" map was taken from Brzezinski, 7. The BOAC map was taken from *Serial Map Service*, v.7 n.6 (Mar. 6, 1946): 63–64.
70. See *Spectator*, v.163 n.5796 (Jul. 28, 1939): 164; v.163 n.5799 (Aug. 18, 1939): iii; v.163 n.5800 (Aug. 25, 1939): 284; v.163 n.5801 (Sept. 1, 1939): 323.
71. Ristow, 72.
72. *Spectator* maps: v.163 n.5806 (Oct. 6, 1939): 463; v.163 n.5807 (Oct. 13, 1939): 495. *Time and Tide* maps: v.26 n.9 (Mar. 3, 1945): 180; v.26 n.10 (Mar. 10, 1945): 200.
73. Gilmartin, 1–3.
74. Judith A. Tyner, "Persuasive Cartography" in *Journal of Cartography*, vol. 81 (1982): 140–144.
75. Ibid.
76. See *Newsweek*, v.24 n.3 (Jul. 17, 1944): 19, and *Time*, v.44 n.4 (Jul. 24, 1944): 23.
77. See *Spectator*, v.162 n.5781 (Apr. 14, 1939): 623.
78. See *Time and Tide*, v.26 n.48 (Dec. 1, 1945): 1006.
79. Ibid.
80. See ad for "*Daily Telegraph* War Map No.5" in *Spectator*, v.166 n.5894 (Jun. 13, 1941): 635.
81. See *Spectator*, v.167 n.5907 (Sept. 12, 1941): 253.
82. See *Spectator*, v.163 n.5801 (Sept. 1, 1939): 340.
83. Harley, 185–187.
84. Reprinted from Susan Danforth's exhibit catalog: *Encountering the New World* (Providence, RI: The John Carter Brown Library, 1991), 40.
85. *Serial Map Service*, v.2 n.2 (October, 1941): map 105.
86. See ad for Canadian Pacific Lines in *Spectator*, v.162, n.5 (Apr. 14, 1939): 78.

CHAPTER 3

Air Age Maps, the Shrinking Globe, and Anglo-American Relations

The Air Age began in the 1920s, reached maturity during World War II, and profoundly changed how Britain and the United States portrayed the world on maps during the Cold War. The ability to envision, and more importantly to map, the spherical earth from high altitudes compelled foreign policymakers, cartographers, and advertisers to depart from using Mercator projections that framed the earth as a flat plane with far-flung landmasses. One of the most prevalent trends in British, and especially American, news journal cartography in the early Cold War era was the use of map projections that illustrated the sphericity of the earth and the close proximity of landmasses in the Northern Hemisphere. This new world-view has assumed many names in modern scholarship. Denis Cosgrove called it the "Apollonian View," which links the modern Air Age conception of a round globe to a cartographic tradition dating back to classical Greece.[1] Richard Edes Harrison called his own innovative maps "perspective maps" since they sought to illustrate the world from the high altitudes. But the most common name for the new perspective in the Air Age was the "airman's view," as opposed to the "mariner's view" promoted by Mercator maps. Although many different types of map projections can achieve this effect, British and American news maps relied on a few standbys that became popular during the height of the Air Age in World War II and remained common throughout the Cold War period.

© The Author(s) 2019   45
J. P. Stone, *British and American News Maps in the Early Cold War Period, 1945–1955*, Palgrave Studies in the History of the Media, https://doi.org/10.1007/978-3-030-15468-4_3

Most Air Age projections were not new—indeed many of them were as old as Mercator himself—but they were retooled for World War II and Cold War geopolitical concerns. Higher latitudinal regions formerly exaggerated or ignored by Mercator maps garnered new interest beginning just before World War II. New air access to the formerly isolated and cartographically neglected Polar Regions, for example, made these areas hot topics for Air Age politicians and cartographers. And although Britain and the United States were the closest of Cold War allies, they often avowed opposing views of these newly mapped regions.

MAPPING THE GLOBE IN THE AIR AGE

As discussed in the previous chapter, the Mercator projection was a product of the maritime Age of Exploration and European colonization. And as long as ships were the dominant vessels of world trade and travel, these flat projection maps were a most helpful way to see the world. But although Mercator maps aptly described certain elements of the world, they did not relate the roundness of the globe, nor could they offer any useful depictions of the Polar Regions. The Air Age simultaneously signified an end to the dominance of the mariner's or navigator's worldview and the birth of the "airman's view," as World War II–era cartographers and politicians recast world geopolitics in light of Air Age technological advances. The ensuing discussion explores British and American maps that were designed to illustrate the sphericity of the globe and foster the perception of a shrinking planet resulting from the advent of powered flight.

Any map that seeks to depict the round surface of the globe on a flat plane is termed an *azimuthal* map in the United States, or a *zenithal* map in Britain. Azimuthal maps are named after the technique of projecting a grid originating on the surface of a globe onto a flat map surface by drawing a series of radii, or azimuths, from a single arbitrary point through the globe surface and onto the map. Azimuthal maps differ fundamentally from Mercator maps which seek to project the globe onto a cylinder that is tangent to the equator. The best way to imagine the complex variables inherent in the creation of azimuthal map projections is to imagine the earth as a hollow sphere defined by a wire frame representing the surface grid of latitude and longitude lines. Now imagine a light bulb that can be placed anywhere in or around the wireframe globe, and a blank screen (a plane) that can also be placed anywhere to catch the shadow cast by the globe. One can imagine an infinite number of possible shadow patterns

POLAR PROJECTIONS

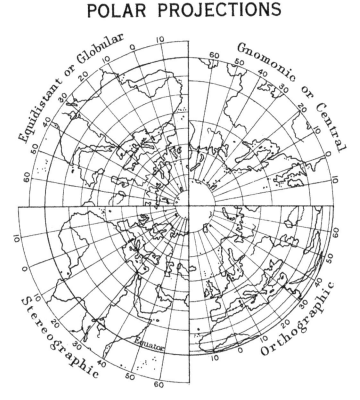

Fig. 3.1 The four most common types of azimuthal polar projections as illustrated in John Bartholomew's *Advanced Atlas of Modern Geography* in 1950

cast onto the plane given the infinite possible positions of the plane and the light source relative to each other and the earth. Thus, there are an infinite number of possible azimuthal map projections.[2]

Most azimuthal projections fall into four general categories as determined by the useful qualities of each (Fig. 3.1). *Equidistant* (or *globular*) projections portray the planet as it would appear if a plane were placed tangential to a point on the globe where it would catch the shadows of a light source placed at a point outside the surface of the planet on the opposite side. This method preserves distances from the center of the map and correctly depicts all azimuths (or directions) from the center. But all land shapes and areas are distorted away from the tangential point. The United Nations employs such a projection as its international symbol. *Gnomonic* (or *central*) projections, with their light source at the center of the planet, map the earth's surface onto a plane that is tangential to a selected point on the globe. This method preserves all meridians (longitude and latitude lines) as straight lines, but less than one hemisphere may be portrayed on any such map, and map distortions increase exponentially away from the tangential plane. *Orthographic* projections aspire to portray the planet as it would appear from space. The light source is placed infinitely far away, which allows only one hemisphere to be portrayed, and land shapes and areas are distorted exponentially away from the center. Finally, *stereographic* projections place the light source on the surface of the opposite side of the globe being mapped, and the resulting shadows are cast onto a plane tangential to the other side. While neither distances nor landform areas are preserved, angles at which landform curves meet are preserved. These azimuthal projections were developed by Greek mathematicians between the fifth and second centuries B.C. and had been casually referenced only occasionally in the last two centuries. They found new popularity in the Air Age due to their ability to relate a round globe.[3]

Norman Thrower, the acknowledged American doyen of twentieth-century cartographic history, would be the first to admit that his standardization of azimuthal projections into three categories (gnomic, stereographic, and orthographic) only hints at the wide array of cartographic experimentation commensurate with the Air Age. At least two deterministic variables account for this. First, generally speaking, there are no hard and fast rules for designing map projections. This reality tends to complicate any attempt to form a comprehensive categorization of them, and any such endeavor will by necessity produce inconvenient hybrids. Thrower's own 1972 study entitled *Maps and Man* elucidated this point. (His survey of twenty-three common map projections classified over a third of them as "miscellaneous.") Second, and more specifically, while his summary of azimuthal projection types serves as a general heuristic, it nevertheless fails to prepare one for the appearance of the many wildly innovative polar projections (and other projections) inspired by the Air Age. As we will see, although most Air Age azimuthal projections did comport to Thrower's three archetypes, many took stranger forms including that of flower petals, outstretched lobes, and twisted geometries.[4]

Until the 1940s, American cartographers had generally ignored azimuthal projections and embraced the Mercator projection, despite its many inherent distortions, as the most useful way to view the world.

Cartographic historian Susan Schulten has argued that American culture, unlike its European counterpart, was not generally familiar with the concept of differing map projections until the Air Age and World War II yanked map readers from their flat maps to their globes. American atlases had dwelled on the Mercator projection until the early 1920s when a few progressive cartographers began designing projections that highlighted the sphericity of the earth. Yet German atlases dating back to the early 1880s regularly contained numerous and varied map projections.[5] It was the American invention of powered flight in 1903, and the rapidly developing Air Age which followed, that ultimately set the stage for a generation of American cartographers to turn away from Mercator maps and design new, innovative map projections portraying an "Airman's view" of the world.

Susan Schulten has traced this American "revolution in cartography" back to J. Paul Goode's 1923 *Goode's Atlas* which rejected the Mercator projection as "damaging to the nation's understanding of geography."[6] And American dissatisfaction with the Mercator projection was in its nascence well before this, and it developed, ironically, as a consequence of maritime travel, not the fledgling Air Age. In the first decade of the nineteenth century, long before air travel was a public enterprise, steamships were still the dominant mode of global travel. Though criticisms of the Mercator projection were rare in this era, they nevertheless appeared sporadically in the American press. In March 1904, for example, the *Chicago Tribune* stated in its "Notes from Manywhere" travel trivia section that "It is a common impression, gained from maps of the Mercator projection, that it is much shorter from San Francisco to Manila by way of Honolulu, but as a matter fact it is several hundred miles shorter by way of Alaska."[7] As early as mid-1910, federal complaints were being lodged by the US Naval Department and various "mercantile marine associations" regarding Mercator maps produced by the US Coast and Geodetic Survey. The projection's oversizing of higher latitudinal landmasses and distances caused confusion when combined with sea charts constructed on polyconic projections, the latter preferred for their more accurate portrayal of the Polar Regions. The *Washington Post* announced "Charts Declared Useless." While naval officers recommended rejecting this "dual system" altogether, no alternative projections were recommended.[8]

Two years later the RMS *Titanic* disaster, and the accompanying public rush to chart its doomed course across the North Atlantic on Mercator

maps, again revealed the flat projection's severe distortions in higher latitudes.[9] The *Washington Post* stated:

> Many a reader of The Post, who has been engrossed in the Titanic disaster
> news and has delved into maps showing the routes of the various steamships
> crossing the North Atlantic, has been struck by the fact that, according to
> such maps, the northern 'lanes,' as they are termed...appear on the maps as
> curving far out of the straightest and nearest path from Europe to America;
> in short, to the eye, these northern lines appear much longer...It is due,
> according to the hydrographic office of the Navy Department, to the fact
> that the maps are made under the Mercator projection.

A representative of the US Navy expounded on the Mercator map
distortions:

> Now just look at this [Mercator] map of the northern portion of the globe.
> You will observe that the meridians of longitude appear in the northern part
> of Greenland as being as far apart as they are at the equator. As a fact, such
> is not the case: they are less than a dozen miles apart; you will see that
> Greenland looks almost as big as Africa, but the distances between those
> meridians up there are only about a fifth of what they are between the same
> meridians at the equator...The maps are stretched out in their northern por-
> tion like India rubber...and in order to accommodate the real travelled lines
> of the boats they have to make a great bend in the lines, when, as a fact,
> there isn't any bend at all.

The article's anonymous author then described how a doubting reader
could reveal the Mercator map's distortions firsthand and, thus, better
comprehend the true course of the *Titanic*:

> To one who has never tried the experiment, it does seem odd that this
> curved line is shorter than the straight line. But all that is necessary to
> understand it is a good-sized globe and a piece of cord. One may then dem-
> onstrate easily how the distance between well-known points in the northern
> parts of Europe and America, which appear in charts and newspaper repro-
> ductions, to be so great, are, by reason of the shrinking in the globe toward
> the pole, reduced to distances far shorter...It was this long curved line
> route, which was, in fact, the shorter, that lured the Titanic into the region
> of icebergs—and death.[10]

As late as 1920, recollection of the *Titanic* disaster was still being used to emphasize the dangers of ice flows made even more treacherous by distortions of the Mercator projection in higher latitudes. In May of that year, the *Boston Globe* stated that "If one looks at an ordinary map, one is surprised to find that Greenland is considerably bigger than South America, which illustrates the distortion of the Mercator projection."[11]

These comments made in the early twentieth century are reminiscent of arguments made against the Mercator projection by later Air Age geographers and cartographers. Yet these criticisms were not inspired by a new "Airman's View" of the world. They were, instead, earlier consequences of an increase in *maritime* excursions into the northern latitudes by military and commercial agencies. This raises important questions about heretofore academic linkages made between the Air Age and the American abandonment of the Mercator projection. Cartographic historians have appropriately asserted that the Air Age "revolution in American cartography" was inspired by the new ability to see the earth from high altitudes as a consequence of powered flight. This causal relationship is evident in the editorial comments of virtually all atlases and academic papers published by geographers of the Air Age. However, one wonders in light of the aforementioned maritime examples if the Air Age was the *only* causal factor in the abandonment of the Mercator projection. Did other federal or private agencies voice dissatisfaction with flat projection maps before the early 1920s? If so, were any alternative projections proposed that better described the higher latitudes? Were any projections proposed that accommodated the sphericity of the earth? What parallels and what contrasts exist between the motivations of aviation-related versus non-aviation-related calls for map reform? At once evident is the similarity between the maritime phrase "shrinking in the globe toward the pole" quoted earlier and the later Air Age catch phrase "the shrinking globe." The former references a maritime concern over the inaccuracies of flat cartography in the higher latitudes, while the latter describes a change in travel times and the perception of distance brought on by powered flight. And at least one example has been found of transcontinental *railroad* travel in higher latitudes prompting a correction in Mercator distortions. Public confusion over the usefulness of a proposed Canadian rail line connecting Winnipeg, Manitoba, to Liverpool, Nova Scotia, spurred the *Los Angeles Tribune* in June 1909 to proclaim:

Most persons will think this a wild sort of scheme. What's the use? The question may easily be answered by looking at a large globe. The ordinary maps on the Mercator projection do not disclose the real truth of the situation. From York Factory, on Hudson Bay, to Liverpool is a shorter line than from New York to the same point.[12]

By the early 1920s, it was largely the advent of powered flight that dominated calls for a reform in American cartography to abandon the Mercator projection in favor of maps that more accurately portrayed the roundness of the globe and specifically depicted the Polar Regions in a more realistic manner. Some replacements for the Mercator projection were actually garnered from older innovations. In 1922 the National Geographic Society adopted the Van der Grinten projection, created in 1898, as the framework for its world maps. The newly employed projection reclaimed the appeal of a spherical earth while correcting many of the spatial distortions inherent in the Mercator projection.[13] The Society would rely on this projection until 1988 when, due to Cold War era concerns over the projection's enlargement of northern latitudinal landmasses—particularly the Soviet Union—it was replaced with the Robinson projection for its more accurate portrayal of landform size.[14]

However, most American Air Age projections were truly innovative solutions to new problems raised by the innovation of flight. Atlases produced by J. Paul Goode beginning in 1923 featured several new projections that rejected the "monstrosity of Mercator." His most innovative and influential creation was the "homolosine" projection, so named for its combining of Mollweide's homolographic equal area projection (created in 1805) and the sinusoidal projection (created in 1570). This was, in theory, an amalgamation of the best of two world projections. Or as Goode stated, he used "the sinusoidal up to the latitude of equal scale, 40° 44' 11.8", and finish[ed] out the polar cusps on the lobes with the homolographic projection." The combination of the two projections more accurately portrayed the true shapes and comparative areas of the continents, preserved true distances up to the 40th parallel, and kept all latitudinal lines parallel with the equator.[15] Moreover, the homolosine projection was the first to remove the United States from the center of world maps—a break from American cartographic tradition dating back over seventy years.[16] Perhaps the most groundbreaking aspect of the homolosine projection was its division of the world into separate "lobes" that could be varied in number and "interrupted" at different intervals to highlight various geographic features such

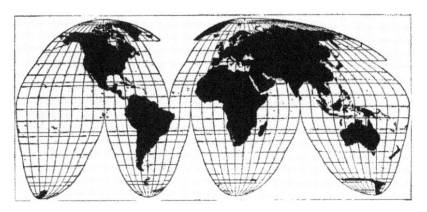

Fig. 3.2 Goode's "homolosine" projection innovatively combined a sinusoidal projection, which described the lower latitudes, and a homolographic projection, which portrayed higher latitudes

as great landmasses and oceans (Fig. **3.2**). Goode argued that his new projection was superior to Mercator maps for portraying "all areal distribution of whatever data," and that "hereafter the use of Mercator's projection for such purposes, in the interests of rational education, should be discontinued."[17] His contention was validated in 1927 when the US Department of Commerce replaced their Mercator maps with sinusoidal maps featuring "three strange looking lobes" inspired by the homolosine projection. Designed by the US Bureau of Foreign Trade and the US Coast and Geodetic Survey, the new world maps responded to a perceived Air Age "growth of American interest in world commerce and the closer contact between the United States and foreign nations." The new projection debuted in the federal government's *Commerce Yearbook* the following year.[18]

The onset of World War II compelled the federal government to enlist the assistance of many notable American cartographers to design maps to aid the war effort. After American entry into the war in late 1941, one of the first such recruited cartographers was Dr. Erwin Raisz, then Lecturer in Cartography and head curator of Maps at Harvard's Institute of Geographical Exploration. Tapped by the director of the Office of Strategic Services (OSS), Colonel "Wild Bill" Donovan, Raisz was contracted to help the US Army "see and measure this new air age world in terms of the medium through which they work." The medium, of course, was maps.

The Hungarian-born Raisz already had a reputation for producing innovative maps since the publication of his *General Cartography* textbook in 1938, which was, by late 1942, the only college cartography textbook printed in English. No doubt his innovative style was influenced by his unconventional background. His doctorate was actually in geology—a discipline which inspired his creation of large, hand-drawn topographic maps of the United States and China. In Raisz's office rested the largest relief model of the United States.[19] As was true of many iconoclastic Air Age cartographers, mapmaking was not his first career. Originally a New England artist, he graduated from the Massachusetts School of Art before specializing in mapmaking. By the early 1940s he was a regular illustration contributor to the *Christian Science Monitor* while he also taught advertising design and technical drawing at New York's College of New Rochelle.[20] Raisz's cartographic work with the armed services was extensive. While designing maps for the government, he taught newly recruited armed services students how to read topographic maps at adult education centers in Boston, Cambridge, and at Northeastern University.[21]

Beginning in the late 1930s, Raisz gained a reputation for breaking from the American Mercator tradition by designing maps with unconventional projections. As pre–World War II tensions mounted, his polar projection maps, most of which centered on the North Pole, stressed the Air Age closeness of the United States to Moscow, Tokyo, and Northern Europe. His seminal work during the war, the 1944 *Atlas of Geography*, utilized unorthodox map projections to promote war mobilization and national patriotism. The book's introduction began with a description of how the first nonstop flight from Moscow to America had changed the world from a cylinder to a sphere on maps. An azimuthal map centered on Japan displayed concentric circles, centered on Tokyo, emphasizing the air strike range of the Axis power, while an accompanying narrative described the nation's use of "an iron hand in ruling and exploiting the native populations." The outer ring ominously overlapped the American soil in Alaska. A large, two-page north polar projection map highlighted the vast size, industrial might, and mobility of the Soviet Union. The most innovative projection in Raisz's atlas was his new "armadillo" projection which, like azimuthal maps, portrayed the roundness of the earth. But unlike azimuthal maps which can display, at most, half the globe, the armadillo projection portrayed almost the complete earth on a torus (Fig. 3.3).[22]

Probably the most original Air Age projection to appear during World War II was a creation of an American economist. Irving Fisher, a professor

Fig. 3.3   The "armadillo" projection developed by Erwin Raisz was one of the many Air Age projections featured in his 1944 *Atlas of Geography*

emeritus of economics at Yale University, designed a map in 1943, based on an icosahedral projection—a flat map projection that can be manipulated to form a twenty-sided polygon (Fig. 3.4).[23] The originality of this projection was not actually in its design. Fisher admitted that the idea of an icosahedron projection dated back at least to British cartographer William Garnett in 1851. Nor was his choice to portray the globe on a twenty-sided polygon an innovation. German artist Albrecht Dürer described the utility of such an object in 1838. Rather, what set Fisher's projection apart was its inclusion in a kit that, once assembled, could transform the flat map into a polygonal spheroid with the pull of a string. The result was a map that, as Fisher explained, would serve as a more realistic replacement for Mercator maps in schools and for laymen in general. Of course, the icosahedron projection was not without its own distortions. When laid flat, the map contained eleven large interruptions which Fisher tried to minimize by placing them "at the least inconvenient points." When in polygonal form, the map's gnomonic projection—whereby all great circles are portrayed as

Fig. 3.4   An icosahedral projection developed by economist Irving Fisher in 1943 typified many Air Age projections which sought to relate the roundness of the globe. Fisher marketed the projection as a map that could be assembled into a polyhedral globe, as seen here on display at the Museum of Modern Art in New York City

straight lines—was "somewhat spoiled when passing from one face…to another." And egregious area distortions occurred at the polygonal vertices and at the poles (which were stretched to infinity due to their placement in the middle of polygonal faces).[24] Ever the entrepreneur, Fisher promoted his map kit in newspapers and academic journals with large diagrams that could be cut out or traced onto hard paper for ready construction. A large working model of his kit was prominently displayed in a larger exhibit of maps and projections at New York's Museum of Modern Art in late 1943. Though the "Fisher projection" as it was called never supplanted the Mercator map in American schools and minds, it serves as a curious example of Air Age American society seeking to better grasp the newly discovered roundness of the globe.[25]

It was not until World War II that American news cartographers came to use Air Age projections with any regularity, and they did this much more frequently than did their British counterparts. The Air Age prompted a stark reevaluation of international relations. Global imagery, which includes globes and global maps, was the best medium to visualize the new world order brought on by powered flight. It was also an effective way to suggest the proximity of a dangerous enemy—or enemies, notably communists. Political analyst Walter Lippmann observed in 1944 that "When we put away the maps of the age of sailing vessels and use a globe for our geography, we realize that to the heart of China the direct routes from the United States by air are over Russian territory."[26] According to historian Joseph J. Corn, the federal government agreed. Shortly after American intervention in the war, the Office of Education and the Civil Aeronautics Administration, with academic consultation by the Aviator Education Research Group (AERG), began publishing a series of twenty texts designed to educate Americans about the global geopolitical implications of the war in the new Air Age. From 1942 to 1945, the group turned out atlases and textbooks highlighting the roundness of the earth with maps that departed from Mercator's flat projection including *Human Geography for the Air Age* (1942) by George T. Renner, and *Science of Pre-Flight Aeronautics for High Schools* (1942) compiled by the AERG.[27] This turning away from Mercator's "squaring" of the globe and toward global map projections had begun prior to World War II, though, in American news journals.

Susan Schulten has linked the rise of Air Age maps to famed American cartographer Richard Edes Harrison who began making maps for *Fortune* in 1935. Harrison, who was trained not in cartography but in interior design and architecture, grew up during the Air Age and was dissatisfied with the Mercator projection as a framework for viewing the world.[28] Influenced heavily by Raisz and other early Air Age cartographers, not only he disliked the distortions inherent in Mercator maps, but he also criticized the cartography profession for becoming too academic and out of touch with the average man who, understandably, interpreted the Mercator view of the world as reality.[29] Harrison preferred visualizing the world literally as one would see it from high altitude or space—as a sphere, not as a flat map—in what have come to be called "perspective" maps.[30] Freed from the rigidity of map conventions, he often presented global landmasses from unusual orientations, hardly relying upon the standard North Pole orientation used in Mercator maps. His emphasis was on landforms and their spatial relationships as viewed from any arbitrary point above the earth's surface. During World War II, Harrison reexamined the vulnerability of the United States which had, until then, held to the assertion that the nation was safely located across wide ocean barriers. For example, Harrison's "Three Approaches to the United States" map that appeared in *Fortune* in September 1940 illustrated what foreign invaders from Berlin, Tokyo, and South America would see, respectively, as they neared the United States from the air (Fig. 3.5).[31] Such perspective maps highlighted geostrategic weaknesses in American defenses as they described a possible Nazi "pincers movement extending from Newfoundland down the New England coast."[32]

Perspective maps represented a new direction in American cartography that was at once very popular with the average news reader and highly criticized in traditional American cartography circles. Harrison probably worried little that a staff cartographer at the National Geographic Society

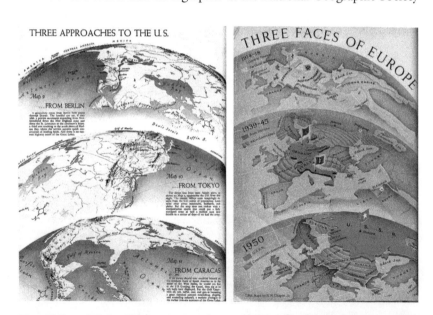

Figs. 3.5 and 3.6   Air Age perspective maps from the World War II era influenced later Cold War–era news maps in the American press. Richard Edes Harrison's perspective map entitled "Three Approaches to the U.S." that appeared in *Fortune* in September 1940 (left) was an obvious inspiration for R.M. Chapin's "Three Faces of Europe" map that appeared in *Time* in January 1950 (right)

labeled his work as "artistic rather than cartographical" since Harrison viewed himself more as an artist than a technician.[33] But he vehemently countered Charles Colby, chairman of the Department of Geography at the University of Chicago, who blasted Harrison's maps for their lack of clear coordinates, north–south orientation, and color gradations.[34] For Harrison, these traditional criticisms reinforced his conviction that American professional cartographers were more concerned with making maps for academic readers rather than for informing the general public. In the end, his perspective maps became top sellers in the popular market during World War II for the same reasons that academics dismissed his work. A fundamental reason that Harrison received such harsh criticism from professional mapmakers was, as cartographic historian J.B. Harley pointed out, because conventional cartography views mapmaking as a *scientific* episteme and devalues anything approaching a new or artistic map quality.[35] This especially holds true for "maps...produced by journalists, where different rules and modes of expressiveness...are evaluated by many cartographers according to standards of 'objectivity,' 'accuracy,' and 'truthfulness.'" News journal maps are, hence, often dismissed as "decorative graphics masquerading as maps."[36] But professional cartographers did not speak for American news readers during World War II.

Harrison's perspective maps sold phenomenally well during the war because they were geared toward the average news reader who was hungry for maps of the war effort but who had no formal training in cartography. His commercial success peaked in 1944, when his *Fortune* maps were collected into an atlas entitled *Look at the World* which sold almost 25,000 copies before it even reached stores.[37] City boosters from Atlantic City, New Jersey, and Nashville, Tennessee, among others, requested perspective maps to promote tourism and citizenship by showing the global position of their cities.[38] Harrison's maps were also very popular with the federal government. Perspective maps by Harrison were used in the US Army to train war pilots, while other maps were reproduced in the nationalistic journals *Newsmap* and *Yank*.[39] More than this, Harrison's works in *Fortune*, *Life* (both owned by Time, Inc.), and the *St. Louis Post-Dispatch* influenced an entire generation of American news cartographers who mapped Cold War geopolitical concerns in all major weekly and monthly news journals.

Easily the most influential American news cartographer after Harrison was Robert M. Chapin, Jr., who studied under Harrison and who was *Time*'s chief cartographer during the early Cold War period. Scarcely a *Time* issue exists from 1945 to 1955 that does not display a map, table, or air-brushed image produced by "R.M. Chapin." Although he never achieved the notoriety of Harrison, Chapin's works were far more numerous. His maps were also far more politically and graphically propagandistic, for they were often designed to warn of the dangers of communist expansion and to rally American support for the Containment policy. Harrison's perspective maps relied on aerial perspectives and text to describe the nearness of the Axis powers during World War II. Aside from these conventions, however, his maps were largely devoid of embellishments. They portrayed landforms as anyone would see them from a high altitude. Chapin often employed Harrison's perspective projection, but he seldom used text blocks to explain geopolitical threats. Instead, Chapin heavily embellished his maps with bright colors, labeling, and icons to relate Cold War threats to the United States and its allies. For example, in January 1950, *Time* published a Chapin map entitled "Three Faces of Europe."[40] This map closely resembled the perspective and layout of Harrison's "Three Approaches to the U.S." from 1940 (Fig. 3.6), but Chapin's perspective map did more: it sought to link communist expansion in Eastern Europe with the aggressive expansion of the Central Powers in World War I and the Axis powers in World War II. With characteristic Chapin flair, it did so using brightly colored international blocs and flags. Gone was Harrison's focus on landforms, terrain, and text blocks, replaced with Chapin's more alarming symbology. And Chapin's maps were exceedingly popular. According to cartographic historian Walter Ristow, the sheer volume and popularity of Chapin's work, which began in *Newsweek* in the late 1930s before he transferred to *Time* in 1938, comprised "one of the major pillars of American journalistic cartography" that lasted well into the 1950s.[41]

British news journals never used perspective maps for news coverage to the extent that American journals did. Nor did the British journals feature maps like those popularized by Harrison and Chapin. British news maps during World War II and the early Cold War period were usually in the form of larger-scale, flat projection locator maps that did not lend themselves to alternate projections. Neither did the *Serial Map Service* use perspective maps. However, examples of perspective maps did appear in several travel ads in British news journals in the early Cold War period when British and American air corporations were heavily competing for postwar air travel revenues. The American-based Pan American (Pan Am) Airlines and the British Overseas Airway Corporation (BOAC) were the most prolific advertisers, with both companies placing ads in both nations' journals.

Although Harrison's perspective maps were merely inspired by the Air Age, air travel ad maps were direct products of it. These ad maps were not designed by iconoclastic mapmakers experimenting with new projections, as did Harrison and Chapin. Rather, air travel ad maps employed projections that best imaged routes taken by their aircraft—projections that showed the curvature of the earth with unconventional directional orientation that matched a pilot's course. In October 1946, for example, Pan Am ran a series of ads in *Time and Tide* and *Spectator* for transatlantic service that used perspective maps very similar to those popularized by Harrison.[42] In January 1947, BOAC ads in *Truth* also used a perspective map with an odd directional orientation and continental placement to highlight the expanse of the corporation's air routes across the British Empire.[43]

These British "airman's view" ad maps which deviated from a true north orientation recall the "mariner's view" flat projection maps discussed in the previous chapter. But while the mariner's view maps favored coastline orientations over true north, these airman's view maps favored air routes and altitude. The curvature of the earth was the prime attractive feature here. The perceived smallness of the globe was another attraction. It now seemed possible to merely "hop" across the oceans to the previously far-flung Commonwealth areas and the Americas. At these altitudes, national boundaries seemed unimportant, as did political turmoil. The ongoing Greek Civil War did not show up on these travel maps, nor did the growing Indian independence or the Chinese Civil War. It was as if British air travel maps simply took American mapmaker Richard Edes Harrison's "perspective" maps and overlaid them with commercial air routes.

Perspective maps popularized by Harrison and Chapin in American journals, and by air travel ads in British journals, were innovative departures from the Mercator worldview as the political world shifted from World War II to the Cold War. These maps portrayed the world not as a flat plane with omitted or grossly distorted sections, but as an observable sphere that imparted a smallness and sense of community to international affairs. Perspective maps that featured the Polar Regions, called *polar projection maps*, also became very common due to the geopolitical and commercial uncertainty associated with these new Air Age frontiers. As a result, many types of polar projection maps came into vogue in Britain and the United States by the early Cold War period.

POLAR PROJECTION MAPS

One of the greatest legacies of the Air Age was the ability to fly to any point on the earth's surface for the first time in world history. This opened up entire regions traditionally neglected by Mercator maps which had focused on areas frequented by maritime navigators. As discussed earlier, the world's Polar Regions were the most neglected areas on Mercator maps due to their historical inaccessibility and their concomitant lack of strategic importance in world colonial affairs. Though many Mercator maps contained polar projection map insets, they were mere abstractions of poorly understood regions. Similarly, polar projection maps have appeared in many British and American atlases through the centuries, but only as rare supplements to the more popular flat maps of maritime regions. Thus the maritime trade imperative marginalized the Polar Regions in favor of warmer oceans and coasts for over 500 years. But in a matter of a few decades, from World War I to World War II, Air Age accessibility to the poles compelled British and American mapmakers to rediscover and chart these regions for the first time in the modern era. Moreover, starting in World War II, cartographers and foreign policy experts began to see the poles as new, viable frontiers for science, territorial expansion and geostrategic importance.

Much blame has been placed at the feet of Gerardus Mercator for inventing a projection that distorted the world by overemphasizing the size of land masses distant from the equator. But Mercator projection maps from the Age of Exploration often displayed polar projection maps as insets to help visualize the higher latitudinal regions. *Life* magazine noted this bygone characteristic of Mercator maps in a 1942 article entitled "History Makes New Maps" (Fig. 3.7).[44] Cartographic negligence of the Polar Regions on Mercator maps, then, is somewhat of a modern trend. It would be up to news cartographers in the United States, and private cartographers in Britain, to bring polar projections back into vogue in the Air Age.

Richard Edes Harrison's perspective maps of the Polar Regions became popular during World War II because these regions were rediscovered, and hence became geopolitically viable, with the advent of the Air Age. But the war itself also made these maps popular because they, unlike Mercator maps, portrayed all lands in the Northern Hemisphere as a ring around the North Pole—a projection that lent itself well to visually unifying the previously far-flung Allied nations. During World War II, Harrison produced

This is Gulielmus Blaeuw's 1630 version of Mercator's projection, great navigation map because all its compass directions are true. Vertical line cutting tip of Brazil is Pope's Line, by which Alexander VI in 1493 halved the world between Portugal (east) and Spain (west). Note polar projections, correcting polar distortion.

Fig. 3.7 Mercator projection maps from the Age of Exploration often displayed polar projection inset maps, as did this seventeenth-century map, but more modern Mercator maps usually did not. This seventeenth-century Dutch map was reprinted in *Life* magazine in August 1942, at the height of the Air Age

many polar projection maps in *Fortune* magazine. These conveyed a sense of global interconnectedness to mobilize American hearts and minds for the Allied war effort. The collection of these maps into a single 1944 volume entitled *Look at the World: the Fortune Atlas for World Strategy* included several interventionist polar projection maps with titles such as "Eight Views of the World" and "One World, One War."[45] At the same time Harrison was popularizing these new projections, though, he often had to correct public misunderstandings about them. In February 1943, for example, an op-ed piece appeared in the *New York Times* entitled "Airplanes and Maps" which detailed how Air Age cartography was outdating the Mercator worldview in favor of map projections that more accurately portrayed true global land relationships.[46] In a reply letter published five days later, Harrison commended the op-ed piece for its "general sense" but corrected its erroneous statement that "you would never guess from a Mercator projection that San Diego…is no nearer Japan than Minneapolis or that the shortest route to Moscow from New York lies through Greenland."[47] Harrison lamented that "through lack of understanding of its limitations, the prophets are misusing the north polar...projection in the same way that Mercator has been misused for centuries."[48] He then corrected the anonymous author by stating that a true reading of the projection reveals that "Minneapolis is about 340 land miles (or 16 per cent) farther from Tokyo than San Diego," while "the shortest route from New York to Moscow misses Greenland cleanly to the south."[49]

Well before America entered the war, Harrison's first perspective maps appeared showing American vulnerabilities to Axis attack. Meanwhile, British polar projection maps of the north polar region, or *north polar projection* maps, were linking the great Western nation to the Allied cause. In January 1941, for example, the *Serial Map Service* published a full-color north polar projection map entitled "Proximity of War to America," which examined the close proximity of the United States to both World War II theaters.[50] Although military maritime and air routes were depicted, it was the *air routes over the Arctic Circle* that provided direct links between American cities and World War II hotspots that heretofore had never appeared. The linking of San Francisco to several cities in the Soviet Union, as this map did, was new, and it was only possible by a new direct flight path over the Arctic Circle.

Ironically, during World War II, most British and American polar projection maps did not deal with the war effort, but rather with the future of international civil air service. This was partly because the air transportation market in both nations was seen as the next big economic boom that was on hold as long as war hostilities continued. But it was also because Britain and the United States had very conflicted designs for the postwar international air services market, and polar projection maps were the most popular medium for illustrating the debate. Despite these differences, the wide usage of these maps in Britain and the United States underscored the perception that the Air Age was primarily an Anglo-American affair.

Mapping the Anglo-American Air Age

Although the Air Age had international origins that date back to before World War I, by the end of World War II, the United States and Britain dominated the world's skies. This dominance was in part due to the utter destruction of the German and Japanese national air forces during the war. But it was also a product of the close, cooperative development of the

British and American military air forces which accelerated the pace of aeronautic science to support the Allied war effort. The most important aeronautical development in the Allied cause was the achievement of global flight, and as cartographic historian Denis Cosgrove has noted, it was an Anglo-American achievement.[51] The combination of the superior American air industry with the far-flung island airstrips that connected the British Empire realized the ability to reach any point on the globe for the first time in human history. Although Britain and the United States both established commercial international flight services before World War II, the war forced an indefinite suspension of these routes. This was dark news to British officials and airline executives who had, until mere weeks before the outbreak of the war, made serious plans to extend international flights into new areas. In early July 1939, for example, the British government predicted the creation of new air routes linking Australia to Western Canada in the following year. Moreover, the impending establishment of England's most ambitious international airline, the British Overseas Airways Corporation (BOAC)—a planned merger of British Airways, Ltd. and Imperial Airways—was set for finalization later that year. In anticipation of future demands, BOAC executives placed an order for fourteen new high-altitude monoplanes, each capable of carrying thirty passengers. Government subsidies to the new company were expected to reach the equivalent of 20 million dollars.[52] And as late as early August 1939, BOAC Chairman, Sir John C.W. Reith, hopefully stated that he did "not think there is likely to be a war in the near future."[53] Unfortunately, he was wrong.

Even as the war raged, air travel corporations from both nations eagerly anticipated peacetime when lucrative air services could be renewed. Though BOAC flights successfully commenced in May 1940 with regular service from London to Lisbon, the fledgling corporation never rivaled the vastly superior American-owned Pan American Airlines with its network of transatlantic "Yankee Clipper" flying boats.[54] Even news of the BOAC's grand inauguration was eclipsed by the reality that it would not have happened without American industrial assistance in the form of 100 aircraft engines built by the Wright-Patterson Aeronautical Corporation headquartered in New Jersey. The *Boston Globe* captured the dour British mood with the statement "Their purchase marks the first time that England, jealously nurturing its own aircraft industry, ever has come to the United States for commercial engines in quantity."[55] While commercial air services in Britain all but ceased under the threat of Nazi air dominance, the number of American air passengers actually increased from

1.5 million in 1939 to 6.6 million by 1945.[56] This increase was due in part to the huge number of war effort-related passengers that more than made up for the loss of American casual fliers. It was also due, according to a December 1939 statement by Pan American Airlines President Juan T. Trippe, to his company's absorption of virtually all European-based airlines to Latin America which had been canceled when the war began.[57]

During the war, both nations' national news journals published innumerable ads for air travel that employed innovative maps designed to jump-start the air travel industry as soon as the war was over. Maps and cartographic imagery in British and American air travel ads utilized innovative projections of the earth's surfaces throughout World War II. While British air travel ads used perspective maps at least as early as Harrison introduced them to news journals in the United States, contemporary American air travel ads were equally innovative. For example, American Airlines ads during the war usually included global perspective maps of the world, while companies such as the Garrett Corporation used north polar projection maps to show the range of their aircrafts.[58] These Air Age ad maps, like Harrison's perspective news maps, imparted a sense of global unity not found on Mercator maps. Ad maps did this by depicting the globe from great distances, by omitting political boundaries, and by eschewing any cartographic symbolism of the ongoing war.

One of the most notable similarities between British and American air travel ad maps was the Anglo-American conception that the new Air Age world was shrinking and borderless. That is, the Air Age inspired British and US airlines to de-emphasize distances, land features, and political borders on maps precisely when regular news maps, which focused on wartime struggles, emphasized these features. In November 1944, for example, the *Saturday Evening Post* published an ad for an American Airlines "Air Globe which presented a world with no land features or political borders whatsoever—only destination cities around the globe (Fig. 3.8)."[59] A similar British ad for Bristol Aeroplane was published throughout the war in *Truth*, which described a world where "national boundaries are losing their significance in this age of flight," and it was accompanied by an image of a featureless globe (Fig. 3.9).[60]

It is interesting to note that American images of a borderless globe de-emphasized political borders, but similar British imagery often highlighted an absence of coastlines. The American Airlines "Air Globe" ad, for example, noted the omission of "innumerable boundary and dividing lines," while the British Bristol Aeroplane ad was titled "World without coastlines."

Figs. 3.8 and 3.9 These two World War II–era ads show a common Anglo-American view of a borderless world inspired by the Air Age. However, while the American Airlines ad (left) highlighted the absence of political borders, the British Bristol Aeroplane ad (right) noted the absence of coastlines. The American ad is from *Saturday Evening Post*, November 1944. The British ad was taken from *Truth*, July 1945

The British cartographic proclivity for coastlines, it will be recalled from Chap. 2, was evident in news journal maps of World War II fronts. Similarly, the *Serial Map Service* often portrayed the British Empire as a world of highlighted coasts, while that journal's maps of the French Empire showed no such distinction.[61] This is probably due to the fact that British international air services, unlike their American counterparts, were World War II–era extensions of maritime services that had existed since the Age of Exploration. In fact, many British air travel ads linked air service with colonial maritime tradition throughout World War II. In 1945, for example, *Truth* published several ads for Bristol Airplanes that superimposed a plane over a colonial era ship with the title "Trade Winds" cleverly altered to read "Trade Wings."[62]

Imagery of borderless globes in travel ads during World War II presented somewhat of an inconsistency given contemporary British and American geopolitical concerns of Axis invasion. Often these optimistic, forward-looking ad maps appeared next to war maps that depicted the world as dangerous and war-torn. But the ad imagery outlasted World War II and continued well into the Cold War. American news cartographers, caught up in the geopolitical bipolarity of the era, often depicted communist regions with political borders while leaving the rest of the world borderless on polar projection maps. This gave the impression that the peoples of the "Air Globe" were aligned in an effort to thwart the Soviets, and then the Chinese after 1949. Such a map appeared in *Fortune* in May 1954 entitled "The Massive Retaliatory Power" which clearly displayed the Soviet Union and China in bright red, clustered in a ring around the North Pole.[63] The rest of the world contained no borders, only city locations as in the travel ad maps, while arrows indicating air strikes proceeded from the exterior (noncommunist) regions inward.

Before the war ended, the British and American governments found themselves at odds over conflicting designs of postwar international civil aviation. Simply put, the United States favored a liberal, unregulated postwar air market, while the British sought to divide international air routes between nations along political lines.[64] Britain hoped that heavy regulation of air services would offset American dominance in the private air market and allow the British to rebuild their private air fleet. During World War II, Britain had an agreement to prioritize the production of military aircraft, while the United States agreed to supply all transport aircraft needed by both nations.[65] As a result, British officials lamented the predicted postwar private travel boom which their military planes were ill-equipped to handle. Meanwhile American airlines, with their cutting-edge transport planes that could be easily converted to civilian use, looked more favorably to the competitive future. Or as a 1944 *Newsweek* ad for Pan Am stated, "Some day soon peace will come...And with it, once again, competition with...twenty or more foreign nations...Pan Am is ready for that competition."[66]

But Britain was not "ready" for the inevitable postwar competition, especially with the United States. World War II–era British maps of international civil aviation routes were nevertheless optimistic in their predictions of the postwar air market, which rested almost solely on a continued strong alliance with the United States. The *Serial Map Service* published several maps immediately after the war that portrayed British and American air routes as a unified system of transportation, although heated debates raged between the two nations over this issue. In October 1945 a polar projection map entitled "Air Junctions Map" was published, showing London-based flights extending nonstop into American airspace and comprising a single network of transpolar air routes that spanned the globe.[67] A similar map, this one with a modified oblique Mercator projection that accommodated both Polar Regions, appeared in November of the same year with even more unified Anglo-American routes (Fig. 3.10).[68]

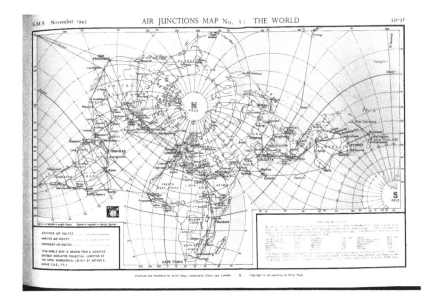

Fig. 3.10 British *Serial Map Service* maps of postwar world air routes, like this one from November 1945, assumed American air carriers would cooperate and form a unified Anglo-American network of global commercial flight. British air routes crisscrossed the United States. Later British air travel maps were not so optimistic

These early postwar British aviation maps recognized the importance of linking London, a major hub of European international service, with New York City, which was then still a growing international air center. For Britain, New York was the main gateway for British flights to the Far East via overland routes across American air space. It was assumed by the British that the Americans would continue to grant Britain the same privileges of air rights after the war that had characterized the wartime Allied Air Command. That, however, would not be the case. The critical Anglo-American debate over postwar civil air services actually outlasted the war itself. This was partially due to both nations' leaders agreeing to table the debate until the war was over. But it was also because Britain had only recently adopted a protectionist stance, whereby postwar international air routes would be divided along political lines, a decided detriment to free competition among carriers. British airline moguls tried furiously to convince the international community (against American designs) to follow this protectionist policy. Indeed as recently as World War I, Britain had lobbied heavily for minimal, not protectionist, regulations on air travel at the Versailles Peace Conference and the Paris Convention on Civil Aviation.[69] But Britain then soon moved toward a protectionist stance in the interwar period when it realized that its greatest rival, the Dutch airline KLM, was undercutting it in productivity and pricing.[70] By World War II, Britain and the United States agreed to loosen prewar protectionist restrictions on air travel in lieu of a 1942 agreement that neither country would make third-party contracts that would restrict British or American traffic.[71]

As long as World War II raged, the spirit of Allied cooperation generally downplayed ingrained differences between British and American plans for postwar civil aviation. Nevertheless, these differences still nourished considerable discord between the two nations—discord that came to involve many other nations around the Atlantic Rim In clear violation of the 1942 Anglo-American agreement not to make third-party air service agreements, the United States independently approached Spain in mid-1944 to obtain landing rights.[72] The British were incensed by this violation, largely because they had a similar pending application with Spain for the same rights.[73] In fact, Britain lobbied the Soviet Union and France independently to foster support for its plans of postwar airline protectionism against American wishes.[74] In the face of overwhelming American commercial power, the British tried in vain to establish an international regulatory body to parcel airline services along political lines. The United States quashed this plan at the international Chicago Conference on civil aviation in November 1944.[75] The greatest strain of Anglo-America relations in this debate occurred when the United States signed—against British wishes—a bilateral agreement for landing rights with Ireland in February 1945.[76] The British were further angered when the United States went on to sign bilateral agreements for the same rights with Egypt, Greece, Iran, and Lebanon—all areas where Britain traditionally had key interests.[77] The British only acquiesced to American postwar civil aviation plans after the United States cut off Lend-Lease aid abruptly in August 1945.[78]

However, American leadership itself had been divided over postwar international air service since 1944 when US Senator Pat McCarran introduced a bill to create a national billion dollar "All American Flag Line" (AAFL) to challenge the BOAC and other foreign competitors.[79] The new airline would have a federal charter, but only US-based international airlines would be allowed to participate. McCarran hoped to revive the Civil Aeronautics Authority—a regulatory body he had chaired until it was supplanted by the Civil Aeronautics Board in 1940—to oversee the AAFL.[80] Of the nineteen American airlines then in service, only two supported the bill.[81] The other seventeen airlines joined with the Secretaries of War, the Navy, and the Army in opposition to the proposed AAFL.[82] They claimed Britain had been "urging, hinting and hoping" the "monopolistic" McCarran bill would pass because it would quash lucrative American free competition and, hence, promote BOAC profits.[83] The bill's narrow defeat in the Senate, however, did not prevent a somewhat amicable resolution between the United States and Britain at the Bermuda Conference on Civil Aviation in early 1946. The United States agreed to regulate international fares so as not to bankrupt the beleaguered British airlines, inducing Britain to accept the idea of liberal, free competition among international airlines.[84] But American–British animosity persisted. After the conference, the British steamed at the American insistence on stopping all international flights at American borders while all American air services could fly over virtually all British lands unimpeded.[85] Simultaneously, the US State Department claimed Britain had secretly urged other nations to restrict American international flights on the eve of the conference.[86]

By mid-1946, after the Bermuda Conference, *Serial Map Service* maps of world airways looked considerably different than they had scarcely a year earlier. British hopes of a unified, global Anglo-American civil air network were gone. The American insistence on stopping all foreign air traffic at its borders cut off direct British air access across North America. A March 1946 map of BOAC air routes from the *Serial Map Service* best illustrates the cartographic implications of these ideological changes in British air services (Fig. 3.11).[87] The 1946 BOAC map was presented on a Mercator projection which centered on the British Empire, not on the Air Age globe. Gone, too, were the Air Age global projections that formerly typified these maps. The United States was cut off the main map almost entirely since British flights could not traverse the nation. The air links between London and New York were downplayed now. The north polar projection map (inset, lower right) labeled London as the "Air Junction of the Future," but its Arctic air routes carefully avoided American airspace. British air services over the Arctic Circle, so proudly displayed in maps a year before, were now gone since these routes depended greatly on American airports and aircraft. It would take many years for Britain, on her own, to build the requisite aircraft suitable for transpolar commercial flight services.

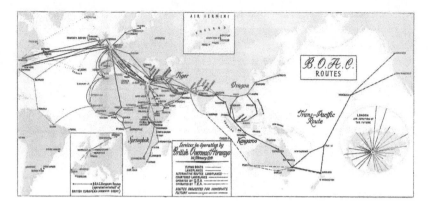

Fig. 3.11 By 1946, British maps of overseas air routes lost their global, unified, Anglo-American themes after the United States cut off all international flights at American borders. This BOAC routes map, from *Serial Map Service* in March 1946, was regional, not global, and the United States was cut off from the main map. The polar projection inset map to the right showed no British flights over American soil

THE POLAR REGIONS IN THE AIR AGE

Maps of the Polar Regions increased dramatically during the Air Age for several reasons. The first and most important of these was technological. Powered flight of the Air Age at last allowed cartographers the needed access to fully map the Polar Regions. Although highly conceptual, maps of Polar Regions date back to antiquity, in the maps of Anaximander of Miletus (610–546 BC) and Aristotle (fourth century BC), but the Poles were not actually visited by man until the twentieth century.[88] Second, the Air Age coincided with World War II and profoundly changed how the Allies regarded polar areas in terms of war logistics. And third, in the early stages of the Cold War, the Polar Regions, especially the North Pole, were deemed likely theaters for any future world war.

THE NORTH POLAR REGION ON MAPS

Air Age maps of the North Pole far outnumbered those of the South Pole in British and American news journals. Since most of the world's landmass is above the equator, and much of the world's population lives above the equator, air access across the "top of the world" profoundly affected most nations' worldviews—these included all the superpower nations in World War II and the Cold War. Understandably, most industrialized nations were concerned with the North Pole for its new importance in postwar commercial aviation. A spirit of international competition was predicted for the new Arctic theater in countless journal articles and advertisements even before World War II had ended. It is perhaps unexpected, then, that some of the most popular imagery associated with the north polar projection maps during the Air Age dealt with world unity rather than international competition.

The consolidation of the Allied war effort after 1941, the drafting of the Atlantic Charter, and the formation of the United Nations between 1942 and 1945 were the driving forces behind the idea of a world peace dominated by northern latitude nations. The United Nations adopted a north polar projection map as its official logo by 1945, and its assembly met in front of a similar, but much more striking, three-story tall map shortly thereafter. When the United Nations first met in October 1946, the *New York Times* published a front-page photo of the gigantic wall map, with President Truman at its base.[89] The use of news maps dropped off considerably in British and American news journals immediately after World War II, and the British journals were almost completely devoid of them. Cartographic images in British ads, such as the map logo of the United Nations, were often the only maps to appear in a given issue.[90]

The spirit of international cooperation and world unity relayed by these north polar projection maps was quickly overshadowed, however, by the breakdown of relations between the United States and Britain on the one hand, and the looming Soviet Union on the other. The Soviet Union, once the reassuring ally across the Arctic Circle during World War II, became a menacing communist threat over the horizon by the late 1940s. More so in the American press, concern over Mercator map distortions of the higher latitudes contributing to public ignorance of a possible Arctic invasion dated back to the early 1940s. Japanese seizure of the Aleutian islands of Attu and Kiska in 1942 prompted the *Hartford Courant* to proclaim:

Unfortunately ordinary maps completely distort the strategic position that the islands occupy. A great circle sailing chart shows that they are directly on the shortest course between Seattle and Yokohama and only slightly north of the course between San Francisco and Japan. Persons whose ideas have been confused by the ordinary Mercator projection can confirm that statement by stretching a string between Japan and our West Coast on a globe. When the string is taut it passes close to Attu.[91]

The fear of a communist attack from across the Arctic Circle was a much greater issue in the American press than it was in the British press for several reasons. First, the British press was less concerned about a Soviet invasion from the Arctic based on simple geographic realities. A surprise Soviet invasion of the British Isles would most likely take a route through Eastern Europe or southern Scandinavia—an Arctic invasion route would be unnecessarily circuitous. Second, in the years immediately after World War II, the British press was preoccupied with Soviet threats to colonial possessions in lower latitudes, such as Greece and Iran. And third, American fears of an Arctic invasion were more pressing since such an act of aggression was more of a geographical likelihood for Americans than it was for the British. The United States, unlike Britain, was bordered by the Soviet Union on two Arctic fronts in the Air Age—to the north across the Arctic Circle and to the west of Alaska.

Although the British did have disputes with the Soviet Union dealing with areas near the Arctic Circle, these concerns were usually more commercial than military. Most north polar projection maps appearing in the *Serial Map Service* in the late 1940s dealt with postwar commerce and commercial aviation. For example, in July 1946, a north polar projection map was used to illustrate the fact that Russia had outbid the British for Icelandic fishing rights.[92] One of the very few military-themed British maps, published in February 1947, dealt with Russian designs to build military bases on Norway's Spitsbergen Islands.[93] The map's accompanying narration made clear, though, that this was a concern for the "United States and most European countries," not for Britain. The map itself excluded all the British Isles except northern Scotland but showed Alaska and Canada prominently close to "Soviet Russia." The American press, by contrast, was far more concerned with the strategic military implications of the Soviet move in the Arctic Circle. A January article in the *Los Angeles Times* speculated that "the Russians are anxious to establish an air and possibly a naval base on the large ice-covered island close to the North Pole." The article's author also linked the Spitsbergen push to Soviet strategic ambitions in North Africa, the Suez Canal, and the Antarctica.[94]

As in journals, north polar projection maps in Air Age British atlases were few, and they often portrayed the Arctic Circle as a nothing more than a blank space. Some British cartographers used the area inside the Arctic Circe to place map legends and text. In 1947, for example, London-based mapmaker George Goodall published the *Cartocraft Geography School Atlas*, which included several north polar projection maps with title blocks covering the area above eighty degrees north latitude.[95] Polar projection maps in general had long been the exception in British atlases, a trend dating back well before World War II. George Philip's 1934 atlas, *Philip's Record Atlas*, contained 128 maps, but only two—the last two in the atlas—were polar projection maps.[96] Although Mercator projection maps were always more popular in British journals and atlases, British cartographers in the Air Age nevertheless continued a tradition of innovative north polar projection design that dates back several hundred years. British cartographers have historically been more concerned with global cartography than their American counterparts due to the global scale of the British Empire. British cartographers may be guilty of neglecting the Polar Regions and their landmasses, but they devised and used myriad types of polar projection maps to chart the far-flung British Empire from the Age of Exploration to the Air Age. A new postwar British affinity for polar projection maps was presaged in the March 1944 meeting of the Royal Geographic Society (RGS) which discussed, among other topics, the limitations of the Mercator projection in civil aviation over the Polar Regions. Speaking before the society, noted astronomer and cartographer Arthur Robert Hinks displayed a large Mercator map of the world and said "The normal Mercator map answers perfectly well for air routes that do not go too far north or south…[but] the scale value of the Mercator map varies so much as you get away from the Equator, you have distances in high latitudes exaggerated and difficult to assess until the device of the transverse Mercator is used." The "device" Hinks was referring to was the transverse Mercator graticule—a combination map grid and numeric table that allowed pilots to chart great circle flight paths in higher latitudes on Mercator maps.

To remedy these cumbersome aviation calculations, Hinks suggested the use of oblique Mercator projection maps which depict "great circle runs very neatly" around the Polar Regions. However, fellow society member Sir Henry Thomas Tizard noted that although the oblique Mercator projection might solve certain technical air navigation problems, it nevertheless retained many of the same cartographic distortions inherent in any Mercator projection. His concerns were centered on the negative effects of all Mercator projections in the public domain. "There is a difference," he said, "between a map suitable for a navigator, and a map suitable for the purpose of educating people who are not navigators. Mercator's projection gives ordinary people a wrong view of the world…[And while] they may be better for the expert navigator…are they suitable for general education?" In the publication of the meeting's notes, the RGS included a zenithal equidistant projection map as a possible compromise between the

Fig. 3.12 The Royal Geographic Society in 1944 suggested zenithal equidistant projection maps as an improvement over Mercator maps for use by pilots in higher latitudes. This map was centered on Valparaiso, Chile

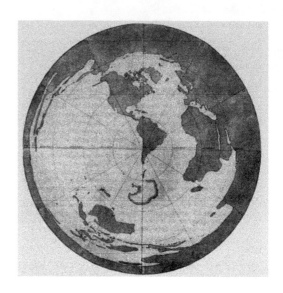

technical needs of air navigation and those of postwar general education (Fig. 3.12).[97] In the last months of World War II, the BOAC concurred by publishing zenithal equidistant projection map of the world, centered on London, which was "designed to 're-teach' geography in a form more suited to the coming 'Air Age.'"[98]

One of the most prolific British cartographers in the postwar Air Age was John Bartholomew, who published several atlases that popularized many self-named polar projections. Bartholomew's 1950 *Advanced Atlas of Modern Geography* displayed three different self-named polar projections: Bartholomew's Nordic Projection, Bartholomew's Regional Projection, and Bartholomew's Atlantis Projection. His "Atlantis Projection" was a self-described "novel application" of Mollweide's homolographic projection invented by German cartographer Carl B. Mollweide in 1805. Although it centered on the North Pole, Bartholomew's Atlantis Projection was popular because it showed *both* poles in a sinusoidal fashion.[99] Many British and American cartographers used the Atlantis Projection throughout the Air Age and the Cold War. In 1955, *U.S. News and World Report* published an article entitled "Secret Cruise of a Russian Submarine," by an anonymous government source. That article was accompanied by an Atlantis Projection map with the description that "This map [was] designed by the author of the accompanying article," but the map clearly employed Bartholomew's Atlantis Projection.[100]

Many north polar projections popular in Britain during the Air Age were directly inherited from earlier times. The Tetrahedral Projection resembled a three-petal flower, with the North Pole at the center, and the Americas, Africa, and Australia featured on the "petals." The projection illustrated the idea of a tetrahedral arrangement of the continents first proposed by British geographer J.W. Gregory in a 1908 article entitled "Recent Literature on the Plan of the Earth" in *Geographical Journal*.[101] Lambert's Azimuthal Projection, named after eighteenth-century French cartographer Johann Heinrich Lambert, resembled a view of the earth from outer space and preserved large land areas. This projection, which was actually a variation of oblique orthographic maps dating from second-century BC Greece and Egypt, gained popularity in the Air Age because it resembled the "Airman's View" of the world.[102] Nevertheless, north polar projection maps of the Air Age were a far more frequent feature of the American press when compared to Britain. Popularized in the Air Age by Richard Edes Harrison in *Fortune* and *Life* magazines in the late 1930s, these maps ushered in a new American awareness of the outside world. Even before the United States entered World War II, while British mapmakers still portrayed the Arctic as a *blank space*, American cartographers used north polar projection maps to analyze the new mobility of the nation's military air forces in the Allied effort. Air Age American airplanes could, for the first time, take advantage of the Arctic shortcut to Europe.[103] In May 1941 a map entitled "New Approach To Convoy: 1,000-Mile Air Patrol From U.S.-Canadian Bases" appeared in *U.S. News and World Report* that illustrated American air patrols protecting shipping lanes from Boston to Greenland to Britain.[104] A similar map, designed by R.M. Chapin, Jr., was published by *Time* in August 1944, entitled "America's Front Door," showing American and Canadian air forces flanking the Arctic Circle as they departed toward the Pacific and European war theaters.[105]

By the conclusion of World War II, many large, colorful north polar projection maps had been published in American news journals glorifying the vast expanse of the Soviet Union, along with articles lauding Joseph Stalin as a "man of the Russian people." One such map, entitled "One-Sixth of the Earth," appeared in *Life* magazine in late March 1943.[106] The map closely resembled Harrison's style, and it included dotted lines showing the expanse of the Arctic Circle occupied by the Soviet landmass. Scarcely three years later, as Cold War tensions heated up, the Arctic became the major corridor for a possible third world war with the Soviet

Union. The north polar region, previously a celebrated gateway to the
Soviet ally, was now a hostile theater for an unthinkable atomic war! It
must be remembered that America and the Soviet Union, as the two most
industrialized nations inside the Arctic Circle, had a unique history of
Arctic competition dating from the turn of the century. In the three
decades after Robert Peary's controversial claim to have been the first man
to reach the North Pole in 1909, American and Soviet researchers flocked
to the Arctic. For the Soviets, the area provided a new and stunning frontier for socialist progress.[107] For the Americans, any communist presence
in the Arctic was a threat to the capitalist way of life. In the early Cold War
period, the United States conducted two major military operations near
the Arctic Circle: "Operation Nanook" and "Operation Frostbite," both
in 1946.[108] These operations generated considerable reaction in the Soviet
press. In 1947 the Soviet humor magazine *Krokodil* published several cartoons that warned of American interests in the Arctic Circle. Several of
these were reprinted in the *New York Times* in October of the same year
(Figs. 3.13 and 3.14).[109]

Figs. 3.13 and 3.14   These two cartoons appeared in the Soviet journal *Krokodil*
in mid-1947 and were reprinted in the *New York Times* in October of the same
year. The cartoon on the left showed Uncle Sam, labeled "Wall Street," making a
grab for Western Europe, but his gaze was over the Arctic Circle, while the
American general warned of Soviet aggression. The cartoon on the right criticized
American imperialistic designs in the same region

Anyone familiar with Soviet-era propaganda would recognize several anti-capitalist tropes at work here. Most reliable was the idea that American capitalist democracy, and by extension Western capitalist democracy, represented an imperialist military threat to world peace. Both cartoons employed this symbolism. The corrupt, tyrannical, and evil "Uncle Sam" was never long for the Soviet press, either, and was usually portrayed with outstretched arms clamoring menacingly over some disputed islands or nation or region. The venomous American union—the military-monopolies bilateral—was what he represented and with no small measure of hypocrisy. He was not just evil, he was a sham. He claimed to be a liberator in one breath and with the next ordered the troops to fire on the helpless. The Soviet depiction (Fig. 3.14) of the "Eskimos" as the most recent victims of American imperialism was not merely coincidental to, or historically subordinate to, communist claims in the Arctic. There is an equally long and more robust communist commitment to the ethnically downtrodden. It is no coincidence that the history of communist movements in the "Third World" is also, at least in part, a history of struggle for ethnic equality. Well before World War II, the Soviet press established a habit of reprinting (at least the approved bits of) major American news items concerning racial violence in the "Land of the Free." Predictably, the worst of America came to represent the best. Uncle Sam was now a card-carrying member of the Ku Klux Klan. The hooded Klansman was quickly as common a symbol in Soviet anti-American cartoons as was the large, black telephone of the bureaucrat. The publication of these cartoons in the Soviet Union, and more importantly their republication in the United States shortly thereafter, is one of several examples offered in this study that further elucidate the sort of unofficial reciprocal relationship that existed between the Soviet and American news presses throughout the Cold War period. Complex and meaningful symbolic exchanges were being conducted concerning geopolitics, human rights, poverty, race, and so forth, which is another reason why this topic deserves further study.

Of course the overarching concern in a potential face-off between Cold War superpowers in the Arctic or anywhere else was the threat of nuclear war. The American press (and US Congress) speculated about a Cold War-type nuclear confrontation well before the Soviets acquired the atomic bomb in 1949. It is not surprising, then, that very suddenly after World War II, American news maps began using north polar projections to speculate about the possibility of a future air war with the Soviet Union over the North Pole. Typical of these maps was an orthographic projection map published in March 1946 in *Newsweek* entitled "Over the Top" which charted possible missile routes, primarily between the United States and the Soviet Union.[110] The ability to strike the Soviet Union over the Arctic Circle with American bombers was colorfully illustrated by *Time*'s R.M. Chapin, Jr., in late 1950, with a stereographic map entitled "Bomber's Reach."[111] These alarmist maps, in stark contradiction with the idea of an Allied cooperation with the Soviet Union, illustrate the considerable significance of the North Pole in the escalation of the Cold War—a process accelerated by Air Age technology.

THE SOUTH POLAR REGION ON MAPS

A discussion of the south polar region in a study of the importance of popular maps in the early Cold War period may seem irrelevant, but South Pole cartography from the era opens a unique window into the broader contemporary relationship between the United States, Britain, and Russia. If the Arctic was "America's Front Door" during World War II and the Cold War, the Antarctic was Britain's backyard during the same period.

Britain has remained unmovable in its claim to have discovered Antarctica with the voyage of Captain Edward Bransfield in late 1820, although the United States and the Soviet Union, each, also lay claim to this discovery.[112] By the 1840s, explorer James Clark Ross's charting and naming of the Ross Sea was a significant step toward "restoring [to] England the honor of the discovery of the southernmost land."[113] British officials claimed a slice of the southern continent in 1908, and by 1920, the claim temporarily expanded to "the whole of Antarctica."[114] Historically, the British colonies of Australia and South Africa had pulled the empire's concerns toward the Southern Hemisphere, as most other European colonizers prioritized the equatorial and northern latitudes. And 100 years after Ross's restorative naval *entrada*, the Brits once again looked longingly at the southern continent. A March 1947 publication in the *New Statesman and Nation* of a jaunty excerpt from "Antarctic Chanty" caught the contemporary flavor of England's recently renewed protective claims to the area against the threat of Cold War competition[115]:

> Now the Yank, Yank, Yankees crash the gate
> And they hoist the Stars and Stripes on British ground,
> While Britain's standing sentry against illegal entry
> By the chilly, chilly, Chileans cruising round.

For we were the first that ever, ever burst
On the Weddell and the Bellingshausen Seas—
Britannia rules the blizzard, and it sticks in Britain's gizzard
When foreign ensigns violate the breeze.

It is surprising, then, that popular British maps of the Antarctic were almost nonexistent during the Air Age. No known maps specifically depicting the Antarctic region are known to have been published in any of the weekly British news journals surveyed for this study. Only the *Serial Map Service* and various British atlases included maps of the southern pole, and then only infrequently. This may be because at the same time that the nations of Chile, Argentina, and Norway were establishing science and weather stations on Antarctica in the late 1940s, British news maps were preoccupied with more pressing geopolitical concerns in warmer climates. The Greek Civil War, the rebuilding of postwar Europe, independence movements in India and Pakistan, and Soviet encroachment in Iranian oil fields, among other developments, dominated maps in the *Serial Map Service* and weekly news journals. Although competitive concerns over postwar civil aviation drew British attention to the North Pole, this was never an issue at the South Pole because no major air service (then or now) traversed its great expanse. The few British maps of Antarctica that were produced during the Air Age were all on south polar projections. They were centered on the pole, and they usually were on a scale large enough to exclude all other landforms except the southern tip of South America. So unlike contemporary maps of the Arctic that usually included nearby nations, maps of the Antarctic continent portrayed the landmass as a remote, isolate wilderness. Unlike the North Pole, which is an imaginary point on a floating ice mass, the Antarctic is actually a landmass—the seventh continent. And although it is the most remote continent, there were several international disputes over Antarctic land rights by the late 1940s that found expression in British maps.

A map of Antarctica published in 1954 in *The Columbus Atlas* by John Bartholomew typifies the few British south polar projection maps that appeared during the Air Age.[116] This map indicated the territorial claims of six nations: Britain, United States, Norway, New Zealand, France, and Australia. But there were actually eight territorial claims to Antarctica—the claims of Chile and Argentina had been suspiciously omitted. (Rival Antarctic claims by Norway, France, and Germany by the 1920s compelled Chile and Argentina to formally cast their lot into the polar arena by 1940.)

Britain had several objections to Chilean and Argentinean claims. She was loath to cede any land to Argentina which had a history of sympathizing with the Axis powers in World War II. Furthermore, Britain was concerned that Chile and Argentina were consorting to form a "Latin front" of solidarity on the southern continent.[117] In fact, Argentina based its claim partially on the 1493 Treaty of Tordesillas papal grant of the Americas (sans Natal) to Spain.[118] The fact that the Chilean and Argentinean claims spatially overlapped Britain's claim exacerbated the situation. Finally, rival Argentinean claims in the Arctic reinforced the ongoing controversy with the British over sovereignty of the nearby Falkland Islands.[119] (The Falklands issue has long outlasted the Air Age and most recently resurfaced in the 1982 Falklands Crisis.) As the Argentineans habitually destroyed British science stations in the Antarctic, the British habitually omitted the Argentinean and Chilean presences on maps of the region.

American interests in the Antarctic date from the Revolutionary War, when, in 1775, British Captain James Cook's first report of finding seals in the region prompted American hunters to venture there.[120] For most of American history, though, the Antarctic had been a realm for unofficial commercial interests rather than an arena to win national prestige. In fact, the first federally sponsored expedition to the region did not commence until 1838, under the command of Lieutenant Charles Wilkes.[121] It was in the Air Age, though, that the United States took the lead in the Antarctic exploration. After World War I, Britain's leading role in the area waned along with the nation's postwar economy, and would-be Antarctic explorers turned to the United States for financing.[122] Indeed, the last major exploration phase in the southern continent's history was financed primarily with American money and carried out by American airplanes in the Air Age.

American navy pilot (later Admiral) Richard Byrd was by far the world's greatest and most renowned Air Age explorer. He barely missed being the first to fly over the North Pole in 1926, and he was the second person to fly solo across the Atlantic Ocean the following year.[123] His first Antarctic expedition in 1928 was by all accounts lavishly equipped and funded by the United States Navy, with three aircraft operating from "Little America"—a prefabricated exploration base with electricity and telephone service.[124] Though American interest in the Arctic was high, the federal government still relied on Mercator maps, with their inherent polar distortions, for exploration. When Byrd requested up-to-date military survey maps of the region, the US Navy responded in mid-December by sending "three sets of Mercator projection plotting sheets" designed by the navy's

Hydrographic Office. Yet when the *New York Times* reported on the event, it used a south polar projection map to illustrate the route of Byrd's expedition.[125] This discrepancy in cartography speaks both to the American journalistic penchant for innovative projections and the federal government's resistance to them. Nevertheless, Byrd pressed on. His 1929 flight over the South Pole was the first in history and earned him a second ticker tape parade in New York City—an honor that has never been repeated in American history.[126] In a little over a year's time, with Air Age mapping, survey, and flight technologies, Byrd was able to accomplish what several hundred years of maritime expeditions had failed to do.

Byrd's historic mapping of the southern continent generated as much controversy abroad as it did praise in the United States. Cognizant of British claims of discovery there, Byrd was careful in April 1929 to respond to a "request of the editors of the *Evening Standard* in London" and stated:

> We are happy to accept your suggestion that we send a message through you to our friends in Great Britain. We wish to be sure that they understand that we approach our problems with respect to those who have preceded us ... Even if international law, vague as to Antarctica, may not be satisfied with their claims of discovery, international courtesy acknowledges them.... Therefore, whatever new land we have discovered or may discover, within the British claims, we see no reason for controversy.[127]

Later that same month, an unnamed Argentinean editor stated that Byrd's discoveries violated the southern nation's claims on the continent. Of course, Argentinean claims there, which were part of larger claims to the Falkland Islands and the South Orkney Islands, had been challenged by the British since the 1830s. Recent publicity over the Byrd expedition, however, had prompted the patriotic editor to revive his nation's "nearest man's sized government" clause.[128] In addition to conflicting with prior British claims, the 1929 Argentinean claim challenged official policy of the United States, begun in the early 1920s, of not recognizing any nation's Antarctic territorial assertions.[129]

The epic international struggle of World War II prompted a new wave of rival claims in the southern continent. Headlines describing the "Battle for Europe" and the "Battle for the Orient" were often accompanied by descriptions of the "Battle of Antarctica." In February 1941 a renewed Chilean claim to lands between the 53rd and 90th meridian based on the "contiguity principle"—a principle, it was rumored at the time, that the United States might support—prompted a negative response by the Argentineans.

This time, though, the stakes of war tempted more rivals. As the *Los Angeles Times* stated, "Of course, there are some other free-style claimants to consider. British, German, Norwegian, and Japanese ship crews have all had offshore glimpses of the icy terrain Argentina and Chile seek."[130] Months before the United States entered the war it joined the "Battle of Antarctica," or so it seemed. Ever the national spokesman for American interests in the region, now Rear Admiral Richard E. Byrd asserted in early May that the United States should establish military naval bases there should the Panama Canal be destroyed by war.[131] His assertions were given more weightage four days later when his exploration party reported that the British had destroyed a Norwegian whaling ship station at Deception Bay to keep nearby German and Japanese ships from taking it.[132] American entry in the war later that year, however, drew international attention away from the South Pole and toward the more traditional battle theaters in Europe and the Pacific. Axis power interest in the Antarctic waned as battlefronts progressively approached the borders of the fascist nations.

Soon after the close of World War II, the strongest American push for continental ground in the southern continent came with the 1946 US Naval "Operation High Jump," led by Admiral Byrd, who overflew the South Pole a second time, commanding a massive aerial survey that mapped over 1.5 million square miles.[133] A postwar international convergence on Antarctica ensued. In the new atomic era, rumors of possible uranium deposits topped interests by the United States, Chile, Argentina, Norway, England, the Soviet Union, and Australia.[134] Amid this fervor for territory, news maps of Antarctica reached their peak popularity in the American press, largely purposed for charting American survey efforts and claim overtures. In January 1947, an orthographic polar projection map of Antarctica entitled "Location of Byrd's Groups" accompanied the *New York Times* article, "Exploration, Training Our Aims In Antarctic."[135] Despite the article's contention that "Britain, Australia, Russia, Chile, Argentina and Norway" were conducting exploration and whaling expeditions in and around Antarctica, the companion map showed only the "Byrd-Ellsworth Claim," which was dominated by the "Little America" station.[136] Renewed Soviet interest in gaining Antarctic territory in the late 1940s prompted the US government to lobby for an international trusteeship of the region.[137] As the 1940s progressed, the *New York Times,* and most American news journals, began omitting indications of American territorial claims while focusing on the claims of the international community. Even as a February 1948 *New York Times* article stated that the

United States would seek to "prevent a possible enemy from gaining a foothold on the frozen continent," the only claims marked on the accompanying map were those of Norway, Australia, France, and New Zealand.[138] The land occupying the "Byrd-Ellsworth Claim" had now been completely redesignated on the map, partly as the "New Zealand" claim and partly as a zone labeled "UNCLAIMED."

In the early years of the Cold War, the spate of international competition for Antarctica spurred by "Operation High Jump" often pitted the Americans against the British more than it did the Americans against the Soviets. The sheer size of the Byrd expedition alarmed British and New Zealand officials who feared an American presence "more permanent than preceding ones" on the Ross Ice Shelf which seemed to threaten both European nations' plans to build airstrips there.[139] Contemporary statements by the American government only fueled European fears. In late December 1946, Undersecretary of State Dean Acheson conveyed an American intent to reserve all rights to future claims in Antarctica while denying rumors that his office had recently asked for a British withdrawal of its expedition there.[140] The following month, the front page of the *Los Angeles Times* reported American officials' announcement of plans to "justly claim at least 1,000,000 square miles and perhaps 800,000 square miles more" upon the return of Byrd's expedition the following spring. That same day British officials countered that its Antarctic interests were tied to those of Australia—a joint claim of roughly one-third of the continent—which, as was pointed out, had the backing of France and Norway.[141]

By spring 1947 the number of competing and overlapping national claims to Antarctica reached an all-time high. A south polar projection map published by the *Boston Globe* in March revealed the international drama (Fig. 3.15). Amid descriptions of repeated lootings of science stations, international naval standoffs, and competing claims of discovery emerged a new southern theater of geopolitical intrigue. The United States was shown to have three Antarctic claims—two of which were challenged by other powers. "Little America" was located squarely inside a British claim, while the "American Highland" interrupted the sole Australian claim. Australia's claim—the largest of all—was also rivaled by a smaller French partition. Another British claim, off the Weddell Sea, retained its traditional rivalry with Chile and Argentina (the latter two claims also overlapped each other). And Norway's claim to Queen Maud Land unintentionally contained a rival German claim.[142]

Fig. 3.15 This south polar projection map published in the *Boston Globe* in March 1947 illustrated the high international competition to claim Antarctica in the early Cold War era. Numerous overlapping national claims dominated the landscape which still had not been fully mapped. Note the incorrectly hypothesized "possible channel" running through the upper left

Conspicuously absent from this early Cold War–era competition to claim Antarctica was the Soviet Union. Even when, in late August 1947, nineteen Western Hemisphere nations emphasized the Antarctic in their agreement to a "New Security Zone" of mutual defense, reactions from the Soviet Union did not materialize.[143] One reason for this was the aforementioned Soviet affinity for the North Pole during this era. Also the new security zone did not, at the time, represent a Cold War threat to the Soviet Union. It was instead seen correctly as simply an extension of the Panama Declaration of 1939, which had been a reaction to a perceived

Axis threat—a move the Allied Soviet Union had supported. Moreover, American officials, most notably Admiral Byrd, had always been careful not to provoke the Soviet Union (or the British) in press statements about national interests in Antarctica. For example, in a three-page commentary in the *Los Angeles Times* by Byrd in January 1947 entitled "Why We're Sailing South," he emphasized American scientific, not strategic, interests. While reassuring that the US "Navy won't lay claims," he pointedly declared that "the hammer-and-sickle flag of the Soviet Union and the British Union Jack will flap in the same wind to which the Stars and Strips will be unfurled." Clearly the old Allied connections were to be preserved, at least for now.[144]

The presidency of Dwight D. Eisenhower beginning in 1953 marked a change in American pursuits in Antarctica. His administration's "New Look" policy of national defense sought to reduce costs of military spending by drawing down on deployment of conventional forces overseas while increasing American reliance on nuclear armaments delivered by air. The new focus on "massive retaliation" also meant a less threatening American stance in the international chessboard of the southern continent. Despite repeated contemporary statements by Admiral Byrd suggesting American intent to claim large sections of the area, Eisenhower consistently assured the international community of the contrary.[145] The American "New Look" at Antarctica stressed its importance as international scientific frontier—a cold frontier where cooperative exploration and experimentation could ease Cold War geopolitical tensions. A similar retreat from Cold War brinkmanship was evidenced in Eisenhower's contemporary "Atoms for Peace" campaign, code-named "Operation Candor," which sought to ease American fears of recent hydrogen bomb tests, promote the benefits of atomic power in Allied nations, and promote world peace.[146] If American statements regarding its desire to obtain Antarctic claims under the Truman administration were conflicted, those of the Eisenhower administration were clear. The United States would not recognize any national claims there in hopes of preserving the continent as a scientific frontier of international cooperation. Beginning in late 1954, American participation in multinational cooperative scientific ventures around the South Pole dominated news about the region. In November the White House announced plans to join a coalition of eight other nations (England, France, New Zealand, Austria, Norway, South Africa, Argentina, and Chile) in a prolonged joint scientific study of the icy frontier. Coordinated by the National Research Council, the study would link twenty-nine

Antarctic survey stations controlled by the member nations from 1957 to 1958.[147] Of course, from these relatively modest beginnings would emerge the massively successful International Geophysical Year (IGY) science program which eventually united 67 nations from both sides of the Cold War.

But while the Eisenhower administration was making overtures for lessening international competition for Antarctic land claims, a new Soviet presence there under the aegis of the IGY prompted considerable American and British concern. Antarctic relations were somewhat stressed in January 1956 when, in preparation for the IGY commencement, Admiral Byrd greeted a newly arrived Soviet expedition at Wilkes Island. Byrd welcomed the Russians with a not so "subtle reminder that the Americans already have flown over much of the territory assigned to the Soviets."[148] The following month, the raising of a Soviet flag at the Mirny research base—located within a traditional British claim—prompted concerns of a possible "forerunner to formal claims to polar continent." The act, which was proudly announced on Radio Moscow, infringed on British assertions of control dating back to Captain James Cook's 1773 voyage to the area.[149] Capitalist suspicions over Soviet designs in the Antarctic were heightened four days later when Soviet Premier Nikita Khrushchev addressed the 20th Congress of the Communist Party in Moscow. Though his address is known today for its denouncement of the cult of Joseph Stalin and subsequent relaxation of Soviet–US tensions, many in the American press saw it as a prelude to Soviet expansion in Antarctica and elsewhere. The *Boston Globe* reported that:

> It is not without significance that the day he began his speech brought word from distant Antarctica that the Soviet expedition there has raised Russia's flag over parts of the south polar continent which have been under British exploration since the 18th century. And that, shortly before that—obviously as a prelude to the party Congress at Moscow—Russia issued its dark warning about the Middle East.[150]

Clearly for some in the American press, the timing of the Soviet flag-raising on traditional British ground was, in coordination with Khrushchev's speech, a clear indication of his "unmistakable program for expansion of the Russian imperialistic drive."

It is of some interest that although early Cold War–era British maps of the Antarctic usually endorsed American land claims there, contemporary American maps seldom returned the favor. Bartholomew's 1954 atlas map persisted in depicting the "Byrd-Ellsworth Claim," which it labeled "(To U.S.A.)." And this was long after American foreign policymakers abandoned any designs on lands of the southern continent. But neither of the aforementioned *New York Times* maps depicted any legitimate British land claims; the 1948 map acknowledged only areas in dispute between Britain, Argentina, and Chile. American news maps that did show British land claims almost always gave equal legitimacy to rival Chilean and Argentinean claims, such as a map entitled "Who Owns Antarctica?" that appeared in the *Saturday Evening Post* in December 1947.[151]

When cartographic historian Denis Cosgrove noted that "the Cold War was aptly named," due to the importance of the Polar Regions in Air Age geopolitics after World War II, he emphasized Soviet–American animosity across the Arctic.[152] But the Antarctic has a longer history as a competitive arena for Cold War antagonists: Britain, the United States, and Russia. These were the three nations that simultaneously claimed first having sighted the southern continent in the early 1800s. Russian explorer Fabian Gottlieb von Bellingshausen, American sealing captain Nathaniel Palmer, and British Captain Edward Bransfield all claimed to have sighted the Antarctic mainland in late 1820.[153] Competition in the Arctic was necessarily deferred until the Air Age since the region contains no actual land to be "sighted" or "claimed," and it cannot be circumnavigated by sailing vessels. Compared to the bipolar nature of American and Soviet animosity in the Arctic, Antarctic geopolitics included many more nations by the beginning of the Cold War. Antarctic competition, however, was roundly nullified in the Antarctic Treaty of 1959, which officially classified the continent as a "global wilderness," and hence *all territorial claims were void*.[154]

NOTES

1. Denis Cosgrove, *Apollo's Eye: A Cartographic Genealogy of the Earth in the Western Imagination* (Baltimore and London: Johns Hopkins Press, 2001), 218–219.

2. Borden D. Dent, *Cartography: Thematic Map Design* (3rd ed.) (Oxford: William C. Brown Publishers, 1990), 43–45; Norman J. Thrower, *Maps and Man: An Examination of Cartography in Relation to Culture and Civilization* (Englewood Cliffs, NJ: Prentice-Hall, Inc., 1972), 162–163.

3. Ibid.; John Bartholomew, *The Advanced Atlas of Modern Geography* (London: Meiklejohn and Son, Ltd., 1950), 8.

4. Thrower, *Maps and Civilization: Cartography in Culture and Society* (Chicago: University of Chicago Press, 1999), 237; *Maps and Man: An Examination of Cartography in Relation to Culture and Civilization*, 162–163.
5. Susan Schulten, *The Geographical Imagination in America, 1880–1950* (Chicago and London: The University of Chicago Press, 2001), 186–187.
6. Ibid., 187.
7. See "Notes from Manywhere," in the *Chicago Tribune*, v.53, n.12 (Mar. 20, 1904): 18.
8. See "Would Curb Survey," in *The Washington Post*, n.12,468 (Jun. 29, 1910): 4.
9. The *RMS Titanic* sank at 41.73° north latitude.
10. "Longest Way Over Shortest Sea Path," in *The Washington Post*, n.13,107 (Apr. 28, 1912): SM4.
11. See "Formation Of Icebergs And Their Passage From North," in the *Boston Globe*, v.97, n.141 (May 23, 1920): 55.
12. See "New Outlet for West," in the *Los Angeles Times*, n.12,070 (Jun. 26, 1909): 6.
13. Schulten, 195–196.
14. John Noble Wilford, *The Mapmakers: The Story of the Great Pioneers in Cartography – From Antiquity to the Space Age* (New York: Alfred A. Knopf, 2000), 100–101; Jeremy Black, Maps and Politics (Chicago: The University of Chicago Press, 1997), 31.
15. J. Paul Goode, "The Homolosine Projection: A New Device for Portraying the Earth's Surface Entire," in *Annals of the Association of American Geographers*, v.15, n.3 (September 1925): 119–125.
16. Schulten, 187.
17. Goode, 124.
18. See "Maps Are Made More Accurate," in the *New York Times*, v.77, n.25,474 (Oct. 23, 1927): X18.
19. Louis M. Lyons, "Shortest Way from Boston to Calcutta Is by Way of the North Pole," in the *Boston Globe* (Nov. 29, 1942): B5. Sunday editions of this newspaper do not have volume and issue numbers.
20. See "Over the Editor's Desk," in the *Christian Science Monitor*, v.36, n.76 (Feb. 26, 1944): WM15.
21. Lyons, B5.
22. Erwin Raisz, *Atlas of Geography* (New York: Global Press Corporation, 1944).
23. This projection went by many names. It was usually and inaccurately called "Fisher's projection" in newspapers. Fisher actually preferred the term "polygnomonic icosahedral projection". But he admitted that "central icosahedral projection" would be easier for the public to accept.

24. Irving Fisher. "A World Map on a Regular Icosahedron by Gnomonic Projection" in *Geographical Review*, v.33, n.4 (October 1943): 605–619.
25. See "Map Problems" in the *New York Times*, v.93, n.31,298 (Oct. 3, 1943): E9.
26. Walter Lippmann, *U.S. War Aims* (Boston: Little, Brown and Company, 1944), 92.
27. Joseph J. Corn, *The Winged Gospel: America's Romance with Aviation, 1900–1950* (London and New York: Oxford University Press, 1983), 125.
28. Susan Schulten, "Richard Edes Harrison and the Challenge to American Cartography" in *Imago Mundi*, v.50 (1998): 174–175.
29. Ibid. Schulten, Geographical Imagination in America, 1880–1950, 223.
30. Schulten, "Richard Edes Harrison and the Challenge to American Cartography," 174.
31. *Fortune*, v.22, n.3 (September 1940): 58.
32. Schulten, 179.
33. Ibid., 185.
34. Ibid.
35. J.B. Harley, *The New Nature of Maps: Essays in the History of Cartography* (Baltimore and London: The Johns Hopkins University Press, 2001), 154.
36. Ibid., 155.
37. Schulten, 180.
38. Ibid., 185.
39. Ibid.
40. *Time*, v.55, n.1 (Jan. 2, 1950): 36.
41. Walter Ristow, "Journalistic Cartography" in *Surveying and Mapping*, v.17, n.4 (October 1957): 384.
42. See Pan Am ad in *Time and Tide*, v.27, n.42 (Oct. 19, 1946): 1005. See *Spectator*, v.177, n.6171 (Oct. 4, 1946): 348.
43. See BOAC ad in *Truth*, v.141, n.3670 (Jan. 10, 1947): 45.
44. "History Makes New Maps" in *Life*, v.13, n.5 (Aug. 03, 1942): 58.
45. Schulten, 175–176.
46. "Airplanes and Maps" in the *New York Times*, v.42, n.31,074 (Feb. 21, 1943): E8.
47. See Harrison's letter entitled "Maps Have Their Limitations" in the *New York Times*, v.42, n.31,079 (Feb. 26, 1943): 18.
48. Ibid.
49. Ibid.
50. See map entitled "Proximity of War to America" in *Serial Map Service*, v.2, n.4 (January 1941): map 64.
51. Cosgrove, 254–255.

52. See "British Wings," in the *New York Times*, v.88, n.29,744 (Jul. 2, 1939): E8.
53. See "British Wings," in the *New York Times*, v.88, n.29,781 (Aug. 8, 1939): E6.
54. See "British to Open New Air Service," in the *Los Angeles Times*, v.59 (Mar. 31, 1940): 2.
55. See "Empire Airlines Get U.S. Motors," in the *Boston Globe*, v.137, n.92 (Apr. 1, 1940): 8.
56. Gilbert C. Fite and Jim E. Reece, *An Economic History of the United States* (Boston: Houghton Mifflin, 1973), 553.
57. See "6 Flights A Week To Lisbon Planned," in the *New York Times*, v.89, n.29,902 (Dec. 7, 1939): 1.
58. See ad for American Airlines in *Newsweek*, v.23, n.3 (Jan. 17, 1944): 50. See ad for Garrett Corporation in *Newsweek*, v.24, n.14 (Oct. 2, 1944): 10.
59. *Saturday Evening Post*, v.217, n.19 (Nov. 11, 1944): 80.
60. *Truth*, v.138, n.359 (Jul. 6, 1945): 9.
61. See map entitled "The French Empire" in *Serial Map Service*, v.7, n.8 (May 1946): map 356–357. An accompanying essay entitled "A Contrast in Empire-Building" stressed the strictly British colonial practice of "extending arteries of sea-borne trade by concentration of land and sea power at strategic points," while "colonial France, on the other hand, has rested on a basis of assimilation." See page 91.
62. See ad for Bristol Airplanes in *Truth*, v.137, n.3587 (Jun. 6, 1945): 467.
63. See map entitled "The Massive Retaliatory Power" in *Fortune*, v.49, n.5 (May 1954): 105.
64. Marc L.J. Dierkx, "Shaping World Civil Aviation: Anglo-American Civil Aviation, 1944–1946" in *The Journal of Air Law and Commerce*, v.57 (Spring 1992): 795.
65. Ibid.
66. See ad for Pan American Airlines in *Newsweek*, v.23, n.8 (Feb. 2, 1944): 44–45.
67. See map entitled "Air Junctions Map No. 2" in *Serial Map Service*, v.7, n.1 (October 1945): map 323–324.
68. See map entitled "Air Junctions Map No. 3" in *Serial Map Service*, v.7, n.2 (November 1945): map 331–332.
69. Dierkx, 796.
70. Ibid.
71. Ibid., 799.
72. Dierkx, 805.
73. Ibid., 806.
74. Ibid.
75. Ibid., 808.

76. Ibid., 816.
77. Ibid.
78. Ibid., 838.
79. "Files Billion Plan For World Airline," the *New York Times*, v.93, n.31,468 (Mar. 21, 1944): 10.
80. Ibid.
81. The only two airlines that supported the McCarran bill were Pan American Airlines and United Airlines—the only two US-based international airlines at the time.
82. Ibid.; "17 Airlines Fight M'Carran's Bill," the *New York Times*, v.93, n.31,474 (Mar. 26, 1944): 36; "Hearings Planned On Air Monopoly," the *New York Times*, v.94, n.31,785 (Feb. 1, 1945): 18; "Army, Navy Oppose One Ocean Air Line," the *New York Times*, v.94, n.31,847 (Apr. 5, 1945): 25.
83. "Competition In Air Urged By 17 Lines," the *New York Times*, v.94, n.31,853 (Apr. 10, 1945): 20.
84. Dierkx, 838.
85. Ibid.
86. "Says Britain Tried To Curb Our Flying," the *New York Times*, v.95, n.32,177 (Feb. 28, 1946): 10.
87. See map entitled "B.O.A.C. Routes" in *Serial Map Service*, v.7, n.6 (March 1946): 63–64.
88. Cosgrove, 35–36.
89. The *New York Times*, v.96, n.32,415 (Oct. 24, 1946): front page.
90. See ad for Hutchinson Publishers in *New Statesman and Nation*, v.31, n.781 (Feb. 9, 1946): 95.
91. See "Japanese In The Aleutians," in the *Hartford Courant*, v.106 (Jun. 17, 1942): 10.
92. *Serial Map Service*, v.7, n.10 (July 1946): 113.
93. *Serial Map Service*, v.8, n.5 (February 1947): 76.
94. Polyzoides, "Spitsbergen Demand Reveals Red Ambition," in the *Los Angeles Times*, v.66 (Jan. 11, 1947): 5.
95. George Goodall (ed), *Cartocraft Geography School Atlas* (London: George Philip and Son, 1947).
96. George Philip, *Philip's Record Atlas* (London: London Geographical Institute, 1934).
97. "The Geography of Post-War Air Routes: Discussion," in *The Geographic Journal*, v.103, n.3 (March 1944): 93–96. See map on page 94.
98. See "An 'Air Age' Map of the World," in *Science*, v.101, n.2626 (Apr. 27, 1945): 425.
99. John Bartholomew, *The Advanced Atlas of Modern Geography* (London: Meiklejohn and Son, Ltd., 1950), 10.

100. "Secret Cruise of a Russian Submarine" in *U.S. News and World Report*, v.39, n.11 (Sept. 9, 1955): 21–26.

101. J.W. Gregory, "Recent Literature on the Plan of the Earth" in *Geographical Journal*, v.32, n.2 (August 1908): 151–156.

102. See the United States Geological Survey website: www.3dsoftware.com/ Cartography/USGS/MapProjections/Azimuthal/Orthographic/.

103. John Noble Wilford, *The Mapmakers: The Story of the Great Pioneers in Cartography – from Antiquity to the Space Age* (New York: Alfred A. Knopf, 2000), 102.

104. *U.S. News and World Report*, v.10, n.18 (May 5, 1941): 9.

105. *Time*, v.44, n.7 (Aug. 14, 1944): 24.

106. *Life*, v.14, n.13 (Mar. 29, 1943): 61.

107. Cosgrove, 218.

108. Kieran Mulvaney, *At the Ends of the Earth: A History of Polar Regions* (Washington, D.C. and London: Island Press, 2001), 136–137.

109. *New York Times*, v.97, n. 32,761 (Oct. 5, 1947): 9.

110. *Newsweek*, v.27, n.11 (Mar. 3, 1946): 40.

111. *Time*, v.56, n.10 (Oct. 4, 1950): 16.

112. Mulvaney, 84.

113. Ibid., 90.

114. Klaus Dodds, *Geopolitics in Antarctica: Views from the Southern Oceanic Rim* (Chichester, West Sussex, England: Wiley, 1997), 79–80. See also Mulvaney, 124.

115. Sagittarius, "Antarctic Chanty" in *New Statesman and Nation*, v.33 n.838 (Mar. 29, 1947): 1.

116. John Bartholomew, *The Columbus Atlas or Regional Atlas of the World* (Edinburgh: John Bartholomew and Son, Ltd., 1954), map 152.

117. Mulvaney, 124–129.

118. Gerald Bowman, *Men of Antarctica* (New York: Fleet Publishing, 1958), 147.

119. Mulvaney, 119–120.

120. Kenneth Bertrand, *Americans in Antarctica, 1775–1948* (New York: American Geographical Society, 1971), 18.

121. Mulvaney, 130–131.

122. Bowman, 96.

123. Ibid., 97–100.

124. Ibid., 97.

125. See "Navy Sends Data To Guide Byrd," in the *New York Times*, v.78, n.25,896 (Dec. 18, 1928): 15.

126. Mulvaney, 132–133.

3 AIR AGE MAPS, THE SHRINKING GLOBE, AND ANGLO-AMERICAN... 95

127. See "Explorer Pays Britons Honor," in the *Los Angeles Times*, v.48 (Apr. 17, 1929): 13.
128. See "Farthest South," in the *Los Angeles Times*, v.48 (Apr. 28, 1929): B4.
129. Ibid., 135.
130. H.M.F. "The Battle of Antarctica," in the *Los Angeles Times*, v.60 (Feb. 19, 1941): A4.
131. See "Byrd Suggests Polar Defenses," in the *Los Angeles Times*, v.60 (May 2, 1941): A11.
132. See "Germans in Antarctic, Byrd Party Reports," in the *Los Angeles Times*, v.60 (May 6, 1941): 2.
133. Bowman, 141. See Mulvaney, 135.
134. See "International Interest in the Antarctic," in the *Los Angeles Times*, v.65 (Nov. 24, 1946): A4.
135. The *New York Times*, v.96, n.32,509 (Jan. 26, 1947): E10.
136. Ibid.
137. Mulvaney, 137–144.
138. The *New York Times*, v.97, n.32,901 (Feb. 22, 1948): E4.
139. See "New Zealand Fears U.S. Force Intends to Stay in Antarctic," in the *Los Angeles Times*, v.66 (Dec. 12, 1946): 7.
140. See "U.S. Reserves Its Claims in Antarctic," in the *Los Angeles Times*, v.66 (Dec. 28, 1946): 4.
141. See "U.S. Plans Claim to Huge Slice of Antarctic Sector," in the *Los Angeles Times*, v.66 (Jan. 6, 1947): 1, 2.
142. K.S. Bartlett, "More Antarctic Surprises Due?" in the *Boston Globe*, v.151, n.82 (Mar. 23, 1947): A5.
143. The agreement was made at the 1947 Inter-American Conference held in Quitandinha, Brazil. See "Entire Western Hemisphere Put in New Security Zone," in the *Boston Globe*, v.152, n.58 (Aug. 27, 1947): 1. All Western Hemisphere nations signed the treaty except Nicaragua and Ecuador.
144. Richard E. Byrd, "Why We're Sailing South," in the *Los Angeles Times*, v.66 (Jan. 12, 1947): E4.
145. See "Ike Won't Claim Any Portion of Antarctica," in the *Boston Sunday Globe* (Aug. 22, 1954): C14. The Sunday edition does not keep volume and issue numbers.
146. Kenneth Osgood, *Total Cold War: Eisenhower's Secret Propaganda Battle at Home and Abroad* (Lawrence, KS: University Press of Kansas, 2006), 156.
147. See "Scientific Study Links 9 Nations Over Antarctic," in the *Boston Sunday Globe* (Nov. 21, 1954): C19.
148. Saul Pett, "Byrd Greets Reds in Antarctica, Says U.S. Has Covered Their Area," in the *Boston Globe*, v.169, n.18 (Jan 18, 1956): 32.

149. See "Russians Hoist Flag on British Antarctic Area," in the *Boston Globe*, v.169, n.45 (Feb. 14, 1956): 7.
150. Uncle Dudley, "Khrushchev's Program," in the *Boston Globe*, v.169, n.49 (Feb. 18, 1956): 6.
151. *Saturday Evening Post*, v.220, n.19 (Nov. 8, 1947): 29.
152. Cosgrove, 219.
153. Mulvaney, 84–87.
154. Cosgrove, 220.

CHAPTER 4

American Spheres, British Zones, and the "Special Relationship"

The complex series of political events that marked the transition from World War II to the Cold War were represented in many ways in British and American weekly news journals. News articles, political cartoons, and advertisements all carried their own levels of political and cultural rhetoric. But news maps were the most effective way to affix weekly news events to geographic locations and hence shape newsreaders' worldviews. Though historians have disagreed on the causes of the Cold War, the most prevalent geopolitical trend of the era was the transition from a polycentric, European-based colonial power structure to a bipolar, global struggle between forces of communism and capitalism. As described in the introduction of this book, this process began during World War II and reached its first era of bipolar, nuclear power-based stalemate by the time of the Geneva Peace Accords of 1955.

During this period British and American politicians, regardless of party affiliation, agreed that international politics was moving from the last vestiges of European colonialism toward a world dominated by the United States and the Soviet Union. British and American news journal cartographers had the daunting task of visualizing an increasingly complex geopolitical world that grew more dangerous after the nuclear arms race began. By 1945, the United States had a long history of visualizing the world in terms of "spheres of influence"—a term that found new importance in the Cold War. As outlined in Chap. 2, British politicians had long relied on the

© The Author(s) 2019
J. P. Stone, *British and American News Maps in the Early Cold War Period, 1945–1955*, Palgrave Studies in the History of the Media, https://doi.org/10.1007/978-3-030-15468-4_4

idea of colonial "worlds" such as the "British World" or the "French World." This concept lost influence in the decolonization that followed World War II, replaced by the British concept of "zones of influence." Though the American "spheres of influence" concept sounds similar to the British "zones of influence," there were fundamental differences between the two. While British and American politicians progressively confronted communism after World War II, their idiomatic and often contradictory worldviews strained the "special relationship." These differences found graphic expression in news journal maps from the period, especially as Cold War rhetoric heated up between the two allies. On the front lines of this Cold War debate were news cartographers who used imagery of cartographic "spheres" and "zones" to report and comment on the latest Cold War developments.

AMERICAN "SPHERES OF INFLUENCE" BY 1945

Historian Edy Kaufman defined a geopolitical sphere of influence as "the high penetration of one superpower to the exclusion of other powers and particularly of the rival superpower."[1] By the end of World War II, a sphere of influence usually described larger sections of the globe—for example, the Americas, the "Communist World," or any large colonial power in American political rhetoric and in the national press. In this way, it was similar to the British and, in general, European concept of a colonial "world" which brought to mind all lands dominated by a colonial power. Following the post–World War II trends of decolonization, multinational stewardship of nations, and Cold War political bipolarity, the idea of colonial "worlds" became increasingly outdated. Conflict between the main two spheres of influence—the "communist world" and the capitalist "free world"—amalgamated formerly separate European colonial worlds in treaties, political speeches, news articles, and maps. This transition happened more rapidly in the United States than in Britain.

Americans have always had a conflicted and hypocritical opinion of "empire." From the earliest days of the American Revolution, national leaders have defined the national spirit as anti-colonial while simultaneously promoting territorial expansion and the acquisition of American colonies. Though many observers have noted this tradition of American hypocrisy, it was eloquently summarized in 1944 by Graham Spry, a Canadian executive for Standard Oil, who stated that "The American people do not like 'empires' or 'imperialism,' though [they are] not unfamiliar with creating an empire and imperialism of their own."[2] Evidence of this double standard flows from the American Revolutionary War. The most revered Founding Father, George Washington, spoke of "our rising empire" while leading the Continental Army against the colonial oppression of the British Empire.[3] Thomas Jefferson likewise saw the war as an opportunity to create an "Empire of Liberty" to serve as a "barrier against the dangerous extension of the British" by the addition of "extensive and fertile country" to the west of New England.[4] These same contradictory ideas of "liberty" and "empire" were crucial motivations for acquisition of the Louisiana Territory under President Jefferson in 1803.

The formal labeling of the American empire as a "sphere of influence" began in 1823 with the Monroe Doctrine which repudiated European colonialism in the Western Hemisphere. Specifically, American diplomats hoped the doctrine would stymie efforts by the kingdoms of the Holy Alliance (Russia, Austria, and Prussia) to intervene in Latin America.[5] This State Department doctrine, endorsed by President James Monroe, stated that no additional European colonies could be created in the Americas, newly independent Latin American nations were to be protected from European control, and the United States would mediate disputes in the Western Hemisphere.[6] Furthermore, the Monroe Doctrine declared that the Western Hemisphere was an official sphere of influence of the United States. It sought to distinguish the democratic societies of the West from the chaos and warfare associated with European colonialism. In its very wording, however, the doctrine subtly juxtaposed familiar American professions of anti-colonialism with visions of American expansion. Historian Jay Sexton recognized this disconnect when he noted, "the key to understanding the nineteenth-century Monroe Doctrine is the simultaneity and interdependence of anticolonialism and imperialism." Though the doctrine did not *explicitly* describe an American right to colonial expansion, its closing description of the "expansion of our population and accession of new states to our Union" as beneficial augmentations to "our resources and...our strength and respectability as a power" *implicitly* endorsed American territorial expansion.[7] Thus it is telling that most American readers, according to historian Walter La Feber, do not consider this last paragraph of the Monroe Doctrine as integral to its understanding.[8] Despite American reluctance to concede the imperialism implied by the Monroe Doctrine, its issuance continued a tradition of national military intervention abroad dating back to the late eighteenth century. Geographer David Slater has noted that from 1798 to 1895, the United States on 103 occasions sent troops overseas to locations "ranging from China and Japan to Chile and Argentina."[9] These deployments began well before the Monroe Doctrine era and before any major overseas lands had been claimed by the United States. Since the 1820s, the Monroe Doctrine has been the longest standing foreign policy in the US history.

From the mid-1820s to mid-1860s, American politicians used the Monroe Doctrine to justify national territorial expansion and dominance in the Western Hemisphere, especially into Latin America. Acquisition of the Mexican Cession after the Mexican–American War (1846–1848) was seen not only as fulfillment of Manifest Destiny, but also as a repudiation of a perceived anti-slavery movement that originated in Britain and Spain.[10] After the American Civil War (1861–1865), national imperial aspirations quickly began to look past the Western Hemisphere. As Gilded Age American industry boomed, the federal government sought greater control in foreign markets, both within and without the Western Hemisphere. The additions of Alaska and Midway Island in 1867 hinted at an increasing American interest in Pacific trade.[11] The Monroe Doctrine was cited as justification for American efforts to annex the Dominican Republic in 1870, and for intervention in Nicaragua a decade later.[12] But it was the publication of Alfred T. Mahan's seminal work, *The Influence of Sea Power upon History*, which first expressed new national military strategic and commercial interests outside the Americas. Written while Mahan was head of the US Naval War College, the book's publication date of 1890 providentially coincided with a federal Census Bureau report that declared the national western frontier was officially closed. If the United States hoped to expand further, it would have to do so in foreign places. Mahan's study was not centered on the United States, but its main points—that all great empires since 1660 have been based on great navies, that great military navies must be supported by equally great commercial navies, and that great imperial navies thrive on overseas colonies—served as a plan to reform the American naval warfare program and foreign policy.[13]

Evidence of a new, extra-hemispherical American expansionism quickly surfaced. In 1893 American privateers representing the Dole Fruit Company temporarily overthrew the Kingdom of Hawaii. And in 1895 Secretary of State Richard Olney invoked the Monroe Doctrine when he imposed American arbitration in the border dispute between Britain and Venezuela.[14] Victory in the Spanish-American War (1898) resulted in the greatest expansion of American territory to date. The United States emerged from the war, ostensibly fought to liberate Spanish colonies from imperial tyranny, as a truly global empire. The island of Cuba came under direct American control.[15] More significantly, the American empire now claimed Puerto Rico and the Pacific islands of the Philippines, Guam, Wake Island, American Samoa, and Palmyra Island.[16]

At the turn of the century, any lingering anti-colonial professions of the Monroe Doctrine were virtually dissolved. Beginning in 1901, US Congress initiated a series of reforms that would, by early 1903, ensure that Cuba remain under American control for the indefinite future. The resulting Platt Amendment allowed for American intervention in future Cuban affairs, as well as the placement of several military naval bases on the island—the most renowned being at Guantanamo Bay. In 1904, control of naval access between the Atlantic and Pacific Oceans was acquired with the Panama Canal Treaty, notably at the expense of Colombia which opposed Panamanian independence.[17] These developments marked a larger change in American foreign policy created during the presidency of Theodore Roosevelt. His "Roosevelt Corollary" to the Monroe Doctrine was both a continuation of and departure from the original doctrine. Whereas the 1823 doctrine sought to keep European powers out of the Americas, as did the new corollary, Roosevelt now reserved the right to intervene in Latin American affairs with a newly built military navy to settle border disputes, protect American commercial interests, and even to collect delinquent international debts. Jay Sexton has argued that the Roosevelt Corollary departed from the Monroe Doctrine in another way. The 1823 doctrine divided the world along longitudinal lines—between Europe and the New World. The corollary, however, envisioned a latitudinal division of the globe—between the "civilized" north and the "uncivilized" south of Latin America.[18]

The Monroe Doctrine has been reinterpreted by each new generation. Its two main tenets—that the United States was the de facto peacekeeping power in the Americas, and that the Americas should be protected against European political instability associated with colonization—have remained intact. These themes have lent themselves well to cartographic imagery. President Theodore Roosevelt's eponymous corollary to the Monroe Doctrine, which emphasized using the new US Navy to enforce American foreign policy in the Americas, found expression in countless political cartoons in the early 1900s (Figs. 4.1 and 4.2).[19] In the early years of World War I, when the American public and Congress were still isolationist, many political cartoons portrayed the Monroe Doctrine as a barrier between the peaceful West and the war-torn East.

Figs. 4.1 and 4.2 Cartographic depictions of the Monroe Doctrine in early twentieth-century political cartoons (left) validated American intervention in Western Hemispherical politics. But by early World War I, the doctrine was mainly valued as a barrier to European wars (right). The cartoon on the left, from 1904, appeared in a collection of Granger cartoons; the cartoon on the right appeared in the *Nashville Tennessean* in 1914

It is probably as predictable that a liberal *Granger* publication would lampoon the Monroe Doctrine as a more conservative Southern newspaper would celebrate it. The 1904 obloquy of President Theodore Roosevelt's "Big Stick Policy" (Fig. 4.1) was based partly on an ad hominem, namely, the politician's known penchant for over-masculinity, but it also derived from more serious liberal concerns about the empire. This cartoon was aimed at those swayed by Mark Twain's then still recent essay, "To Those Sitting in Darkness," and not to equally recent fans of Rudyard Kipling. It was fewer than twenty years ago that the United States had first flexed her modern naval might off the bothersome coast of Venezuela, and only six years since her great naval victory over Spain which had won for her all the boons and bothers of a globe-spanning empire. The Venezuelan bit had been done to mediate a foreign squabble, but then the intercessor became the oppressor. The cartoonist's placement of Cuba in the foreground recalled the begrudging half-independent status recently imposed on the island, caught as she now was in limbo between the Teller and Platt Amendments. Teddy Roosevelt's foot hovering over Cuba was prescient. Two years after the cartoon's publication, the US Marines would return to install William H. Taft to govern the island with martial law for the remainder of the decade. Still, the Cubans fared better under American rule than did the followers of Emilio Aguinaldo in the Eastern Pacific whom Twain had lamented. And the vultures seen pacing the US Navy reminded anti-imperialists that—all implied parallels aside—the colonies were no longer dealing with the "Great White Fleet" of the United Fruit Company.[20]

Despite media coverage (albeit "yellow") of the problems and the native sufferings in the colonies that so provoked the left, it was the conservative view that held sway in the early twentieth century, especially after the outbreak of European war in 1914. The *Nashville Tennessean*'s view (Fig. 4.2) of the Monroe Doctrine as *the* barrier to the ravages of European colonial wars could have been drawn by the ghost of John Quincy Adams, or found in the papers of a young Simón Bolivar. But this was not the anti-imperial isolationism of George Washington; it was Progressive Era isolationism which tended to view war itself as the greatest threat. The *Tennessean*'s depiction of war-torn Europe did not distinguish friend from foe; in fact, no armies were seen at all. The entire Eastern Hemisphere was simply ablaze as the only real victor—death itself—hovered above. So long as this sort of bipolarity dominated American foreign policy, the Monroe Doctrine would be viewed as both peacekeeper and policeman of the American Sphere.

However, the settlement of World War I brought the concept of spheres of influence into question, especially in American society. Spheres were negatively linked to the European imperialism and "power politics" seen to have caused the war.[21] President Woodrow Wilson promoted international liberalism in his designing of the Fourteen Points, which favored "universalism" of democratic ideals designed to be protected in the League of Nations.[22] His administration's intervention in Mexico, the Dominican Republic and Haiti notwithstanding, Wilsonian foreign policy generally sought to assuage concerns of "Yankee imperialism" in the Latin America. Restoration of the Dominican government under President Calvin Coolidge, and the contemporary partial recall of US Marines from Nicaragua which had been deployed there since 1912 to support the rule of Adolfo Diaz, similarly evinced a general American retreat from regional power politics. Perhaps the apex of American antipathy for the Monroe Doctrine in Latin America during the interwar period developed in the early years of the Great Depression, with the issuance of the Clark Memorandum in 1930. Announced during the presidency of Herbert Hoover, Secretary of State J. Reuben Clark's memorandum on the Monroe Doctrine—though never considered an official change in American foreign policy—repudiated American intervention in Latin America as a right of the Monroe Doctrine which, it may be recalled, had been intended to counter European imperialism. Rather, Clark argued that intervention south of the border—past and future—should be viewed as an extension of American *national* security.[23]

Occasionally, Latin American nations unified to challenge the Monroe Doctrine. In 1910, Argentina, Bolivia, and Chile formed the "ABC Alliance," which briefly served as a mediating party between President Woodrow Wilson's administration and Mexico.[24] Wilson had been faced with the deploying of US Marines to Veracruz in 1914 with the purpose of thwarting the German-backed regime of General Victoriano Huerta.[25] However, Wilson's intervention in Mexico worked to sour the multilateral flavor of his proposed Pan-American Pact in 1915. The pact would have cemented Wilson's prescient "Good Neighbor" leanings into official policy seeking to balance US and Latin American power and influence. Ultimately, Wilson's proposal for equanimity and respect among nations failed realization. A cynical House of Representatives deemed the pact a thinly veiled attempt "to broaden the Monroe Doctrine so that it may be upheld by all the American republics instead of by the United States alone."[26] Delayed vindication for Wilson's vision of US fairness with Latin America would later take form in Franklin Delano Roosevelt's pre–World War II Good Neighbor Policy, denouncing "the right...of the United States to intervene alone" in the affairs of Latin American nations.[27]

President Franklin Delano Roosevelt's World War II–era internationalism, however, reenvisioned spheres of influence, each to be maintained by a superpower "policeman" nation as the most effective way to guard against fascism after the war. The American-led United Nations granted only the five policemen nations of the world—United States, France, Britain, Russia, and China—permanent membership on the Security Council, as well as veto power.[28] Article 21 of the United Nations charter recognized that "the Security Council should encourage the settlement of local disputes through...regional arrangements or...regional agencies."[29] By the end of World War II, American politicians, journalists, and news cartographers viewed spheres of influence very subjectively. They reconciled universalism with Monroe Doctrine ideology by claiming that the American sphere was an "open" sphere in which American supremacy did not violate the sovereignty of Western Hemispheric nations.[30] The European colonial worlds, and later the communist "Soviet sphere," were seen as "exclusive" spheres, which described a "direct control of policy, the suppression of civil liberties, and the intrusive management" of member nations by the dominant nation.[31] For example, even before World War II ended, the American press labeled Eastern Europe part of the "Soviet sphere" or the "Russian sphere"—a conceived monolithic, communist, fascist region dominated by Stalin's will to power.

Needless to say, these distinctions of "open" and "exclusive" spheres of influence were somewhat hypocritical given America's history of intervention in Western Hemispherical affairs. As historian Thomas G. Paterson has pointed out, Latin Americans familiar with American dealings in Panama and Cuba in the early twentieth century probably would not agree they were living under an "open" sphere of American influence.[32] Toward the end of World War II, British officials were aware of the hypocrisy as well. In 1943 the British Ministry of Information distinguished American and British "empires," in continental terms for the former and oceanic terms for the latter.[33] After World War II, in response to expanding American power in Eastern Europe and Asia, British Tory Minister Harold Macmillan commented that "these Americans represent the New Roman Empire."[34]

But Americans have always been reluctant to acknowledge that they inhabit anything resembling an empire. This reluctance is not just a product of the anti-imperial national sentiment described earlier. It is also a result of American ethnocentricity and cultural provinciality. Barring brief periods of international war, American society has largely been geographically illiterate about areas outside its own borders. While it is true that the nation was a relatively young (political) world power by 1945, the size, breadth, and importance of American overseas possessions had already been monumentally influential on national industry and trade for almost half a century. The American Empire effectively began in 1898 when the United States gained from Spain the Midway Islands, the Philippines, Guam, the Samoan Islands, and Puerto Rico. That same year, the nation annexed the Hawaiian Islands. The US Virgin Islands were acquired in 1917. As a result, by 1945, the United States controlled about 15,000 square miles of overseas islands stretching around the world. The nation also had control of the Panama Canal Zone (since 1903) and shared joint control, along with Great Britain, of Canton Island (since 1939). Yet American-made maps portraying the United States and its overseas possessions are almost impossible to find in the public media before and after World War II. In this survey there were far more American-made maps (news maps and atlas maps) portraying the British Empire than the American Empire. In fact, from 1945 to 1955, no national news maps were made describing anything resembling an American Empire.

The *Atlas of World Affairs*, published in 1946, included one of the few atlas maps of the "United States Empire" known to exist from the early Cold War period (Fig. 4.3).[35] It illustrated the centrality of the Pacific Ocean in the empire after World War II and connected the United States with the Far East. Though the Orient has significantly influenced American culture, especially in the American West since the early nineteenth century, American atlases rarely made such East–West connections.[36] Latin America, and the Western Hemisphere in general, were relegated to the western border of the map which rendered irrelevant any claims that the Monroe Doctrine only applied to the Americas. Tellingly, this rare American empire

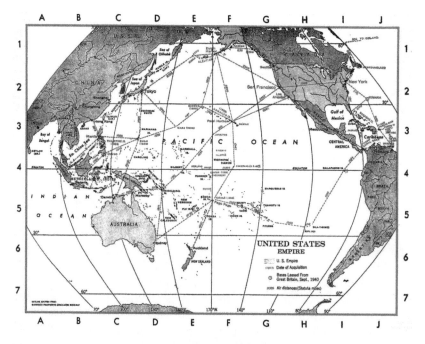

Fig. 4.3   A rare map of the "United States Empire" published in the 1946 *Atlas of World Affairs* stressed the importance of Alaska and the Pacific Islands in American colonial power. Courtesy of the Special Collections Department, University of Texas at Arlington Central Library

map is an equally rare example of Americans not placing their nation at the center of a world map. The far-flung Caribbean and Pacific territories necessitated placing the United States to the right (east) side of the map. It may seem ironic that this map was published in 1946 when the national foreign policy, albeit briefly, still favored international isolationism after World War II. However, the American Empire would have appeared much more domineering if the mapmaker had included all the areas under military and/or administrative control by the nation after the war. Though Caribbean bases leased by Great Britain were shown, South Korea, Japan, and Okinawa could have been added to the American-controlled areas of the Far East. Inclusion of the Monroe Doctrine area would have encompassed all of the Americas and the recently claimed areas of Greenland and Iceland (see earlier in the chapter). Also, the American-controlled areas of Germany and Austria would have necessitated the inclusion of Europe as part of the American Empire. So the empire could have appeared much more imperialistic than it did. Moreover, even this expended version of the American Empire pales in comparison to the American-led "Atlantic Community" and the "Anglo-American Sphere" endorsed by Winston Churchill and many American political analysts during and after 1946.

BRITISH "ZONES OF INFLUENCE" BY 1945

Though the British refer to the "British World" to this day, the importance of colonial worlds was slowly overshadowed after World War II by the idea of geopolitical "zones of influence," or "zones," in the British press. For the British, a "zone" described any nation's political or industrial interests in an area—a concept that differed from the American sphere of influence in two fundamental ways. First, whereas a "sphere" described larger regions of the globe in the American press, a "zone" had no restrictions on the size of region it described for the British. Eastern Europe was called the "Soviet Zone" as often as Britain's oil concessions in Iran were called the "British Zone" of Iran. The British colonial world was often seen as a collection of zones of varying size. Second, while Americans defined spheres with comparable subjectively by 1945, the British viewed all national zones of influence the same—namely, as arrangements of indirect control by the dominant nation. Whereas Americans feared a multinational monolithic Soviet sphere by 1945, the British press generally viewed the Soviet "zone of influence" in Eastern Europe in gradations of allegiance to Stalin from country to country, and it was usually seen as separate from the Soviet Union proper. But this relatively simplistic worldview was to be overshadowed by the complex power politics settlements of World War II.

For example, in the various treaty negotiations of World War II, British leaders were compelled to frame their postwar agenda in terms of spheres of influence or risk being alienated by the two postwar superpowers—the United States and the Soviet Union—both of which saw spheres as a viable paradigm for postwar peace. Understandably, the transition from notions of zones to spheres was not without friction in British political circles. During World War II, British leaders generally assumed they would retain their prewar empire. In fact, Prime Minister Winston Churchill (Conservative-Tory) believed a close alliance with the United States was the way to achieve this given the British war debt and ravaged economy.[37] But as postwar negotiations proceeded, other Conservative ministers became concerned that the American foreign policy, rooted in spheres of influence ideology, was threatening the future of the British Empire. Minister Lord Halifax stated in 1945, "the trouble with these [Americans] is that they are so much the victim of labels...'Power politics,' 'spheres of influence,' 'balance of power,' etc....As if there was ever such a sphere of influence agreement as the Monroe Doctrine."[38] Halifax was reacting specifically to American insistence on expanding the system of multilateral trade that dominated the Monroe Doctrine-controlled Americas to the European colonial realm after the war.[39] But he was also reacting to a perceived naïveté and inconsistency in American foreign policy that had developed between both World Wars. His denunciation of the Monroe Doctrine reflected a historical British consensus. As Jay Sexton has argued, the doctrine's 1823 implementation began "a near-century-long struggle for hemispheric ascendancy between Britain and the United States."[40] Halifax's comment found resonance with sentiments expressed by the British Foreign Office dating back at least to the mid-nineteenth century. When American Ambassador to England, James Buchanan, invoked the Monroe Doctrine as necessary for Latin American stability in 1856, British Foreign Secretary, Lord Clarendon, countered that "Her Majesty's government cannot admit that doctrine as an international axiom which ought to regulate the conduct of European states."[41]

By the end of the nineteenth century, however, the British mood began to change. The dual ascendance of American industrial and military naval power toward the end of the Gilded Age, coupled with a contemporary rapprochement of British and American foreign policy in Latin America, compelled the British Foreign Office to reconsider the Monroe Doctrine as a possible complement to the British Empire. A turning point occurred in 1895 during negotiations over the disputed boundary between British Guiana and Venezuela. The discovery of gold in the region reawakened a border crisis dating back to the early 1840s and threatened British claims based on the careful surveys of Sir Robert Schomburgk.[42] The eponymous "Schomburgk Line" had clearly claimed British control of the disputed borderlands, but by the 1890s, the government of Venezuela disagreed. Due in part to statements by the US Ambassador to Venezuela, William L. Scruggs, who argued that British border claims infringed on Monroe Doctrine hegemony in the region, British officials agreed to an American-led arbitration. A resulting tribunal of American, British, and Russian diplomats largely upheld the "Schomburgk Line," and Britain retained roughly 94 percent of the disputed lands.[43]

American victory in the Spanish-American War of 1898 gave the nation its first truly global empire. The announcement of the Roosevelt Corollary six years later, and British support of it, completed the new Anglo-American rapprochement in foreign policy that now encompassed the entire *world*. The corollary was Theodore Roosevelt's extension of the Monroe Doctrine avowing the United States right to intervene on behalf of European nations wronged through instability, indebtedness, or malfeasance of any Latin American country. The payoff for the United States acting as "policeman" in Latin America was to minimize any chance for retaliatory European presence in the Western Hemisphere. In December 1904 the British journal *Economist* proclaimed "The rest of the world, and this country in particular, cannot fail to regard with satisfaction to [the message] of the President of the United States." A contemporary editor of the *London Times* similarly stated that "The process indicated by the President is one that has been carried out again and again—in Turkey, in Egypt, in China, in Cuba, in Asia by ourselves and others." For the British, the Monroe Doctrine had now become a perceived aide to the beleaguered British Navy in its pursuit of imperial order in the world that would endure, with a few exceptions, throughout the twentieth century.[44]

But the gradual deterioration of the British Empire, and the concomitant increase in American and Soviet influence by the end of World War II, strained British affinity for the Monroe Doctrine. Although British foreign policy was largely deemed a success from 1945 to 1955, British officials often voiced concern that they were being left out of spheres of influence negotiations between the United States and Russia during and after World

War II.[45] This realization sometimes compelled Churchill to broker bilateral spheres of influence agreements with the United States and Soviet Union separately, and without consulting other superpower nations until after the fact. The most notable of these agreements occurred between Churchill and Stalin shortly after the Teheran Conference of 1943 in which the "Big Three" (United States, Soviet Union, and Britain) had resolved to let the Soviets have military dominion over Eastern Europe.[46]

After the Soviets liberated Bulgaria and Romania by late 1944, however, Churchill sought to protect nearby Greece and Yugoslavia from Stalin's influence with the famous "percentages" deal with the communist leader.[47] In October 1944, Churchill and Stalin unceremoniously agreed that the Soviet Union should have 90 percent control in Romania and 75 percent in Bulgaria, in exchange for Britain retaining 90 percent control in Greece. The two leaders agreed to divide their interests in Yugoslavia and Hungary equally.[48] For all its import, the "percentages" agreement was strictly an oral one with no resulting treaty or official record—aside from a notated napkin which now resides in the British National Archives. Churchill thereafter referred to the dubious arrangement as the "naughty document" given its almost flippant ambiguity and informal establishment.[49] And it was received differently by Soviet and American leaders. Soviet Foreign Minister Vyacheslav Molotov held British Foreign Minister Anthony Eden to the agreement throughout the rest of 1944.[50] But American Ambassador to the Soviet Union, Averell Harriman, who also owned *Newsweek* magazine, wondered why Churchill made such an agreement especially since it was never brought up at the later Yalta Conference of 1945.[51]

By the time Churchill's coalition government was voted out of office in mid-1945, the British were witnessing an eclipsing of their international influence by the Americans who favored the spheres' political paradigm. The new Labour government's Foreign Secretary, Ernest Bevin, predictably lamented in late 1945 that "this sphere of influence business" seemed irreversible.[52] Indeed, though out of office, Conservative leader Churchill's now famous "Iron Curtain" speech the following year was one of the first overt examples of British statesmen employing "spheres" terminology:

From Stettin in the Baltic to Trieste in the Adriatic, an iron curtain has descended across the Continent…Behind that line lie(s)…what I must call the Soviet sphere.[53]

It must be remembered, though, that Churchill was speaking in Fulton, Missouri, with President Harry S. Truman in attendance, and his rhetoric was designed to appeal to American, not British, fears of communism.

Spheres and Zones in News Maps During and After World War II

Since almost all the World War II warfronts were located outside the Americas, and while the United States remained tenuously neutral in the first two years of the war, Allied and Axis powers alike generally endorsed the Monroe Doctrine as a precedent for their newly proclaimed spheres of influence.[54] Cartographic historians Guntrab Henrik Herb and Mark Monmonier have shown how Nazi Germany, for example, developed very specific notions of spheres of influence that were illustrated in propaganda journal maps published in the United States in the early 1940s.[55] Third Reich endorsement of the Monroe Doctrine, however, contrasted sharply with the animosity held by Second Reich leaders over the American sphere. Historian Nancy Mitchell has pointed out that while German Chancellor Otto von Bismarck attacked the doctrine as a "special manifestation of American arrogance," his imperial ambitions in Latin America "moved delicately, careful not to step on the hypersensitive toes of Uncle Sam."[56]

Continuing the tradition of using maps "to define and popularize the 'just' extent of the German nation" that developed during the Weimar Republic, Nazi mapmakers brought propaganda maps to a high art by World War II.[57] In April 1941, for example, the New York City-based Nazi journal *Facts In Review* published a Mercator projection map of the world divided into four spheres of influence.[58] In the map, the Americas were shown to be the domain of the United States, while Europe, Scandinavia, and Africa were depicted as the European sphere. The Russian sphere consisted of the Soviet Union, which is noteworthy since the map did not acknowledge any Nazi designs for invading the area. The Far East was seen to be the dominion of fellow Axis power Japan—a claim that overlapped British colonial possessions in India, China, and the South Pacific, and French Indochina. Notably, on the eve of Japanese imperial expansion in the western Pacific Rim area, the Japanese ambassador to the United States, Hiroshi Saito, suggested that his nation's impending conquests, like those of Nazi Germany, were also inspired by the Monroe Doctrine. His 1934 proposal to US Secretary of State Cordell Hull to recognize separate Japanese and American spheres of influence in the Pacific "to establish a reign of law and order in the regions geographically adjacent to their respective countries" became known as the "Japanese Monroe Doctrine." Hull's cordial rejection of the proposal was no doubt influenced by its implication of Japanese dominance in China and its possible negative associations with American imperialism.[59]

Supporting the Monroe Doctrine on Nazi propaganda maps helped the German cause in many ways. First, despite criticism from American president Franklin Delano Roosevelt over Nazi expansion in Europe, German news journal maps could portray national expansion as simply a necessary step in the creation of a German sphere of influence modeled after the United States' own precedent. Second, validation of German expansion could be found in the Monroe Doctrine's assumption that the most industrialized and powerful nations in a region have a right to protect the region from outside instability and encroachment. It must be remembered that at the onset of World War II, the United States and Germany were arguably the two most industrialized nations in the world, which made German–American parallels of hegemony easy to argue. And third, illustrating the Monroe Doctrine on Mercator maps such as this one gave ample space between the Americas and the rest of the world to delineate the extent of the doctrine's hemispherical boundaries. The more evident this delineation, the more convincing was the argument that the United States should stick to its own western sphere and not impede in European matters during World War II.[60]

Linking Nazi territorial expansion to the Monroe Doctrine had another implicit benefit—an Allied precedent for imperial racism. David Slater has argued that the Monroe Doctrine and the preexisting British imperialism both exhibited racist tendencies. American colonial white supremacy reached an apex under President Theodore Roosevelt. In 1902, two years before his eponymous corollary, his disdain for non-white natives surfaced in his description of national victory in the US–Filipino war as a "triumph of civilization over forces which stand for the black chaos of savagery and barbarism."[61] Roosevelt's sentiment seemed to be an acceptance of British poet Rudyard Kipling's famous 1899 call for America to "take up the white man's burden" in the Philippines. For Britain, this racial imperative also applied to her contemporary colonies in Africa. As historian Caroline Elkins's 2005 study, entitled *Britain's Gulag*, demonstrated, British colonial ventures in Africa were dominated by "a single imperial ethos, the 'civilising mission'...to bring light to the Dark Continent by transforming the so-called natives into progressive citizens."[62] Moreover, a synthesis of Anglo-American colonial white supremacy was evident in President Theodore Roosevelt's feelings about the Boer War when he stated in 1899 that "The downfall of the British Empire I should regard as a calamity to the race, and especially to this country."[63] And as late as 1943, a British Foreign Office subcommittee report reinforced the racial superiority component of the American empire "with its subject negro and American Indian inhabitants."[64]

It is interesting to note, then, that at the same time Nazi journal maps were supporting the Monroe Doctrine in its original form, American news journal maps were illustrating the need to revise it in light of World War II developments. When the Monroe Doctrine was issued, it described "the Americas" in very general terms—no longitudinal delineations for the Western Hemisphere were given. Most interpretations of the doctrine over time saw the Americas consisting of, and restricted to, North, Central, and South America, and the Caribbean Islands. By 1941, however, as the Battle of the North Atlantic raged, the United States began establishing naval military bases progressively eastward to protect Lend-Lease era shipping routes to and from the British Isles. A new interpretation of the Monroe Doctrine was needed; otherwise, the United States would appear to be meddling outside its own sphere of influence. In actuality, the idea of expanding the realm of the Monroe Doctrine outside of the traditional area of the Americas was not entirely new. It must be recalled that Theodore Roosevelt's 1904 corollary was partly based on the idea that "the United States might have a 'manifest destiny' to intervene in extreme humanitarian disasters, whether or not they occurred inside America's sphere of influence."[65]

In early April 1941, the United States brokered a deal with the Netherlands to establish military naval bases on the southern tip of Greenland to repel German naval attacks.[66] Concomitant with this move was a new American assertion that the Western Hemisphere (and hence, the Monroe Doctrine area) now included Greenland. It may be recalled that the Nazi map in *Facts In Review* excluded Greenland from the American sphere that very same month. American national news journals immediately illustrated the expanded claim with numerous maps. In April, *U.S. News and World Report* published a map inked in black and, appropriately, green, showing the new hemispherical line that now put Greenland under the aegis of the Monroe Doctrine (Fig. 4.4).[67] The new line, placed at twenty-five degrees west longitude, was painted green, as was Greenland,

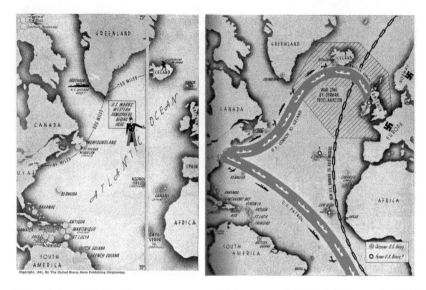

Figs. 4.4 and 4.5   These two maps, which appeared in *U.S. News and World Report* in 1941, illustrated the American desire to expand the Monroe Doctrine sphere of influence to include Greenland

which linked Western Hemispheric defense to the large landform. An icon of Uncle Sam pointed to the line with the text "U.S. Warns: Western Hemisphere Begins Here." The map illustrated many French, Dutch, and British colonies to be protected in the Caribbean with text and point of interest icons although, curiously, the absence of a map legend detracted from the impact of these.

In July 1941, American forces began replacing British and Canadian troops further east in Iceland—a Danish protectorate lying just east of (hence, outside) the new Monroe Doctrine line. That same month, *U.S. News and World Report* covered the maneuver with a colorful, full-page map in the "National Week" section which accompanied several articles on Allied strategy in the North Atlantic (Fig. 4.5).[68] This map (the "July" map) was a reprint of the previous map (the "April" map) in most respects, but telling changes were made. Both maps shared the same Mercator projection and placement of continental landmasses, although the July map was slightly larger in scale. But the July map showed no indication of the new Monroe Doctrine line. If it had, it would have appeared that American forces had crossed over the line to get to Iceland, which could be viewed as a violation of a recently publicized limit on national authority. Instead, the July map replaced the recently touted new Monroe Doctrine line with military shipping and supply lanes that now linked both hemispheres. The April map had been careful not to show any American military presence east of the line. The July map, however, now portrayed the North Atlantic as a borderless open theater that, with American naval and air dominance, protected the many European colonies in the West while it liberated Iceland and the British Isles from the ominous "War Zone By German Proclamation." The implication was clear. Military necessity had extended the American sphere of influence so far past Greenland as to render any delineation of the Monroe Doctrine a mute exercise during the remainder of the war. A contemporary statement by Assistant Secretary of State Adolf Berle that "for the first time, the Monroe Doctrine has to be implemented militarily on a frontier" underscored the nebulous scope of the new policy.[69]

The "New U.S. Barrier To Axis Raiders," illustrated in the July map as a chain running north and south, was east of the Azores and Cape Verdi Islands; moreover, it was no longer a straight line—it curved eastward toward the higher latitudes. This curvature further invalidated—or rather expanded—the previously drawn Monroe Doctrine line. The July map also hinted at future American expansion eastward in the map legend. The red, circled star icons denoting "Outlying U.S. Bases" in the Caribbean and off the coasts of Canada, Greenland, and Iceland were joined by several similar black icons marking "Future U.S. Bases?" Two of these proposed bases were indicated at the Azores and Cape Verde Islands—inside the previous Monroe Doctrine line—but other bases were shown across the line in Ireland and Scotland.

For their part, British leaders generally approved of a stronger American military presence outside the Western Hemisphere during World War II since the fate of Britain was seen to depend on American intervention. They had no qualms about Americans expanding the Monroe Doctrine jurisdiction. In fact, British leaders have a history of disregarding the idea of spheres of influence in international politics. The tremendous size of the British Empire ensured that her colonial possessions overlapped virtually every imagined sphere of influence on the planet. Given this, the British could never realistically assert it had a sphere of influence, for it would encompass virtually the entire colonial world. On British maps, the "British World," which stretched from the Middle East to Australia (see Chap. 2) by World War II, actually excluded all British colonies in the

Western Hemisphere.[70] Even outside the Monroe Doctrine area, in places where British colonies were in close proximity with other European colonies such as in Africa and the Far East, British leaders have traditionally not claimed hegemony to any larger regions.

Churchill's few spheres of influence negotiations notwithstanding, British press favored the zones paradigm, rather than spheres, well after World War II. As a result, British and American news maps often portrayed geopolitical developments very differently. The aforementioned Teheran Conference of late 1943, for example, was the first meeting of the Big Three during World War II, and it occurred amidst great concern over the future of tripartisan occupation of Iran, especially given the abundance of oil there. But American and British news maps portrayed Soviet oil interests in Iran in very different ways. Even during World War II, when the Soviets were still celebrated allies in the American press, US national news maps often viewed the "Russian sphere" in Eastern Europe and the Middle East much more suspiciously than the British press saw the "Russian zones." For example, in October 1944 *Newsweek* published a map of international oil concessions in the Middle East (Fig. 4.6).[71] The oil claims of Britain, America, Iraq, and Kuwait were denoted by differing line patterns of identical black ink. These geographic claims were similarly labeled as "concessions" in a map legend in the lower left corner. The Soviet oil claim, however, was colored with attention-grabbing light-green ink and was labeled part of the "Russian 'Sphere Of Influence'." The Russian oil concession was not listed in the map legend with the non-communist concessions. With the "U.S.S.R." shown bordering Iran to the north, the Russian "sphere of influence" label effectively singled out Soviet oil concessions as an attempt to claim Iranian soil. Contemporary British news maps, however, portrayed Iranian oil fields much less ideologically than did the American press. On these British maps, the oilfields were mutually divided between the "Big Three" and local Arab economic concerns. This is partly because the British press emphasized the economic benefits of the empire's zones of influence, while Americans focused on the political implications of expanding communism.

About the same time that British Conservatives, led by Churchill, were starting to use spheres of influence rhetoric in foreign policy negotiations and later in speeches, the party was voted out of office and replaced by the Labour Party in mid-1945. The Labour Party was elected in large measure on its promise to end the war-torn economic devastation through socialist

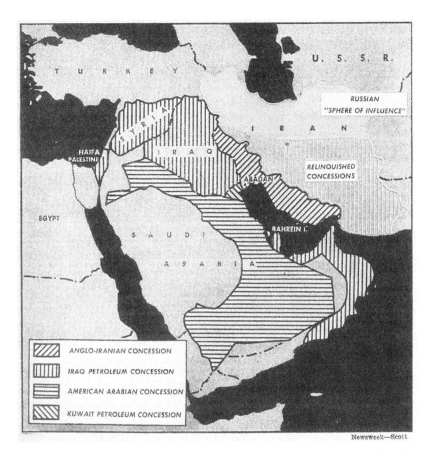

Fig. 4.6 This World War II–era news map, which appeared in *Newsweek* in late 1944, legitimized all international oil concessions in the Middle East except those of the Soviet Union, which were portrayed as an extension of the Russian "sphere of influence"

reforms, but its promise to offer better relations with the Soviet Union was also a factor. One of the party's 1945 campaign slogans, after all, was "Left can speak to Left," which drew a connection between British socialism and Soviet communism—a philosophical position that contradicted, or at least downplayed, any idea of competing international spheres of influence.[72]

The British presence in Iran was stronger than that of the Americans, and the newly elected Labour government under Clement Atlee sought better relations with the Soviets in general.[73] British maps of Iran from the early Atlee period downplayed recent Anglo-Soviet disputes over oil concessions there. Only a few months before Atlee's election, Iranian attempts to squash an Azerbaijani independence movement were blocked by Soviet troops. Foreign Secretary Ernest Bevin publicly railed against Russian interference in Iranian affairs. According to historian Randall Bennett Woods, at risk was no less than "Britain's lifeline in the eastern Mediterranean and its strategic and economic position in the Middle East."[74] Yet in June 1946, the British *Serial Map Service* portrayed Middle East oil concessions in a much more even-handed way than did *Newsweek* three years earlier. In a map entitled "Middle East Oil Map," all major international oil operations were illustrated as similarly drawn pipelines, not as oil fields as in the 1944 *Newsweek* map (Fig. 4.7).[75] This made the multinational oil concessions seem less like land claims, which in turn downplayed the geopolitical implications of claims to territory in the region. In fact, it is impossible to tell from the map which pipelines were owned by which nations. Moreover, although the British map denoted the area of Soviet concessions in northern Iran, the area was labeled "Soviet-Persian Oil Company Concession." Absent were any symbols or text relating to a perceived Soviet sphere of influence, much less of threat.

Other factors besides the new Labour government's "Left Can Speak to Left" optimism for improved postwar Anglo-Soviet relations account for the cartographic downplaying of Soviet troops in traditionally British-controlled Iran. In the spring of 1946, the American Congress was still debating a proposed massive postwar British loan of 3.75 billion dollars—a loan which, in British eyes, would not only help prop up the empire in general, but also would specifically ensure British dominance in Iran. Historian Justus D. Doenecke has explained how British officials saw the loan as necessary to prevent the Soviet Union from seizing further valuable Iranian oil in the near future.[76] But portraying Iran on maps as a postwar theater of Anglo-Soviet animosity ran the risk of alienating American readers already returning to prewar isolationism. After all, only five months before the publication of the "Middle East Oil Map," the inaugural meeting of the United Nations had seen American Secretary of State James F. Byrnes downplay British Foreign Secretary Bevin's recent accusations of Soviet interference in Iran. The American State Department was still wary of spoiling US–Soviet agreements in Europe. Any hint that

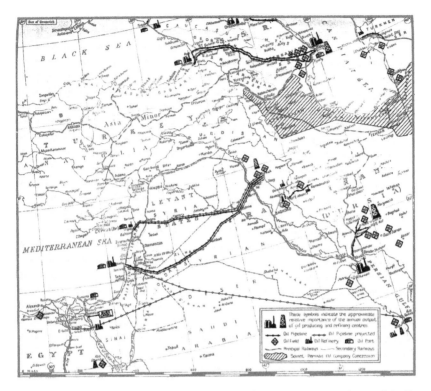

Fig. 4.7 British news maps of Middle East oil concessions were less politically charged than American maps of the same area. This 1946 *Serial Map Service* map labeled all international pipelines identically, and no attempt was made to link Soviet oil interests in northern Iran to Communist territorial expansion

a British loan would lead to Anglo-Soviet animosity in Iran might jeopardize the much needed relief.[77] And as historian Fraser J. Harbutt has noted, despite Bevin's suspicions of Soviet actions in Iran, he no doubt remembered that American detachment in Europe in mid-1945 had "precluded a vigorous British response to the developing Soviet challenge" there.[78]

British mapmakers (and politicians) had another reason to downplay anxieties over the Soviet presence in Iran, which was also related to the pending American loan. Since the early 1940s, American aid to England had been contingent on the expectation that the postwar British Empire would abandon its practice of exclusive trade zones such as the British zone in Iran. Randall Bennett Woods has summarized the tradeoff whereby "U.S. policymakers...would seek in return for wartime and postwar aid the breakup of the sterling bloc and the elimination of imperial preferences."[79] Article VII of the Lend-Lease Act of March 1941 had prohibited exclusive trade policies in both the United States and the British Empire.[80] In the Atlantic Charter issued five months later, the British had agreed to lower postwar trade barriers and promote freedom of travel on the high seas.[81] Moreover, postwar multilateral trade had been viewed by President Franklin Delano Roosevelt's administration as an important aspect of a successful United Nations. During the war, American economists Herbert Feis and Clair Wilcox, and U.N. Trusteeship Council member Francis B. Sayer, Sr., among others, endeavored to dismantle exclusive bilateral trade agreements such as those valued by traditional British mercantilism. In their place were instituted lower barriers to trade and less discriminatory shipping practices.[82] But as historian Susan A. Brewer has pointed out, for the British, the idea of multilateral trade, or "free trade," was code for a new American dominance in the Sterling Area. And while British officials viewed free trade as a threat to their empire, they nevertheless felt compelled to accept it or risk losing American aid if the nation slid back into traditional postwar isolationism.[83] It is noteworthy that Randall Bennett Woods has argued that the American stipulation of postwar multilateralism in British aid has been largely ignored by modern scholarship. Surely the same can be said of British news maps which, in this case, hint at a new British reluctance to glorify its trade dominance in traditional colonial areas.

Contemporary British tolerance of communist ideology also contributed to non-confrontational portrayals of Soviet aspirations on maps of the Middle East. Generally speaking, communism was much more palatable in Britain than in the United States throughout the early Cold War period. Although not a major political force in this period, the Communist Party of Great Britain (GBCP) existed from the 1920s to the fall of the Soviet Union in 1991.[84] The GBCP gained popularity in British trade unions during World War II, and it supported Atlee's Labour Party in its victorious "Left Can Speak to Left" campaign of 1945.[85] Despite the growing British anticommunism after World War II, British news journals published Soviet-friendly material throughout the early Cold War period. In 1953, the *Sunday Times* saw the United States House on Un-American Activities Committee's search for communists as "witch-hunts."[86] As late as 1955, London's *News Chronicle* promoted travel to the Soviet Union, while the *New Statesman and Nation* sold over fifteen Soviet journals including *Krokodil, Izvestia*, and *Pravda*.[87]

It is telling that in the more Soviet-friendly British press, no news map is known to exist from 1945 to 1955 that labeled any part of the world a Soviet "sphere of influence." Although British maps from this period did recognize Soviet "zones of influence" in places such as Eastern Europe and the Middle East, these maps were careful to denote boundaries between the Soviet Union proper and regions of communist control. For example, in August 1945, the *London Tribune* published three maps from J.F. Horrabin in a collection entitled "The European Chess-Board, 1925–1945," the last of which addressed Soviet expansion since 1939.[88] Although the map imagery and key described the "Russian Zone of Occupation in Germany" and the "Countries in U.S.S.R.'s 'zone of influence,'" it carefully delineated these areas from the Soviet Union with differing hatch mark patterns. And a bold black border separated Russia from the areas under its dominion. The implication was clear. Russian presence here was less of a threat than a resolution to Germany's terrifying expansion in World War II.

Contemporary American news maps, however, were much more purposeful in their linking a Soviet wartime presence in Eastern Europe to the idea that Stalin was seeking to expand the Soviet Union itself. In May 1945, *U.S. News and World Report* published a map of Europe showing all areas under Soviet military control, including parts of the Baltic Sea, as a singular "red blackout."[89] This presented Europe as a bipolar realm, with Stalin on one side and Britain and the United States on the other—a notion underscored by the placement of each nation's leaders on the top border of the map. The border between Russia and Eastern Europe was upstaged by the dangerous red coloring that stretched from the Elbe River in Germany to the eastern extent of the map. A similar map entitled "Trouble Spots" created by R.M. Chapin, Jr., appeared in *Time* magazine that same month.[90] It described the "Soviet Sphere of Influence" as an extension of Stalin's personal grab for territory. Stalin himself, literally facing westward, was superimposed over Russia, from which lines of power thrust to the western border of Eastern Europe and terminated into Soviet stars. Areas of Soviet expansion were shaded only slightly lighter than Russia itself. Whereas the *U.S. News and World Report* map showed the British and American leaders opposing Stalin atop the map, the *Time* map visualized Anglo-American resistance to Stalin's advance with a "British-U.S. Chain of Interest" arcing from southern Norway to Syria. This chain symbolism is reminiscent of the "New U.S. Barrier To Axis Raiders" evident in the 1941 *U.S. News and World Report* map discussed earlier. Moreover, it presaged Containment policy symbolism so popular in American news maps by the late 1940s.

POLARIZATION AND THE "SPECIAL RELATIONSHIP" IN NEWS MAPS

Historian Richard H. Ullman has noted that "the Anglo-American 'Special Relationship' has been about security—specifically, about the threat to security posed by the Soviet Union."[91] Indeed, the term "special relationship," as applied to Anglo-American relations, was coined by Winston Churchill in his "Iron Curtain" speech designed to rally Americans to fight communism in British-controlled Greece, among other places. But although the "Iron Curtain" speech was delivered in March 1946, most historians agree that the special relationship began with the Anglo-American cooperation in the Allied cause of World War II. As historian David Reynolds has argued, the idea of a special relationship was first conceived by British Foreign Secretary Lord Halifax shortly after the fall of France to Nazism in 1940, when he voiced interest in "the possibility of some sort of special association with the U.S.A."[92] Conceived during World War II and cemented in the Iron Curtain speech, it is not surprising that the idea of a special relationship began to interest historians in the same ten years that comprise this study. H.C. Allen's 1954 study entitled *Great Britain and the United States*, still considered "the classic historiographical expression of the 'special relationship,'" examined Anglo-American relations from the end of American Revolution to the Korean War and concluded that the two nations had developed a unique bond in three ways.[93] First, a "ripening of friendship" was seen to develop between the War of 1812 and the creation of NATO. Second, while embracing the special relationship, British officials in the early to mid-twentieth century still hoped their empire's obvious decline was not total and was only relative to the rapid and recent rise of the American empire. Finally, Allen detailed the nature of the special relationship as a blending of realpolitik and common cultural heritage. Leon Epstein's study, also published in 1954, challenged Allen's "ripening" of Anglo-American relations between World War II and the Korean War, arguing instead that the interwar period marked a period of British dissatisfaction over its new role as junior partner to the Americans.[94]

Toward the end of World War II, American news journal maps envisioned the world with the same Anglo-American unity and interventionism that characterized maps of the Allied war effort. Gone were most cartographic references to Monroe Doctrine hegemony, American exceptionalism, and anti-colonialism that were so prevalent on maps years before the war. Whereas the Western Hemisphere had been portrayed as the protected sphere of the United States, as the war drew to a close, news maps saw the hemisphere as yet another part of a larger international society. One of the most influential daily newspapers on the East Coast during this period was the *New York Herald Tribune*, which had a long tradition as an internationalist paper with a pro-British attitude.[95] Star columnist and noted author Walter Lippmann worked for the paper, and in 1944, he released a book entitled *U.S. War Aims* which was reviewed in *Newsweek* that July.[96] Lippmann, whom the *New Statesman and Nation* called "the most instructed of American columnists," supplied a map to illustrate various points of his book for *Newsweek*'s review column.[97]

The 1944 Lippmann map was an interesting blend of cartographic imagery that on one level portrayed the Western Hemisphere as a separate region and yet still promoted internationalism. The map employed Goode's projection, which graphically separated the Western Hemisphere from the rest of the world. But Lippmann's coloring of the Western Hemisphere with the same green as was used for Africa, Western Europe, Greenland, Britain, Norway, and Australia emphasized the scope of his conceived "Atlantic Community." This was a graphic linking of the United States with most western European nations and their colonies. Although France was included in this community, its pre–World War II colonial holdings in French Indochina were shown as part of the "Chinese Orbit." But when Lippmann wrote his book in early 1944, France was still under the Vichy government, and its Southeast Asian colonies were in serious question. At this time too, the United States and the Soviet Union were still nominal allies. Separate recognition of the "Russian Orbit" and "Chinese Orbit" followed the ideology of the nascent United Nations—they were two of the four "policemen" of the new world order—but it was also a religious distinction. The "Potential Hindu-Moslem Orbit," which included all lands south of Russia and China, stretched from Turkey to India and underscored the religious criterion. Linking Southeast Asia with China was also religiously convenient. The importance of religion in Cold War power politics grew stronger as the Christian Anglo-American "special relationship" coalesced to confront communist atheism.

Lippmann's vision of a multilateral world shared by four spheres of influence did not long endure, however. According to Randall Bennett Woods, Lippmann revised his geopolitical worldview shortly after Joseph Stalin's February 1945 pre-election speech was publicized. The speech, which blamed both World Wars on capitalism, garnered the label of the "two-camp thesis" in the American press. It was largely this speech that prompted George F. Kennan's famous "Long Telegram" in late February to recommend that American officials abandon the idea of a Soviet-friendly "one world" view of international cooperation. That same month after a meeting with US Secretary of State Dean Acheson, Deputy Chief of "Mission in Moscow" Elbridge Durbrow, and Director of European Affairs H. Freeman Matthews, Lippmann forever embraced to the "two worlds" concept of Cold War geopolitics.[98]

Anglo-American relations cooled somewhat immediately after World War II as Americans, weary from four years of war, drifted back into isolationism. Moreover, as evident in State Department briefings of the July 1945 Potsdam Conference, American leaders were also weary of repeatedly being drawn into Anglo-Soviet disputes over empire in the Middle East and Greece, among other places.[99] American suspicions of British imperialism, Atlee's new Socialist government, and British intentions in Palestine also hurt the "special relationship" in this period.[100] American news maps visualized these new concerns. The international unity evident in Lippmann's 1944 map was quickly replaced in the American press with world maps suggesting isolationist themes after World War II. It may be recalled from Chap. 2 that *Newsweek*'s "Three Worlds and their problem spots" map of February 1946 divided the world among the "Big Three," with the Western Hemisphere once again portrayed as a separate realm of "US Influence." The map was a catalog of politically unstable areas of decolonization which, on its Mercator projection, showed the United States being pulled into matters outside its geopolitical responsibility. One week prior, *Time* magazine published a map by R.M. Chapin, Jr., entitled "Reshuffle," which featured the African landmass and parts of the Middle East with similar isolationist themes.[101] Chapin painted all "World War I Mandates" bright red, which made them appear dangerous against the otherwise gray African landmass. Next to Palestine was a text block that candidly read "Britain wants U.S. to share this headache."

As American foreign policy drifted back toward isolationism and Monroe Doctrine rhetoric, British politicians, journalists, and news cartographers reacted negatively. Although the Labour government had promoted better

Anglo-Soviet relations in early 1945, by the end of the year, Atlee was pushing for a stronger stance from the Americans toward the Soviets.[102] In fact, many American foreign policy practices frustrated the Labour government and British news analysts from the end of World War II to early 1946. These included America's refusal to share atomic secrets, the rapid termination of Lend-Lease aid, the insistence on multilateral trade in the Sterling Areas, and a perceived American irresponsibility over the Palestine question.[103] These political concerns were founded largely on the British realization that its economic recovery, which the Brits always assumed to be tied to unilateral trade in the "British World," was being thwarted by American insistence on multilateral trade in *all* colonial areas. In geopolitical terms, the British were lamenting a perceived American extension of Monroe Doctrine trade ideology, through international trusteeships, that could erode traditionally exclusive British trade access in China, Greece, and the Middle East.[104] When British politicians and news journals discussed foreign policy in this era, they usually couched their rhetoric in terms of what it meant for the British economy.

It is not surprising, then, that during this period, most British news maps were more concerned with economic, rather than political, aspects of the British Empire and world politics. The *Serial Map Service* published several maps assessing the economic state of the postwar British Empire and other empires throughout 1946. The journal's maps of the British Overseas Airways Corporation, the British and French Empires, and European Passenger Transport were explained largely in economic terms.[105] The aforementioned 1946 "Middle East Oil" map was more about the importance of oil than international posturing.

Mapping the world in economic terms was nothing new for the British, of course. British cartographers have a long history of portraying colonial lands in terms of trade goods found there. Even during the darkest days of World War II when most maps concerned the war effort, the *Serial Map Service* produced economic maps of Commonwealth areas, with icons denoting industrial products for export to the British Isles.[106] The end of the war brought a precipitous decline in the frequency of news maps in general, but this was countered by a revival of advertising maps promoting international economic expansion to benefit the beleaguered British Empire. Compared to ad maps in the World War II era, British postwar ad maps were relatively apolitical as they sought to downplay the many international crises facing the Foreign Office—even as they promoted overseas travel, investments in Commonwealth trade, and a general sense of world unity.

Chapter 3 examined how British air services began omitting national boundaries in ad maps to promote a sense of accessibility to foreign places in the postwar Air Age. However, ads promoting business in specific British colonies often included maps describing only the colonies them- selves and the British manufactured products sold there, with no reference to nearby non-British colonies. One of the more prolific advertisers in this regard was Barclay's Bank of London, which produced cartographic ads throughout the early Cold War period in *Spectator* magazine. Barclay's Bank ads promoted investments in its "dominion, colonial and overseas" branches in places such as South Africa and Anglo-Egyptian Sudan with maps of the colonies, tables of goods sold there, and images of native inhabitants.[107]

The disparate trends of British and American news maps in the immedi- ate post–World War II period, with the former promoting international economic activism and the latter endorsing geographic isolationism, began to converge in light of a perceived communist threat by early 1946. Heightened American and Soviet economic interests in Iran, Stalin's con- solidation of the East German and Soviet economies, and a Soviet push for governance of the Turkish Dardanelles promoted a tougher anti-Soviet line from American and British leaders.[108] It was these events, or more importantly, the American and British interpretations of them, that began the closer Anglo-American unity and gradual process of bipolarity that characterized the rest of the Cold War. Nevertheless, an analysis of 1946 political rhetoric shows that British and American foreign policy experts still interpreted this unfolding process of bipolarization in different ways, effecting differences in how they visualized the world on maps.

Easily the most influential American foreign policy document of 1946, and of the entire early Cold War period, was the "Long Telegram" sent by George Kennan, the American ambassador to the Soviet Union. Kennan, who had served in the Moscow embassy since the 1930s, composed the 8000-word telegram on Soviet foreign policy at the request of American officials who were recently convinced that Stalin could no longer be trusted.[109] In February, Kennan concluded that the Kremlin's recent aggres- siveness was the product of Marxist–Leninist ideology, but also it was evi- dent throughout older Russian traditions.[110] Although the Soviet Union was fundamentally weak and insecure, it would seek to expand in the future to combat a perceived encirclement by capitalism.[111] Kennan's telegram was well received by American foreign policy planners for its insight, timeliness, and clear recommendation to contain communism abroad.[112] His ideas, eventually maturing into the American policy of Containment, were echoed less than two weeks later in Churchill's "Iron Curtain" speech which saw Containment as best achieved by a closer Anglo-American alliance.[113] Kennan's and Churchill's early 1946 rhetoric has been addressed by virtually every Cold War historian. Much less known, though, is the British version of the "Long Telegram" issued by Frank Roberts, British ambassador to the Soviet Union, less than a month after Kennan's missive. Though largely ignored by modern scholarship, the "Roberts telegram" offers insight into differences between American and British worldviews at the beginning of the Cold War—differences eventually eclipsed by a preponderance of American power after 1946.

Roberts and Kennan were constituents who served together at the Moscow embassy, and Roberts was aware of Kennan's ideas before composing his own summary of Soviet intentions for the British Foreign Office.[114] Kennan and Roberts agreed that aggressive Soviet foreign policy was a continuation of pre–communist Russian tradition, and that more recent Marxism gave new impetus to Soviet insecurities about their capitalist neighbors.[115] But unlike Kennan, Roberts stressed the importance of Anglo-American unity to protect British interests.[116] And whereas Kennan predicted an inevitable future dominated by spheres of capitalism versus communism, Roberts more optimistically held that zones of British, American, and Soviet interest could be maintained.[117] In general, by endorsing zones of influence rather than spheres, Roberts "presented a picture with softer edges than that projected from the American embassy."[118]

Roberts's worldview at the onset of the Cold War, composed of multilateral zones of influence, more closely described the imagery and ideas expressed on British news maps than did Churchill's bilateral spheres rhetoric that so appealed to American leaders. But as America began to assume a leadership role in world affairs, and especially in Anglo-American relations, British politicians, journalists, and news cartographers slowly adopted the spheres terminology. However, the British interpretation of geopolitical spheres of influence remained more complex and multilateral than in the American mind. Long after Churchill's 1946 speech, British news journalists and cartographers usually distinguished gradations of Soviet control in Eastern Europe, yet they often used anti-Soviet catch phrases popularized by Churchill and by the American press when distinguishing grades of communism. The result was news articles and maps with titles as provocatively bipolar in nature as those in the American press, but with text and maps that described Soviet power as complex and polycentric.

For example, in July 1947, the *Serial Map Service* published a map of Eastern Europe with commentary from Sebastian Haffner, a diplomatic correspondent for *The Observer*.[119] Haffner's essay entitled "The Communist Curtain: 'Russian Sphere of Influence in Europe'" recalled Churchill's 1946 rhetoric and implied a monolithic Soviet threat. But the essay described Eastern Europe as divided into "three degrees of Communism."[120] Finland and Czechoslovakia, in the first group, were not occupied by the Russian Army. They had parliamentary democracies, free elections and press, and communist parties.[121] The second group, consisting of Yugoslavia and Albania, were "the most completely communist states outside Russia."[122] Under fanatical regimes that were products of native communist struggles against World War II Germany and Italy, these nations squashed all political opposition. Yugoslavia's Marshal Tito was recognized as a frequent "embarrassment of the Kremlin."[123] The third group included Poland, Romania, Bulgaria, and Hungary. They were under a "less complete" form of communism which was based on Russian military occupation.[124] Haffner then described the differing states of affairs in each of the four countries of this third group. The accompanying map was, in many ways, a color version of the 1945 *London Tribune* map.[125] "Soviet Russia" proper was colored green (not a menacing red as on most colored contemporary American maps), with a dark border between it and Eastern Europe. Eastern and Western Europe were colored the same— white, with light-green symbols indicating surface features. Text labels for all European nations were the same as well. Only the darker green Russian occupation zones of East Germany and eastern Austria denoted a Russian presence in Eastern Europe. No *spheres* of influence label appeared on the map, but four *zones* of influence were shown. And most notably, there was no cartographic reference to the "Iron Curtain."

It is important to note that despite the influence of Churchill's "Iron Curtain" speech in the United States, from 1946 to 1955, only one British news map is known to exist which depicted that conceived barrier. In April 1949, *Time and Tide* published an article entitled "Ports and Politics" that was accompanied by a black and white map of central Europe.[126] But the article and the map were actually used to describe the permeability of the "Iron Curtain," not its significance as a European barrier. Journalist Aldo Cassuto described a "deep rift" between the Soviet Union and Marshal Tito which allowed Marshall Plan aid to cross the "Iron Curtain," through the Yugoslavian port city of Trieste, to reach Czechoslovakia and Hungary, among other places.[127] On the article's map, the "Iron Curtain" appeared as a permeable dotted line.

In American press maps, however, "Iron Curtain" symbolism was much more popular and explicit. As noted previously, Churchill's "Iron Curtain" speech was delivered on March 5, 1946. The first news map with "Iron Curtain" symbolism appeared thirteen days later. On March 18, *Time* magazine published a map by R.M. Chapin, Jr., entitled "Behind the Iron Curtain," which portrayed Europe as divided by a menacing red chain curtain with a hammer and sickle in the center.[128] The cable that controlled the curtain was tethered in Moscow. As the Cold War progressed, the "Iron Curtain" became a powerful symbol for visualizing a progressively bipolar world order on American news maps. Beginning in June 1946, the *New York Times* began publishing so many "Iron Curtain" maps that it developed a standard base map that was simply reprinted with different hatch mark patterns and text blocks to suit different news articles.[129] The 1948 Berlin crisis prompted a shift in the "Iron Curtain" westward to include East Germany, and was symbolized by a large chain on a *Newsweek* map entitled "Playing With Fire" published in July of that year.[130] *American* magazine, a popular nationalist monthly journal, published several large, colorful maps with "Iron Curtain" symbolism in the late 1940s and early 1950s.[131]

Arguably the most popular and visually striking way American news maps portrayed the Cold War process of geopolitical bipolarization, though, was through their depiction of competing spheres of influence. Churchill's "Iron Curtain" speech and Kennan's "Long Telegram" predicted that multilateral international politics would soon give way to a bipolar struggle between forces of communism and capitalism that would divide the globe into two ideological worlds. For politicians, journalists, and news cartographers, the concepts of "spheres of influence" and geopolitical "worlds" became interchangeable as concepts of bipolarization crystallized in the American mind. The idea of a bipolar world was not new to the American press, though. This chapter has already shown how early World War I–era cartographic political cartoons divided the world into two camps in the Monroe Doctrine tradition—the peaceful, democratic American sphere and the war-torn, European colonial sphere. But when American news maps began visualizing a bipolar world in mid-1946, they did so according to Churchill's recent oratorical characterizations.

Churchill had insisted that communism would best be thwarted by stronger Anglo-American unity, which he viewed primarily in military terms. But the underlying concerns for Churchill, and the British press, were always more economic than militaristic. Simply put, the British could not afford a world-spanning military after World War II. And while Churchill was rattling sabers in the United States, the British press was touting a stronger economy to fight communism. As an anonymous British journalist noted in 1947, "power these days means...industrial power...If Britain could produce enough to raise the economic level on the Continent, then the present division of Europe...might be replaced by a united Europe."[132] Unfortunately this did not happen. The British Empire continued to decline. More importantly, hope for a unified post-war Europe was rapidly overshadowed by escalating Cold War tensions between Western capitalist nations and the growing power, number, and maneuvers of communist forces linked to the East.

THE RISE OF THE COLD WAR'S "TWO WORLDS"

The most profound and stark geopolitical development of the early Cold War era was the idea that world affairs were crystallizing into a bipolar contest between the United States and its capitalist allies, and the Soviet Union and its communist allies. Though the roots of a Cold War-inspired "two worlds" concept of geopolitics predated the late 1940s, most notably in the rhetoric of early twentieth-century communist ideologues who predicted a world revolution against oppressive capitalism, it was not until after World War II that communist internationalism posed a genuine threat to world peace in the minds of capitalist leaders. Even before the "fall" of China (as the Western press termed it) to communism in 1949, the perceived gradual bipolarization of world affairs presaged ominous consequences for those who championed international cooperation in the still new United Nations. Moreover, the rise of "two worlds" rhetoric on both sides of the Cold War threatened the already tenuous division and military occupation of postwar Europe. Even so, rare was the observer who by the late 1940s could have predicted that Cold War bipolarity would come to dominate global geopolitics for the next forty years.

The idea that all the world's governments and peoples, or at least the major ones, could be categorized in a bipolar context did not begin with the rise of communism. In their 1997 study of "metageography," authors Martin W. Lewis and Karen E. Wigen argued that European culture and politics have long distinguished a Western world from that of the East. Though the specific delineation of "West" and "East" naturally varies considerably over time, western European kingdoms have traditionally defined themselves and their colonies as culturally "Western" while simultaneously seeing other cultures, especially those lying to the east, as "non-Western."[133] In this sense, West and East were defined by the West—all things non-western were lumped together as eastern. The first manifestation of West versus East was religious in nature; Latin Christendom of the Western Roman Empire contrasted sharply with the Eastern Orthodoxy of the Byzantine Empire. Next, in the eighteenth and nineteenth centuries, the "supra-European West" comprised Western Europe and its Atlantic colonies. Cold War geopolitics birthed a third incarnation of global bipolarity. No longer determined solely by geography, capitalist economies squared off against those of communist nations. Though Lewis and Wigen argued that Cold War geopolitical bipolarity did not dominate world affairs until the 1960s, American news maps began portraying the phenomenon as early as the mid-1940s.[134]

The first American news maps to characterize Cold War bipolarity appeared shortly after Churchill's speech, and they usually divided the world along economic lines. In late May 1946, *U.S. News and World Report* published a map entitled "Two Worlds" which divided the world between the "Soviet Sphere" and the "Anglo-American Sphere."[135] The map was a vision of two economic worlds, as it accompanied an article entitled "Line-up of U.S., Soviet Blocs: Greater Resources of the West."[136] The Soviet Sphere, colored deep red, included Russia, Finland, Eastern Europe, and Mongolia. Manchuria, where the Soviets were extracting Japanese-made heavy machinery, was colored pink. The rest of the Mercator map landforms were labeled the "Anglo-American Sphere"—a misleading but portentous term since it encompassed all the multinational lands without communist economies.

The idea of an Anglo-American sphere of influence did not last very long in the American press, however. This was partly due to an innate American distaste for all things colonial as evidenced by protesters shouting, "Don't be a ninny for imperialist Winnie!" when Churchill appeared in New York ten days after his "Iron Curtain" speech.[137] But it was also due to an American preference for geopolitical "universalism"—meaning liberal international trade and an open political world—rather than spheres of colonial interest.[138] It is not surprising that between 1945 and 1955 no American news map is known to exist that labels any part of the world as an American "empire." Nevertheless, many news maps were published, cataloging the affairs between the American sphere and other spheres. An analysis of these maps produces a sort of cartographic barometer of Cold War hostilities in the international arena. The 1946 "Two Worlds" map notwithstanding, American news maps generally progressed from a period of multiple spheres of influence at the end of World War II to a bipolarization of world affairs by 1955.

Recall that Walter Lippmann's 1944 map had foreseen a postwar world divided along religious lines into four spheres—the Anglo-American-dominated Atlantic community, the Russian orbit, the Chinese orbit, and the "potential Hindu-Moslem" orbit. Cartographic multilateralism reached its height three years later when a *New York Times* map, entitled "Focal Points on the World Map," claimed there were five spheres, namely, the American, Russian, French, British, and Dutch powers. Most early postwar maps, however, saw the world dominated by the three victorious Allied nations of Britain, Russia, and the United States. Three of the most influential news journals—*Newsweek*, the *New York Times*, and *Time* magazine—followed this trend until the late 1940s.[139]

While American news journals frequently published world maps to put power politics into a global perspective, contemporary British maps preferred to examine political hot spots on a case by case basis. As previously noted, the frequency of British news maps dropped dramatically after World War II. The few maps that were produced continued the World War II tradition of describing national or smaller regional areas. Aside from the *Serial Map Service*, no regular weekly or monthly British news journal is known to have published any maps of the world from 1945 to 1955. Nor did any such journal publish a map of the entire British Empire during the same period. The result was British maps in such large scale that they were unable to convey any grand picture of spheres of influence, competing worlds, or global bipolarity so prevalent on American maps. Although Chap. 5 will examine cartographic portrayals of Cold War Germany, a brief comparison of how the British and American press saw the Berlin crisis reveals the importance of *scale* in news maps.

After Germany was divided among the victorious Allies following World War II, the nation remained a test case for Cold War tensions. The first major rift between Western capitalist powers and the Soviets began in mid-1948. In June of that year, the Western powers introduced a new German currency in their zones of occupation, which seriously undermined the value of the older money still used in the Soviet zone.[140] Stalin answered by introducing a new East German currency, while simultaneously blockading all land access to Berlin.[141] The American-led Berlin Airlift nullified Stalin's attempt to use the blockade as a bargaining tool for more control over German affairs, and he reopened access to the city by May 1949.[142]

The fate of Germany after World War II was always more important to the British than to the Americans.[143] Not only was Britain geographically closer to the former Nazi, and now communist, threat than the United

States, but the British zone of Germany was also a source of economic recovery for the war-torn empire. Although British news articles frequently warned of a Stalinist threat in the Soviet zone of eastern Germany, contemporary news maps almost never made that connection. Moreover, the small scale of British news maps during this period depicted most political events as local or regional issues—not as facets of a larger struggle between the "free world" and the "communist world." In April 1949, just as roads between the British and Russian zones were reopening, London's *Daily Express* published a front-page article and map describing the state of affairs in Germany.[144] The map was very large in scale and described only the border immediately between the British and Soviet zones. No cartographic imagery linked the Soviet zone to Russia proper, or to any larger Soviet empire. Nor could the economic unification of the three western zones of Germany be portrayed at this scale. Although a broad black border separated the British and Russian zones, a major highway and five rail lines were shown to traverse it and converge in Berlin. This was only the second British news map published depicting the Berlin crisis. The first was the aforementioned "Iron Curtain" map that appeared in *Time and Tide* two weeks prior, which, although it portrayed all of central Europe, was devoid of national boundaries.

A striking contrast, both in frequency and in style, is evident between British and American maps of Germany during the Berlin crisis. Despite American isolationism after World War II, the nation's press published numerous news maps of postwar Germany. Between 1945 and 1946, American maps recounting the Allied push for Germany, postwar economic relations there, and the growing Soviet presence in East Germany were popular themes.[145] As discussed earlier, Churchill's "Iron Curtain" speech inspired many maps depicting Germany as the front line between the capitalist and communist worlds. The Berlin crisis caused a similar wave of news maps centering on Germany as the latest Cold War hot spot.[146] Typically, American news maps of the Berlin crisis were smaller in scale than contemporary British maps. This gave ample room to link the Soviet zone to Stalin directly with icons, text, and color. For example, in late July 1948, *Newsweek* published a map entitled "Playing With Fire?" which portrayed Berlin as a dangerous powder keg of possible war between the four occupied German zones.[147] A large arm entering from the East, and holding a torch under Berlin, was implied to be Russian in origin. The question mark in the map title consisted of a sickle and Soviet star. The international importance of the crisis was underscored with flags representing the British,

French, American, and Russian zones. But ultimately this crisis was seen as a bipolar struggle as the three western zones' airlift planes converged in Berlin—across the "Iron Curtain" symbolized with a large steel chain isolating the Soviet zone.

The year 1949 saw many events that furthered the notion of a bipolar Cold War world. The North Atlantic Treaty Organization (NATO) was created in April and guaranteed that an attack on any one of the twelve founding capitalist nations would be met with response by all. The Soviets detonated their first atomic bomb in August, which ended the American monopoly on nuclear weapons. And by early October, Germany was formally divided into two separate states. But predictably, British and American news cartographers expressed this increasingly bipolar world in very different ways.

By the late 1940s, the American press was quick to link any communist regime, no matter where it resided, to Joseph Stalin and the Soviet Union. The "fall of China," as the American press termed it, to communism in 1949 affirmed in the American mind that Stalin's promise to start a world revolt against capitalism was more than rhetoric. It was in these dark days of capitalism that NATO, it was hoped, would serve as a mutual defense bulwark against communist aggression. Much less remembered today, however, is Republican Senator Robert A. Taft's contemporary alternative plan for NATO to serve as an extension of the Monroe Doctrine—to provide a "military umbrella" over Europe. Not satisfied with the proposed NATO scheme to merely supply weapons to capitalist European members, Taft hoped that any future communist aggression there would be met by massive unilateral military action from the United States.[148]

By 1950, many American leaders and a majority of the public saw communist China as an extension of Stalin's power.[149] Despite the many differences between Soviet and Chinese models of communism, and never mind the strong tradition of Chinese nationalism, numerous news maps were published from 1949 to 1950 portraying the Soviet Union and China as a unified "Communist World."[150] Although all weekly American news cartographers had access to a wide palette of colors, they usually employed only red coloring on "Two Worlds" maps by the late 1940s and early 1950s to denote areas under communist political and military control while leaving all other areas uncolored. This presented an alarmingly polarized world not only due to, as graphic design expert Edward Tufte has noted, the exceptionally high reflectivity of red coloring on maps and displays.[151] And for the American public in the late 1940s, attention-grabbing red ink usually denoted threatening areas of communist control. The Soviet Union was usually colored darkest red, while nearby communist areas, including China, and Eastern Europe, were in lighter shades. This coloring tactic presented a communist advance radiating outward from the Kremlin to Eastern Europe and Asia while also cultivating and reinforcing the popular contemporary American opinion that all communist regimes were mere puppets of the Soviet Union. "Two Worlds" maps in this fashion found new popularity following Kennan's 1947 Containment policy because they presented multinational communism as a unified threat to be confronted. In December 1948, a *Time* magazine map by R.M. Chapin, Jr., entitled "Lost Horizon?" linked communist victories in China to Stalin, with a unifying red Soviet star and with railroads linking northern China to Moscow.[152] A map entitled "War of Two Worlds: Results of the Summer Campaigns," published by *Newsweek* in late October 1949, colored the Soviet Union, Eastern Europe, and China the same despite article text differentiating between these locations, and between Yugoslavia.[153]

The onset of the Korean War in late June 1950 prompted American news cartographers to begin lumping North Korea into the Soviet sphere as well. While modern scholarship has shown that Joseph Stalin did, in fact, supply considerable military leadership, weapons, and eventual consent to the North Korean invasion of South Korea, when the war began, American assertions of Soviet sponsorship were merely speculative.[154] President Harry S. Truman's 1951 State of the Union Address, which blamed the war on Soviet imperialism, was certainly unfounded.[155] Still, the American media ran wild with accusations that the Korean War was yet another example of Soviet aspirations to rule the world by violent means. As historian Marilyn B. Young has argued, the outbreak of war even prompted many Americans to advocate nuclear war against the Soviet Union.[156] The American film industry, still reeling from the 1947 House Un-American Activities investigation hearings on suspected communist influence, raised the alarm as well. In 1950, 20th Century Fox studios released a thirty-minute documentary entitled "Why Korea?" which blamed the Soviet Union not only for the Korean War but also for civil unrest in the United States, Europe, China, Greece, Iran, and Italy.[157] Though by today's standards the film reeks of propaganda, it nevertheless won an Academy Award in 1951 for Best Short Subject Documentary.

Historians Kenneth Osgood and Andrew K. Frank have argued that the Korean War was confusing to many Americans, and for several reasons. The lack of an official declaration of war by the National Congress engendered a multitude of labels including the "Korean conflict," "police action," and "non-war." Compounding this confusion was a general public ignorance of the location of the Korean peninsula. Unhindered, American news maps quickly employed bold iconography and coloring to implicate a Soviet hand in the war. Osgood and Frank noted how news maps favored "thick arrows moving relentlessly across clearly defined borders" which became "familiar markers on the geography of the American imagination."[158] These maps not only implied a Soviet hand in North Korea, they offered Russian involvement as proof of Stalin's wish to control all of Eurasia.

A map entitled "What We're Up Against," published in *Newsweek* in July 1950, represented the Korean War as one of "a dozen communist threats all around the borders of the red-inked Eurasian landmass."[159] Eastern Europe, China, and North Korea—all colored pink—appeared as Soviet provinces. Arrows indicating communist expansion, colored dark red to match the Soviet Union, appeared in Eastern Europe, the Middle East, and along the southern border of China. This gave the impression that Soviet influence traveled unimpeded through all communist nations as it sought to expand into "threatened areas." Despite the fact that most American politicians agreed that the Soviet Union was not seeking war, by the 1950s, "two worlds" maps were frequently used to illustrate the theoretical military might of a unified communist world. These were usually polar projection maps which effectively related proximity of the perceived "monolithic," Soviet-dominated Eurasian landmass to the United States. In September 1952, the *Saturday Evening Post* published a large polar projection map that accompanied an article entitled "Stalin's Secret War Plans."[160] The map was centered on the Soviet Union and showed potential air strike paths of over sixty "Red Air Bases" situated on the periphery of the Soviet-Sino-Eastern European landmass. A similar, but reciprocal, polar projection map outlining the "massive retaliatory power" of NATO forces upon the communist world was published by *Fortune* in May 1954.[161] *U.S. News and World Report* added Tibet and Finland to the communist world in a polar projection map illustrating Soviet submarine maneuvers near the South Pole in September 1955.[162]

As mentioned earlier, British news maps of the world were very rare, possibly non-existent in the early Cold War period. But many contemporary political cartoons containing cartographic imagery were published, which reveal British conceptions of the Cold War world. That said, British cartoons did not employ cartographic symbolism as often as their American counterparts. British cartoonists have followed a tradition of representing foreign nations and the British Empire itself with animals and political caricatures more often than with actual cartographic imagery. British Commonwealth nations were often depicted with symbols of exotic animals found there. Cold War nations comprising multilateral zones of influence, such as Germany and China, usually took the form of indecisive women being wooed by foreign leaders. The few political cartoons with cartographic imagery show that by the early Cold War period, British newspapers were very concerned about the effects of geopolitical bipolarity on the empire and the world. Absent were any images depicting Stalin or the "Communist World" trying to conquer the globe, even as these same images were popular in the American press. Rather, the Stalinist threat to the British was one of destabilization of world trade and peace. In January 1948, for example, *Time and Tide* published a cartoon showing Stalin feeding a box of "suspicion" to two fish named "East" and "West" in a fishbowl fashioned from a transparent globe.[163] That same year, the British government, under Clement Atlee's Labour Party, created the Information Research Department to disseminate propaganda championing British Social Democracy over American capitalism and Soviet communism.[164]

Communist advances in 1949, however, compelled British officials to realign their foreign policy and economics with American interests. In that year, the Soviets detonated their first atomic bomb, China became communist, and NATO was formed. Waning ideas of an exclusive British World were now lampooned in British news cartoons. In October 1949, outspoken Tory Lord Beaverbrook was criticized by his own paper, the *Daily Express*, with a cartoon poking fun at his outdated worldview which promoted an exclusive "British World" of trade.[165] The cartoon showed Beaverbrook speaking to a Shadow Cabinet, composed exclusively of his clones before a "Map of the World (Up to Date)" (Fig. 4.8).

On the Mercator map, the entire world's nations were omitted except the United States and those in the British Commonwealth. But while the Commonwealth nations were inked in solid black, the United States was rendered in white with fragmented borders—it was "disappearing" from the map. The Colonial Secretary addressed the Shadow Cabinet with his arms raised, and the caption read, "The Shadow Cabinet meets, and solves the crisis in the twinkling of an eye." Beaverbrook's simplistic solution to American insistence on free trade in the Commonwealth was to erase the nation from the world map. While this cartoon was humorous in light of a renewed British need for American military support in the late 1940s, Beaverbrook's map of the world resembled *Serial Map Service* maps from the mid-1940s that centered on the British Empire and often excluded the

The Shadow Cabinet meets, and solves the crisis in the twinkling of an eye.

Cummings—London Express

The Beaver's own newspaper kids him about the way he lays down policies . . .

Fig. 4.8   By the late 1940s, British fears of Soviet destabilization of world peace and trade prompted closer ties to US foreign policy. Ideas of an exclusive British Empire became outdated and were often criticized in cartoons with map imagery. This cartoon appeared in the *Daily Express* in October 1949. The map satirized Liberal Unionist Lord Beaverbrook's passé nationalist foreign policy

United States. The caricature of Beaverbrook was no doubt humorous to Americans, too, when the cartoon was reprinted in *Newsweek* roughly two weeks later.[166]

A Case Study in "Two Worlds" Symbolism: The "Atoms for Peace" Stamp

Due to factors discussed in the Introduction, the presidency of Dwight D. Eisenhower coincided with the first thaw (a not entirely straightforward respite) in the Cold War. Within two years of his election, a new national security policy emerged, known as the "New Look," which sought to balance Republican concerns of federal overspending in defense while seeking more effective global air superiority in the nuclear age. But this new policy was fraught with inherent contradictions. His 1952 campaign promise to bring Americans home from the Korean War—a welcomed de-escalation from a foreign war that was already being viewed as a stalemate—was quickly overshadowed by the horrific implications of nuclear "massive retaliation" associated with the New Look policy. His promise to scale down conventional American armed forces in Europe was countered by new, massive propaganda and espionage programs in the same region. Undaunted by these inconsistencies, the Eisenhower administration endeavored to convince the American people and the world of the beneficial political, economic, and social implications of his new atomic foreign policy, employing a massive propaganda campaign of speeches, press releases, and, of course, cartographic imagery.

Osgood and Frank have shown that Eisenhower promoted the New Look in three phases. The first phase, which began in mid-April 1953 barely a month after Stalin's death, commenced with his "A Chance for Peace" speech before the American Society of Newspaper Editors. There, Eisenhower described the Cold War as a global moralistic struggle between evil communists and good capitalists—apropos generalizations, indeed, to engender sympathy for a new "Two Worlds" view.[167] The second phase begun later that year was the "Atoms for Peace" campaign. Beginning with Eisenhower's December speech at the United Nations, this campaign sought to assuage American and international fears of his administration's recent hydrogen bomb tests while extolling the virtues of newly acquired atomic power among political allies. The funding and administration of this second phase fell under a larger federal program wishfully called "Operation Candor."[168] The "Open Skies" initiative comprised the last phase of selling the New Look to the world. Capitalizing on the chance to address the new leader of the Soviet Union, Nikita Khrushchev, at the 1955 Geneva Summit, Eisenhower proposed a new US–Soviet agreement to allow both sides to overfly each other's air space. The hope was that such cooperation would allow each superpower to validate the other's compliance with nuclear arms control and thereby reduce Cold War geopolitical tensions.[169]

The Eisenhower administration relied heavily on friendly relations with the American press to publicize the goals of the New Look policy. In Osgood's 2006 study of the administration's propaganda campaign, he noted that "Eisenhower could count on *Time-Life* publications [including *Fortune* magazine] to sell his Cold War policies to the American public and the wider readership abroad." By the mid-1950s, the friendly press included the *New York Times*, *Newsweek*, and the *New York Herald Tribune*.[170] To spread the

Fig. 4.9 The 1953 US
"Atoms for Peace"
stamp was commissioned
by the Eisenhower
administration to
promote the idea that
American atomic power
could be used for more
positive ends than
nuclear war

word about the "Atoms for Peace" initiative, the administration also utilized the prolific and patriotic tradition of the US Postal Service to commission a commemorative postage stamp. In December 1953, the resulting "Atoms for Peace" stamp relied heavily on cartographic imagery to promote a new world vision which sought to portray heretofore alarming nuclear technology as an agent of peace and social progress (Fig. 4.9). The stamp employed cartographic imagery to portray the New Look world as united by the atomic "inventiveness of man," with both halves of the globe ringed by stylized orbits of subatomic particles. In Osgood's description of the stamp, he noted that its imagery "depicted a world encircled by the symbolic energy."[171] But his reading of the imagery may be too straightforward.

At first glance, the "Atoms for Peace" stamp imagery does appear to portray a unified, peaceful world in the new atomic age. However, a more nuanced reading of the cartographic imagery exposes subtle Cold War–era geopolitical bipolarity characteristic of the Eisenhower era. Osgood's description of the imagery as a *single* world encircled by atomic energy is somewhat misleading. Actually, the stamp depicted *two* worlds—two *separate* spheres meant to convey Cold War bipolar global society. As this study has shown, there were many traditional and recently designed Air Age cartographic projections that could have been employed, which would have related a unified single globe with greater effectiveness (see Chap. 3). Instead, the stamp's designers chose to portray two globes—Cold War bipolarity in its simplest form. The orientation of the two globes' landmasses further reinforced 1950s' American foreign policy concerns. The globe on the left, through its selective continental positioning and shading, emphasized the United States as the dominant nation in the Western Hemisphere. Latin American nations south of Central America were obscured by dark shading and bright lettering. With both globes oriented with true North at the top of the stamp, the globe on the left—the *western* globe—might be viewed as the Western capitalist world. Visible on the western globe was not only the United States but also all of its major Western capitalist allies including Canada and the western European nations. The western globe reinforced its Western capitalist identity as it effectively portrayed all the founding nations of the North Atlantic Treaty Organization (NATO), except Italy. If the stamp designers had rotated the western globe westward to reveal Italy, it would have had the unintended consequence of depicting the most populated section of the Soviet Union and much of communist-controlled Eastern Europe. And obscuring the Southern Hemispheres of both globes— regions dominated by the industrially underdeveloped and (largely) politically neutral Third World—reminded readers that the Cold War geopolitical battle was largely a North Atlantic exercise. The orientation of both globes also relegated the entire African continent to the southern periphery. As Lewis and Wigen argued, this was not new to the Cold War era as earlier cartographic depictions of West versus East saw Africa as "threatening to fall off the map."[172]

The globe on the right side of the stamp's map—the eastern side— seems to conform to the prevailing contemporary American view that the Eastern world was a separate communist world dominated by the Russians. Although the majority of Russian people have resided west of the Ural Mountains and closer to western Europe than China, viewing Russians as an eastern people was nothing new. Lewis and Wigen have pointed out that western Europeans have traditionally seen Russians as "only vaguely European" and "certainly not Western" due to the popularity of the Russian Orthodox Church, Russian's intermittent isolation from western Christian society, and the people's historic contact with Mongolians and Turks. And a sort of geographic determinism has underscored the western idea that Russia's history of totalitarianism was derived from its close proximity to Asian cultures.[173] Early Cold War developments reinforced these concepts. Soviet occupation of Eastern Europe prompted labels of "Soviet Europe" and "Eastern communism" as distinct from Western capitalist society. Churchill's "Iron Curtain" speech, the Berlin Crisis, the Chinese communist revolt, and the onset of the Korean War convinced the American press that the postwar Eurasian landmass embodied a new Soviet communist colonial realm. American news maps began frequently referring to Eurasia as a "Lost Horizon," a "Soviet sphere," and a continent "in the shadow of the sickle" by the early 1950s.[174]

The "Atoms for Peace" stamp's cartographic portrayal of the eastern globe graphically reinforced the idea that Eurasia was a separate world dominated by communism. Eurasia comprised Eastern Europe, the Soviet Union, China, Southeast Asia, and India—all regions where communist political or military threats had been feared in the American press for several years. Africa's presence was once again consigned to the periphery as it was on the western globe. Capitalist NATO allies otherwise visible in the eastern hemisphere were obscured or hidden. American-occupied Japan was partially covered by one of the stylized atomic orbital paths. And the massive capitalist continent of Australia was completely eclipsed by the same shading and bright lettering that covered Latin America on the western globe. The Antarctic Continent, then still a region of unresolved conflict between capitalists and communists (see Chap. 3), was similarly obscured on both western and eastern globes.

The Eisenhower administration's cartographic portrayal of the Cold War world on the "Atoms for Peace" stamp thus presented a substantial contradiction between the program's stated goal of promoting global unity and deft imagery that reinforced preexisting American views of a contentious, bipolar Cold War world. In his 2014 study entitled *Diplomacy at the Brink: Eisenhower, Churchill, and Eden in the Cold War*, historian David Watry argued that Eisenhower's "New Look" foreign policy itself contained a similarly confusing contradiction. While Eisenhower publicly spoke to the benefits of building closer ties with capitalist European allies to thwart the growing communist threat, he nonetheless began a pattern of unilateral overt militarization and covert espionage campaigns in the same region.[175] The administration's public promotions of a more multilateral Containment policy were countered by the reality of Eisenhower's unilateral actions in Europe. Similarly, the administration's propagandistic message of global unity obvious in the promotion of the "Atoms for Peace" program was betrayed by the subtle "two worlds" cartographic symbolism in its commemorative stamp.

NOTES

1. Edy Kaufman, *The Superpowers and Their Spheres of Influence: The United States and the Soviet Union in Eastern Europe and Latin America* (London: Croom Helm, 1976), 11.
2. Susan A. Brewer, *To Win the Peace: British Propaganda in the United States during World War II* (Ithaca and London: Cornell University Press, 1997), 163.

3. Jay Sexton, *The Monroe Doctrine: Empire and Nation in Nineteenth-Century America* (New York: Hill and Wang, 2011), 16.
4. Julian P. Boyd, Charles T. Cullen, et al., eds., *The Papers of Thomas Jefferson* (Princeton: Princeton University Press, 1950), 237–238. Quote taken from a letter from Thomas Jefferson to George Rogers Clark, dated December 25, 1780.
5. Sexton, 49–60.
6. For the wording of the Monroe Doctrine, see http://www.yale.edu/law-web/avalon/monroe.htm.
7. Sexton, 5, 61–62.
8. Walter La Feber, ed., *John Quincy Adams and American Continental Empire* (Chicago: Quadrangle Books, 1965), 109–115. See also Sexton, 62.
9. See David Slater's essay entitled "Space, Democracy and Difference: For a Post-colonial Perspective" in David Featherstone's and Joe Painter's (eds.) book, *Spatial Politics: Essays for Doreen Massey* (West Sussex, U.K.: John Wiley and Sons, Ltd., 2013), 72.
10. Lester D. Langley, *America and the Americas: The United States in the Western Hemisphere* (Athens, Georgia and London: University of Georgia Press, 1989), 57–58, 60–61.
11. Ibid., 90.
12. Sexton, 163–165, 182–183.
13. Alfred T. Mahan, *The Influence of Sea Power upon History, 1660–1783* (Boston: Little, Brown and Co., 1890).
14. Wilfrid Hardy Callcott, *The Western Hemisphere: Its Influence on United States Policies to the End of World War II* (Austin and London: University of Texas Press, 1968), 58–61.
15. Ibid., 66.
16. Ibid., 66–67.
17. Ibid., 80–81.
18. Sexton, 237.
19. Both images in Fig. 4.1 were taken from online archives located at: http://www.authentichistory.com/images/1900s.
20. Mark Twain. "To Those Sitting in Darkness" in *North American Review*, v.531 (February 1901): 161–176.
21. Ross Hoffman, "Europe and the Atlantic Community" in *Thought*, v.20 (1945): 25.
22. Elizabeth Spalding, *The First Cold Warrior: Harry Truman, Containment, and the Remaking of Liberal Internationalism* (Lexington, KY: University Kentucky Press, 2006), 2.
23. Julius W. Pratt, *A History of United States Foreign Policy* (2nd ed.) (Englewood Cliffs, N.J.: Prentice-Hall, Inc., 1965), 367–369.
24. Callcott, 140.

25. Langley, 114–115.
26. Callcott, 141–142.
27. Ibid., 285.
28. John Lewis Gaddis, *Strategies of Containment: A Critical Appraisal of American National Security Policy during the Cold War* (New York: Oxford University Press, 2005), 10.
29. Originally quoted in Hoffman, 25–26. See United Nations charter, Article 21, Chapter VIII, Section C.
30. Ibid., 52–53.
31. Ibid., 53.
32. Ibid.
33. Brewer, 163.
34. Ibid., 42.
35. Clifford H. MacFadden, Henry Madison Kendall and George Dewey, *Atlas of World Affairs* (New York: Thomas Y. Crowell Co., 1946), 31.
36. See Richard Francaviglia's book *Go East, Young Man: Imagining the American West as the Orient* (Logan, UT: Utah State University Press, 2011).
37. Robert Hathaway, *Great Britain and the United States: Special Relations since World War II* (Boston: Twayne Publishers, 1990), 10–11.
38. Daniel Yergin, *Shattered Peace: The Origins of the Cold War and the National Security State* (Boston: Houghton Mifflin, 1978), 61.
39. Neil Smith, *American Empire: Roosevelt's Geographer and the Prelude to Globalization* (Berkeley: University of California Press, 2003), 359.
40. Sexton, 63.
41. Dexter Perkins, *The Monroe Doctrine: 1826–1867* (Baltimore: Johns Hopkins Press, 1933), 193–252. See also Sexton, 133.
42. For an excellent account of Schomburgk's survey, see D. Graham Burnett, *Masters of All They Surveyed: Exploration, Geography, and a British El Dorado* (Chicago and London: The University of Chicago Press, 2000).
43. Ibid., 199–200.
44. Sexton, 238.
45. C.J. Bartlett, *British Foreign Policy in the Twentieth Century* (New York: St. Martin's Press, 1989), 62. See also Hathaway, 13.
46. J. Robert Wegs and Robert Ladrech, *Europe Since 1945: A Concise History* (4th ed.) (New York: St. Martin's Press, 1996), 6–7.
47. Ibid., 7.
48. Ibid.
49. Robin Edmonds, *The Big Three: Churchill, Roosevelt and Stalin in Peace and War* (New York and London: W.W. Norton, 1991), 388.
50. Ibid., 389.
51. Ibid., 388.

52. Thomas G. Paterson, *On Every Front: The Making and Unmaking of the Cold War* (2nd ed.) (New York and London: W.W. Norton and Company, 1992), 42.

53. For the wording of this speech, see http://www.fordham.edu/halsall/mod/churchill-iron.html.

54. Japan's expansion in the Pacific is the major exception to this statement. Japanese World War II–era military attacks on the US possessions of Alaska and Hawaii underscored this exception.

55. Guntram Henrik Herb, *Under the Map of Germany: Nationalism and Propaganda, 1918–1945* (London and New York: Routledge, 1997), *passim*, and Mark Monmonier, *How to Lie with Maps* (2nd ed.) (Chicago and London: University of Chicago Press, 1996), 99–107.

56. Nancy Mitchell. *The Dangers of Dreams: German and American Imperialism in Latin America* (Chapel Hill: University of North Carolina Press, 1999), 3, 41. Sexton, 225.

57. Herb, 2.

58. *Facts In Review*, v.3, n.13 (April 1941): 182. See Monmonier, 107.

59. Pratt, 353–354.

60. See J.B. Harley's essay "Deconstructing the Map" in John Agnew's *Human Geography* (New York: Blackwell, 1996), 422–443.

61. Slater, 72.

62. Caroline Elkins, *Britain's Gulag: The Brutal End of Empire in Kenya* (London: Pimlico Press, 2005), 5.

63. Howard K. Beale, *Theodore Roosevelt and the Rise of America* (Baltimore: Johns Hopkins University Press, 1956), 134. Sexton, 238.

64. Brewer, 163.

65. Sexton, 237.

66. "Greenland: A Warning to Axis—What Occupation of Danish Colony Means to Hemisphere Defense" in *U.S. News and World Report*, v.10, n.16 (April 14, 1941): 16–17.

67. Ibid., 17.

68. *U.S. News and World Report*, v.11, n.3 (July 18, 1941): 11.

69. Warren F. Kimball, *Forged in War: Roosevelt, Churchill, and the Second World War* (New York: William Morrow and Co., 1997), 203.

70. British colonial areas in the Americas by 1945 included the Bermuda, Jamaica, the Windward and Leeward Islands, Barbados, Trinidad, Tobago, the Bahamas, British Guiana, and British Honduras. This is excluding the contested areas of the Falklands Islands and a short-lived claim to a section of Antarctica.

71. *Newsweek*, v.24, n.17 (Oct. 23, 1944): 68.

72. F.S. Northedge and Audrey Wells, *British and Soviet Communism: The Impact of a Revolution* (London: Macmillan Press, 1982), 103.

73. Sydney Morrel, *Spheres of Influence* (New York: Duell, Sloan and Pearce, 1946), 92–93. Morrell argues that although outgoing Prime Minister Churchill pressed for continued hegemony in Iran, the British presence there was largely commercial and not heavily regulated, while the British government's involvement continued to be indirect.

74. Randall Bennett Woods, *A Changing of the Guard: Anglo-American Relations, 1941–1946* (Chapel Hill and London: University of North Carolina Press, 1990), 291.

75. See map entitled "Middle East Oil Map" in *Serial Map Service*, v.7, n.9 (June, 1946): map 360.

76. Justus D. Doenecke, *Not to the Swift: The Old Isolationists in the Cold War Era* (London: Associated University Presses, 1979), 58–59.

77. Woods, 291.

78. Fraser J. Harbutt, *The Iron Curtain: Churchill, America, and the Origins of the Cold War* (New York and Oxford: Oxford University Press, 1986), 133.

79. Woods, 10.

80. Ibid., 30.

81. Brewer, 164–165.

82. Woods, 13–14.

83. Brewer, 165.

84. GBCP membership was 12,000 in 1941, and rose to 65,000 in 1942. See Northedge and Wells, 152.

85. David Childs, *Britain since 1945: A Political History* (New York: St, Martin's Press, 1979), 35. The GBCP won two seats in the 1945 general election. See Northedge and Wells, 104.

86. See ad for *Sunday Times* reporter Rebecca West's article entitled "Facts Behind the Witch-Hunts" in the *New Statesman and Nation*, v.45, n.1150 (Mar. 21, 1953): 345.

87. See ad for the *News Chronicle* in the *New Statesman and Nation*, v.50, n.1277 (Aug. 27, 1955): 241; see ad for Collet's Bookshop in *New Statesman and Nation*, v.50, n.1287 (Nov. 5, 1955): 578.

88. See J.F. Horrabin's map set in the *London Tribune*, n.450 (Aug. 10, 1945): 7.

89. *U.S. News and World Report*, v.18, n.21 (May 5, 1945): 13.

90. *Time*, v.45, n22 (May 28, 1945): 21.

91. See Richard H. Ullman's essay entitled "America, Britain, and the Soviet Threat in Historical and Present Perspective" in William Roger Louis and Hedley Bull (eds.), *The 'Special Relationship': Anglo-American Relations Since 1945* (Oxford: Clarendon Press, 1986), 103.

92. David Reynolds, "Rethinking Anglo-American Relations," *Royal Institute of International Affairs*, v.65, n.1 (Winter, 1988–1989): 94.

93. H.C. Allen, *Great Britain and the United States: A History of Anglo-American Relations (1783–1952)* (London: Odhams Press, 1954); Reynolds, 94.

94. Leon D. Epstein, *Britain – Uneasy Ally* (Chicago: University of Chicago Press, 1954); Reynolds, 94.

95. Louis Liebovich, *The Press and the Origins of the Cold War, 1944–1947* (New York and London: Praeger, 1988), 2.

96. Walter Lippmann, *U.S. War Aims* (Boston: Little, Brown and Co., 1944); see *Newsweek*, v.24, n.2 (Jul. 10, 1944): 96.

97. *New Statesman and Nation*, v.31, n.783 (Feb. 23, 1946): 131.

98. Woods, 293.

99. Bartlett, 68.

100. Hathaway, 12–13.

101. See map entitled "Reshuffle" in *Time*, v.47, n.4 (Jan. 28, 1946): 26.

102. Hathaway, 13.

103. Ibid., 14–15.

104. Neil Smith, *American Empire: Roosevelt's Geographer and the Prelude to Globalization* (Berkeley: University of California Press, 2003), 359. See also Bartlett, 69–70, 74.

105. See these maps in the following issues of *Serial Map Service*: "BOAC," v.7, n.6 (March, 1946): 63–64; "British Empire," v.7, n.7 (April, 1946): map 352–353; "French Empire," v.7, n.8 (May, 1946): map 356–357; and "European Passenger Transport," v.7, n.12 (September, 1946): map 370–371.

106. A good example is the economic map of Australia in *Serial Map Service*, v.2, n.5 (February, 1941): map 67.

107. See ad for Barclay's Bank of London in *Spectator*, v.183, n.6331 (Oct. 28, 1949): 569.

108. Paterson, 62–66.

109. Gaddis, 301–302.

110. Melvyn P. Leffler, *A Preponderance of Power: National Security, the Truman Administration, and the Cold War* (Stanford: Stanford University Press, 1992), 108.

111. Ibid.

112. Ibid., 108–109.

113. Ibid., 109.

114. Sean Greenwood, "Frank Roberts and the 'Other' Long Telegram: the View from the British Embassy in Moscow, March 1946" in *Journal of Contemporary History*, v.25, n.1 (January 1990): 110.

115. Ibid., 111.

116. Ibid., 114.

117. Ibid.

118. Ibid., 115.
119. Sebastian Haffner, "The Communist Curtain: 'Russian Sphere of Influence in Europe'" in *Serial Map Service*, v.8, n.10 (July 1947): 162–163.
120. Ibid., 162.
121. Ibid.
122. Ibid., 163.
123. Ibid.
124. Ibid.
125. Ibid., map 416.
126. Aldo Cassuto, "Ports and Politics" in *Time and Tide*, v.30, n.15 (Apr. 9, 1949): 345.
127. Ibid.
128. *Time*, v.47, n.11 (Mar. 18, 1946): 24.
129. See map entitled "How The Communist Vote Has Varied In Europe's Elections" in *NYT*, v.95, n.32,278 (Jun. 6, 1946): E5; see map entitled "The Split In Europe Between East And West" in *NYT*, v.97, n.32,796 (Nov. 9, 1947): E1.
130. *Newsweek*, v.32, n.4 (Jul. 26, 1948): 30.
131. See map entitled "Marshall Plan Giveaway To Europe" in *American*, v.148, n.2 (August 1949): 24–25; see map entitled "Voice Of America" in *American*, v.150, n.1 (July 1950): 26–27.
132. *Time and Tide*, v.28, n.35 (Sept. 13, 1947): 976.
133. Martin W. Lewis and Karen E. Wigen, *The Myth of Continents: A Critique of Metageography* (Berkeley: University of California Press, 1997), 6.
134. Ibid., 49–51.
135. *U.S. News and World Report*, v.20, n.22 (May 24, 1946): 21.
136. Ibid., 19–21.
137. Gaddis, 309.
138. Paterson, 52.
139. See map entitled "Three Worlds and their problem spots" in *Newsweek*, v.27, n.5 (Feb. 4, 1946): 35; see map entitled "Marking Time" in *Time*, v.48, n.16 (Oct. 14, 1946): 31; see The *New York Times*, v.96, n.32,558 (Mar. 16, 1947): E1.
140. Ladrech and Wegs, 17.
141. Ibid.
142. Ibid.
143. Greenwood, 117.
144. Charles Wighton, "Buses Pass Blockade: German Railwaymen Get Order, 'Be at the Ready,'" in *Daily Express*, n.15,248 (Apr. 29, 1949): 1.
145. See maps entitled "The Occupation of Germany," *U.S. News and World Report*, v.18, n.24 (Jun. 15, 1945): 23; "Master Strokes: Overlord, Anvil," *Newsweek*, v.26, n.16 (Oct. 15, 1945): 56; "Berlin: Allied Zones

of Occupation," *Time*, v.46, n.2 (Jul. 16, 1945): 29; "Chart of U.S. Zone," *Time*, v.47, n.25 (Jun. 24, 1946): 26.

146. See maps entitled "Cold War Crystallized: Western Union v. Russian Satellites," in *Time*, v.51, n.5 (Feb. 2, 1948): 16; "Piece by Piece," in *Time*, v.51, n.10 (Mar. 10, 1948): 26; "Russian Travel Barrier in the Berlin Area," *Time*, v.51, n.15 (Apr. 12, 1951): 35; "Marshall Plan Giveaway to Europe," in *American*, v.148, n.2 (August, 1949): 24–25; "Watch on the Rhine," *Newsweek*, v.34, n.24 (Dec. 12, 1949): 34.

147. See map entitled "Playing With Fire?" in *Newsweek*, v.32, n.4 (Jul. 26, 1948): 30.

148. Doenecke, 162.

149. D.F. Fleming, *The Cold War and its Origins, 1917–1960* (Garden City, NY: Doubleday and Co., Inc., 1961) vol. 2, 584.

150. Roderick Farquhar and John K. Fairbank, *The Cambridge History of China* (Cambridge: Cambridge University Press, 1989) vol.14, "The People's Republic, Part I: the Emergence of Revolutionary China, 1949–1965," 64.

151. Edward R. Tufte, *The Visual Display of Quantitative Information* (Cheshire, CT: Graphics Press, 2001), 154.

152. See map entitled "Lost Horizon?" in *Time*, v.52, n.23 (Dec. 6, 1948): 28.

153. "War of Two Worlds: Results of the Summer Campaigns" in *Newsweek*, v.34, n.18 (Oct. 31, 1949): 24.

154. Kathryn P. Weathersby, "Should We Fear This?: Stalin and the Danger of War with America," Cold War International History Project: Working Paper No. 9 (Washington, D.C.: Woodrow Wilson International Center for Scholars, 2002), *passim*.

155. Kenneth Osgood and Andrew K. Frank, *Selling War in a Media Age: The Presidency and Public Opinion in the American Century* (Gainesville: University Press of Florida, 2010), 97.

156. Ibid., 116.

157. Ibid., 120–121.

158. Ibid., 114–115.

159. See map entitled "What We're Up Against" in *Newsweek*, v.36, n.3 (Jul. 17, 1950): 14.

160. *Saturday Evening Post*, v.225, n.12 (Sept. 20, 1952): 37.

161. *Fortune*, v.49, n.5 (May 1954): 105.

162. *U.S. News and World Report*, v.39, n.11 (Sept. 9, 1955): 23.

163. *Time and Tide*, v.29, n.3 (Jan. 17, 1948): 65.

164. Greg Barnhisel and Catherine Turner (eds.), *Pressing the Fight: Print, Propaganda, and the Cold War* (Amherst and Boston, MA: University of Massachusetts Press, 2010), 112.

165. *Daily Express*, n.15,390 (Oct. 12, 1949): 4.

166. *Newsweek*, v.34, n.17 (Oct. 24, 1949): 36.
167. Osgood and Frank, 153.
168. Kenneth Osgood, *Total Cold War: Eisenhower's Secret Propaganda Battle at Home and Abroad* (Lawrence, KS: University Press of Kansas, 2006), 156.
169. Osgood and Frank, 157–161.
170. Osgood, 82, 137 and 164. See also Hanson W. Baldwin's article "Military 'New Look'" in the *New York Times*, v.103, n.35,073 (Feb. 2, 1954): 11.
171. Osgood, 165.
172. Lewis and Wigen, 6.
173. Ibid., 57.
174. See maps entitled "Lost Horizon?" in *Time*, v.52, n.23 (Dec. 6, 1948): 28; "Two Worlds" in *Time*, v.55, n.1 (Jan. 2, 1950): 34–35; and "In the Shadow of the Sickle" in *Newsweek*, v.36, n.14 (Aug. 14, 1950): 25.
175. David M. Watry, *Diplomacy at the Brink: Eisenhower, Churchill, and Eden in the Cold War* (Baton Rouge: Louisiana State University Press, 2014), *passim*.

CHAPTER 5

Cold War Germany in News Maps

The defeat of Nazi Germany was the focus of the Allied effort in Europe during World War II. After 1945 the postwar Allied division and occupation of the nation made Germany a barometer of early Cold War tensions between capitalist Western democracies (England, the United States, and France) and the communist Soviet Union. However, while British and American news journals acknowledged that "a study of the map of [postwar] Europe must … begin with a study of Germany," their respective national political leaders had very different ideas about the place and importance of a divided Germany after 1945. We will examine just how British and American news journals expressed these differences in their own idiomatic ways on maps.

Four major themes characterized and differentiated British and American views of Cold War Germany on news maps. First, the very shape of the mapped image of Germany was far more important in the American press. Second, the advent of Iron Curtain rhetoric profoundly changed how both nations perceived the occupied zones of Germany. Third, both national presses, in their own way, sought to link sections of Cold War Germany to Nazi heritage. And fourth, by the late 1940s and early 1950s, American and British news journals found ways to link East Germany to geopolitical events in the Far East.

© The Author(s) 2019   151
J. P. Stone, *British and American News Maps in the Early Cold War Period, 1945–1955*, Palgrave Studies in the History of the Media,
https://doi.org/10.1007/978-3-030-15468-4_5

ONE OR TWO GERMANYS: NOT THREE

Germany underwent an astounding series of territorial changes in the five years between the end of World War II (when Nazi Germany was a large monolithic threat) and 1949 (when East and West Germany were officially created as separate states). In general, Germany was transformed from a large, monolithic nation in the Nazi era, to a bipolar, occupied region symbolizing Cold War tensions between East and West. Though both American and British news cartographers followed the transition from "one Germany" to "two Germanys," they proceeded in very different ways.

By the end of World War II, American news mapmakers had a rich history of equating the mapped image of a Nazi Germany with danger and aggression. Unlike the Japanese threat, however, which actually reached American soil at Pearl Harbor and the Aleutian Islands during the war, the immediacy of a German threat was somewhat more obscure in the American mind. Throughout the war, the Allied campaign against Hitler, fought in the North Atlantic Ocean, Europe, and North Africa, was not generally seen as a campaign to save the American homeland. To rally support against Hitler, news cartographers found creative ways to convince Americans that although Germany was a continent away, it still represented a threat to America. In the minds of some, the most direct way to bring the Nazi threat across the Atlantic Ocean with news maps was simply to superimpose a map of Nazi Germany over a map of the United States. This not-so-subtle maneuver, however, had the counter potential to portray a less menacing Germany by drawing attention to the obvious size disparity between the two nations. And to the uninitiated among Americans, geographic size on maps could easily (and often erroneously) equate with imperial power.

In any cartographic comparison of Nazi Germany to the United States designed to portray a German threat, American mapmakers had to overcome the reality that an accurate geographic portrayal of the two nations would likely communicate a preponderance of American power. Simply put, the numerous American overseas possessions notwithstanding, the continental United States dwarfed Nazi Germany. So to convince American news readers that Germany was a real threat, mapmakers had to do some heavy map manipulation. For example, in February 1945, *U.S. News and World Report* published a map entitled "Suppose Pittsburgh Were Berlin." This map showed the eastern half of the United States overlain by a map of Germany.[1] The eastern United States was a pale tint with black borders, contrasting with the menacing red German nation that stretched from Tennessee to New Hampshire. As the accompanying article truthfully stated, "Germany ... is a small country that could be set down in one corner of the United States."[2] And accurately comparing a map of Germany to a full map of the United States would have made the Nazi nation seem overmatched and non-threatening. The intent mapmaker compensated for this by omitting the American states west of the Mississippi River Valley. Similarly, the long, peninsular state of Florida and northern New England were left off the map because they would have presented large landforms free from the shadow of the Nazism.

Equally interesting was the portrayal of Germany on the map. Although by the time the map was published, the German region of East Prussia had come under Allied control, the mapmaker's inclusion of this area as a fascist component of the unified German state greatly exaggerated the extent of Nazi power. The placement of East Prussia over New York City—the most populated city in the United States—certainly made the map more alarming. Interestingly, this positioning also placed Germany over the most industrialized portion of the United States; this was yet another way of implying the threat that Germany posed. Also, the inclusion of non-German warfronts in Budapest and Bologna, which overlapped southern Georgia and Cape Hatteras, respectively, made Germany appear to extend 200 miles south and west of its actual borders.

In reality, this mapped image of Nazi Germany would have been even larger and more intimidating if the mapmaker had included all areas acquired by Hitler after 1936. After militarizing the Rhineland in that year, Germany had taken control of Austria and the Sudetenland by late 1938.[3] The following year, Bohemia, Moravia, Slovakia, Poland, Danzig, and Memel fell under Nazi control. Moreover, a map of Nazi military power, which eventually stretched from the Soviet Union and Scandinavia in the north to North Africa and the Mediterranean Rim in the south, would have dwarfed a map of the United States. However, American news cartographers generally followed the national political preference of not recognizing Nazi political or territorial expansions as legitimate. For American news readers, the shape of the Nazi menace on maps was bound by 1936 German borders throughout the war. The designers of the *U.S. News and World Report* map thus reduced the area of the underlying US map so that the overlaid map of 1936 Germany, with added warfront extensions, would look more dangerous by comparison. By relating the size of a mapped region to its inherent power, cartographers employed a practice that was at once misleading and non-objective. Although World War II–era German leaders would take issue with the cartographic manipulations evident in *U.S. News and World Report*, Nazi propaganda maps frequently used the similar tactics to defend German expansion throughout the war.

As Mark Monmonier has shown, in early February 1940, the German periodical *Facts In Review* published two black ink maps entitled "A Study in Empires" which compared the apparent size of Nazi Germany with that of the British Empire.[4] The German state, colored solid black, included the Rhineland, the Saarland, the Sudetenland, Austria, and northwest Poland. The protectorates of Central Poland, Bohemia, and Moravia were delineated with black borders only. Still, Germany appeared miniscule compared to the numerous landmasses controlled by Great Britain which were noted to cover "26% of the World." The mapmaker colored all areas of Great Britain, colonial regions, and the British Commonwealth identically in solid black, but labeled the map "Great Britain" above the British Isles. This technique centralized and legitimized vast British imperial power at the British Isles and contrasted with diminutive Nazi territorial claims on the nearby map. The island of Ireland was properly shown to be divided between the Protestant Northern Ireland (allied with Great Britain) and the independent and Catholic Irish Free State (IFS). However, because the IFS was officially neutral in World War II, it was outlined in the same fashion that signified Nazi protectorates on the map of Germany.

Nazi Germany may have been dwarfed by the British Empire on maps, but it was certainly much larger than the British Isles. During World War II, British news cartographers could have overlapped maps of Germany and the British Isles to alert citizens of the Nazi threat. But there was no need to warn English news readers of something they dealt with every day. Whereas Americans had to be convinced to join the war, the British were drawn into it to survive. For them, the Nazi threat was not an abstract foreign concern, but a domestic one, especially after Hitler began bombing England in late 1939. It is not surprising, then, that no cartographic comparisons between Great Britain, or her empire, and Nazi Germany have been found in the British national press during World War II. One recalls that British wartime news maps tended to detail small areas in large scale, a practice which precluded any size comparisons of warring nations. British maps catered to a public already familiar with European and German regions and place names; smaller-scale maps of larger regions were seldom needed to put German warfronts in geopolitical perspective. Consequently, unlike in the United States, the cartographic image of Hitler's Germany apparently never became an alarmist symbol of anti-Nazism in British society.

American news journals during World War II, however, found it beneficial to exaggerate the size of Nazi Germany on maps as a means to
heighten the American fighting spirit. This cartographic tactic worked as
long as Germany itself was perceived as a monolithic threat. However, the
end of the war saw a defeated Nazi Germany carved up among the four
victorious Allies and Poland. At Yalta, and later at Potsdam in July 1945,
Germany was divided into four Allied zones, as was Berlin.[5] The former
German territory of East Prussia was also divided—the northern zone
went to the Soviet Union, the southern zone to Poland (Fig. 5.1).
Poland's borders were shifted 200 miles westward, at Germany's expense,
and the new Polish–German border followed the Oder and Neisse Rivers.

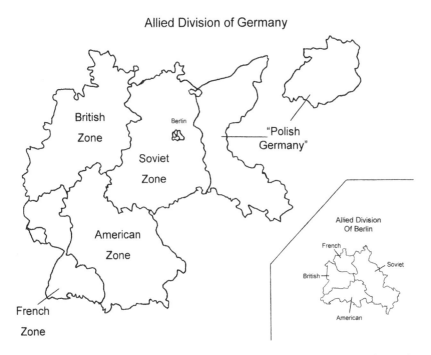

Fig. 5.1 The post-World War II division of Germany presented a complex multinational chessboard of Allied and Polish interests. The bulk of the former Nazi
nation and its capital of Berlin were divided between the four Allies—England, the
United States, France, and the Soviet Union. Most East German lands were given
to Poland. (Map compiled by author)

Did a credible postwar German threat still exist? And if so, how could American news mapmakers portray this threat, especially since the victorious Allies now controlled the divided nation?

The postwar German threat to the United States (although it took a few years to develop) came to be the communist, Soviet-controlled zone of Germany. In the anticommunist fervor that developed in Western nations after World War II, Germany was seen as the crux of a developing Cold War bipolarity. American anti-Soviet sentiment, which never completely disappeared during World War II, surged in response to Joseph Stalin's territorial ambitions in Iran in 1946, and to the Stalinization of Eastern Europe that followed World War II.[6] The beginning of the Greek Civil War, Winston Churchill's subsequent Iron Curtain speech, and George Kennan's famous "Long Telegram" spurred many American news journals by 1947 to reassess the vulnerability of Germany to communist influence.[7]

Unlike similarly divided Austria, the four Allied zones of Germany had been moving toward an east–west polarization since the end of World War II. Great Britain transferred its financial dealings in the British zone to American control in late 1946; France did the same by February 1948.[8] The American and British zones were combined into "Bizonia" in January 1947.[9] However, it was not until the 1948 Berlin crisis that the American citizenry began seeing the Soviet zone of Germany as a serious threat to postwar peace and as a sort of barometer of Cold War tensions. The introduction of a new West German currency in 1948 threatened to seriously undermine the economy of East Berlin, and Stalin responded by blockading all land access to between the whole of Berlin and the West. The Soviet message was a categorical declaration that all Allied control in West Berlin was thereby defunct. The resulting Berlin Airlift of supplies and necessities to the cut-off West Berliners by the Western powers was duly celebrated in the American press, especially after Stalin, apparently recognizing the futility of his strategy, reopened access to Berlin the following year.[10] Stalin's blockade of Berlin quashed all hope in the American press that the Allies could realistically affect an autonomous, unified Germany. The land was partitioned into two states in October 1949. The combined Western capitalist zones now comprised West Germany, or the Federal Republic of Germany (FRG), and West Berlin. The Soviet zone became East Germany, or the communist German Democratic Republic (GDR), and East Berlin. Throughout the remainder of the Cold War, almost all American news maps would portray Germany in terms of its bipolarity—FRG versus GDR—or the "two Germanys."

Unlike during World War II, when the mapped image of Nazi Germany was a symbol of Nazi aggression, postwar maps of the GDR never commanded the same importance in the early Cold War American press. Given that the FRG was roughly three times larger than the GDR, size comparisons of these states on maps would have suggested the GDR to be the weaker of the two. Consequently, the American press rarely made such size-oriented cartographic comparisons of the two Germanys. However, if American news cartographers had been more sensitive to how *West Germans* perceived Cold War Germany—that there were, in fact, "three Germanys," not two—size comparisons between capitalist and communist Germanys would not have cast East Germany as the underdog. In the West German view, the "third" Germany consisted of all the lands east of the Oder–Neisse line taken in 1945 from Nazi Germany and given to Poland and the Soviet Union. Since the majority of these lands were transferred to Poland, this area has often been called "Polish Germany" on maps, obviously ignoring the northern section of East Prussia given to the Soviet Union. Although Allied leaders embraced the transfer of these lands to Poland as just compensation for Nazi aggression, and to balance eastern Polish lands given to the Soviets, the FRG government staunchly resisted the concept that Germany's eastern border ended at the Oder–Neisse line.[11]

In 1953, FRG Chancellor Konrad Adenauer vowed that the German people would never accept the Oder–Neisse line as the eastern boundary of Germany.[12] This sentiment, no doubt, derived from the precedent of aggressive German occupation in Poland. After 1945, however, this occupation was reversed with the forced westward evacuation of millions of ethnic Germans. Adenauer was also voicing a general FRG adherence to a 1937 German law that defined citizenship in the Reich as including all of Polish Germany.[13] As late as 1955, official FRG atlases relied on the 1937 citizenship law to define German borders. On a West German atlas map from 1955, the FRG, the GDR, and Polish Germany were clearly defined from each other with dark borders (Fig. 5.2).[14] Berlin was divided, and the Saarland was separated from the FRG. But similar yellow coloring of the "three Germanys" linked them across border lines, as did a wider, light-brown border that circumscribed the entire original 1937 German state. Text labels describing Polish Germany as German lands under Polish and Soviet administration, and the appearance of a unified East Prussia (no longer divided between Poland and the Soviet Union), contrasted sharply with contemporary American and Soviet maps which adhered to Allied partition treaties.

Fig. 5.2 This map from a 1955 West German atlas rejected the Allied division of postwar Germany. Instead of a polarized Cold War Germany, this map reminisced about the former "Three Germanys" which included West, East, and "Polish Germany." The mapmaker found ways to unite German-speaking peoples across Cold War lines separating the three Germanys, mainly with border shading, uniform toponym design, and a diminished set of Cold War partition borders

Despite the importance of the FRG as a bastion against the GDR after 1949, the FRG idea of "three Germanys" was never endorsed by the American or British governments, or by their respective national presses. All Allied nations (including the Soviet Union) held firm to the German borders established at Yalta and Potsdam for the duration of the Cold War. In the American press, only one map is known to exist from 1945 to 1955 that described "three Germanys." Entitled "Three Germanys," this map by Robert M. Chapin, Jr., was published by *Time* magazine in August 1953, and it did not accompany any particular news article (Fig. 5.3).[15] It was

Fig. 5.3   In the only map of "three Germanys" known to exist in the American news press, published in *Time* magazine in 1953, primacy was given to Cold War geopolitics that downplayed pan-German heritage. Communist East Europe, colored red, was dominated by East Germany. "Polish Germany" was seen to be lost to communist advancements

printed with an extensive caption, and when contrasted with the 1955 West German atlas map, it highlighted how very differently Americans and West Germans each viewed Cold War Germany. While the 1955 FRG map utilized similar shades of yellow to "reunite" all German lands recognized under the 1937 citizenship law, *Time's* 1953 "Three Germanys" map left no doubt that World War II and Potsdam had profoundly redefined, even literally reshaped, Germany. *Time's* map painted the GDR a menacing blood red to denote communist occupation and to link it to Eastern Europe which (sans Poland) was colored a muddier red. Polish Germany and Poland were tinted a lighter red, but were still visualized as part of the communist bloc. Only on *Time's* map did bold fractures separate all "Three Germanys," as well as the two sections of East Prussia. Unlike the FRG map, the American view of the "Three Germanys" did not preserve the *Germanness* of the regions but rather viewed them in terms of Cold War anticommunist rhetoric by mapping them in the framework of European bipolarity.

Since the Soviets controlled East Germany and Polish Germany, American news cartographers could have easily lumped them together on maps as a singular communist German landmass. The resulting region would have offered a larger, and hence more menacing, threat to West Germany and Western Europe than did East Germany alone. Polish Germany, located between East Germany and Moscow, could have provided an alarming continuous land bridge between the center of Soviet power and the Iron Curtain. Moreover, fused "East Germany-Polish Germany" maps could have reinforced preexisting American notions that Nazis and Soviet communists were more alike than different. However, these *Pan-Germanism* concepts contradicted prevalent Cold War ideology of a bipolar Germany and Europe. They detracted from the conceived monolithic Soviet threat centered in Moscow, not Berlin.

In the British national press, as in the American press, the mapped image of "Three Germanys" was very rare in the early years of the Cold War. The *Serial Map Service* (*SMS*), however, occasionally published maps discussing the fate of Germany after World War II which portrayed the three sections. One such map, published in October 1947, dealt exclusively with the issue of the "Three Germanys" and offered a starkly different view than did Chapin's map discussed earlier (Fig. 5.4).[16]

The most obvious difference between Chapin's map and the *SMS* map is, again, the use of coloring. Chapin's map virtually exploded off the page in three shades of red, with "Russia's Germany" boldly inked in the brightest shade. The message sent by such coloring was, of course, that red equals dangerous communism. The *SMS* map of the "Three Germanys" was printed exclusively in black and white. It must be recalled from Chap. 2 that the *SMS* had access to, and often employed, a varied palette of colored inks in its monthly maps. The absence of red coloring to denote communist lands was an artistic choice and not a result of printing limitations suffered by the British weekly national press. Cartographic historians often discuss *absences* or *silences* on maps in terms of geographic formations, political boundaries, cities, and so forth, omitted to downplay the importance of those features.[17] But in this case, the selective absence of *color*, specifically the provocative Cold War–era red, is an equally telling omission. The *SMS* map is at first reading much less anticommunist than Chapin's map.

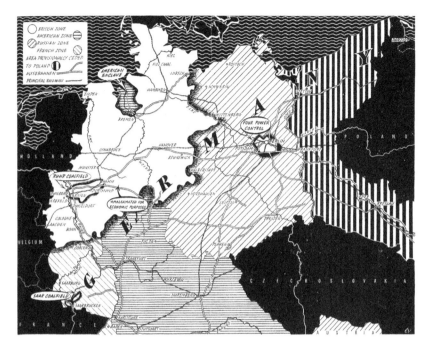

Fig. 5.4   This 1947 British *Serial Map Service* portrayal of the "Three Germanys" minimized Cold War bipolarity in the region. No ominous red ink was found in the communist areas. Line shading patterns distinguished the Allied zones but did not group communist and capitalist areas together. And all other European nations were colored the same basic black

The *SMS* map of the "Three Germanys" differentiated the five political zones of the region (the four-part Allied occupation zones and "Polish Germany") with black and white ink and line shading patterns. But no discernible concordance of shadings visually linked the communist zones or capitalist zones together. A partial explanation for this may be that the British Labour government at the time faced almost as much criticism from the Americans for its proposed socialist reforms in the British quarter of Germany as did the Soviets for their communistic reforms in Soviet Germany. As historian Julius W. Pratt has argued, before the British, French, and American governments reached a capitalist *modus vivendi* on occupied Germany, "[the] Labour government talked little of free enterprise and much of nationalizing the Ruhr industries."[18] Similarly, although the "Four Power Control" of Berlin was delineated (it was not on Chapin's map), the four city zones were melted together in a uniform white. From the map's portrayal, Berlin seemed rather immune to the surrounding political strife. Moreover, all European nations outside the "Three Germanys," both communist and capitalist, were colored with the same solid black ink—quite unlike Chapin's vivid portrayal of a divided Europe. Also noteworthy, the *SMS* map's depiction of major transportation modes—the Autobahn and railroads—gave an equal treatment to communist and capitalist occupied zones, a point to be discussed in greater detail at the end of this chapter.

The Iron Curtain Falls Across Germany

Arguably, the most powerful concept to shape Western ideas of post–World War II Germany was the Iron Curtain. Popularized by Winston Churchill's "Sinews of Peace" speech (popularly known as the "Iron Curtain" speech) in early March 1946, the Iron Curtain described the menacing "Soviet sphere" as the land east of a line "from Stettin in the Baltic to Trieste in the Adriatic."[19] This description was somewhat misleading since the Soviet sphere, according to Churchill himself, included the Soviet zone of East Germany—an area directly *west* of Stettin. Nevertheless, Churchill's Iron Curtain concept eventually became one of the most recognizable metaphors for the division of Cold War Germany and Europe in the American and British news presses.

Churchill's speech was delivered in Fulton, Missouri, with President Harry S. Truman in attendance—in fact, the setting was Westminster College, the president's alma mater—and was couched in alarmist terms that appealed more to American, rather than British, fears of communism. The idea of an Iron Curtain, however, was not immediately received favorably in American political circles. While moderates and conservatives accepted Churchill's evaluation of a Soviet threat, they contended his negative rhetoric and his plan for closer Anglo-American military ties were not beneficial to US interests. Left-wing politicians saw Churchill's comments as unduly antagonistic and lampooned the idea that the American military should support British imperialism.[20] Secretary of Commerce Henry Wallace's comment that "Churchill undoubtedly is not speaking either for the American people or their government or for the British people or their government" reflected a leftist fear that any Anglo-American bilateral maneuvers could undermine Rooseveltian multilateral cooperation in the newly formed United Nations.[21]

Many in the American press, however, immediately embraced the concept of an Iron Curtain in Europe. Lord Halifax responded to Churchill's speech in March 1946 by observing that the term "Iron Curtain … has given the sharpest jolt to American thinking of any utterance since the end of the war."[22] And historian Fraser J. Harbutt has noted the favorable reporting of Churchill's rhetoric in the *New York Times*, the *Wall Street Journal*, the *Christian Science Monitor*, the *New York World Telegram*, the *St. Louis Globe Democrat*, and, of course, *Time* magazine, which he described as "Churchill's most wholehearted supporter."[23] American news journalists readily put to work Churchill's catchy anticommunist phrases such as "Iron Curtain" and "Soviet sphere" in the headlines of countless articles. Consequently, news agencies quickly devised new Iron Curtain symbolism for maps to illustrate a growing communist threat in Europe.

Two weeks after Churchill's speech, *Time* magazine published a map entitled "Behind the Iron Curtain," which gave a perceived Soviet perspective on the ever unfolding "German question" (Fig. 5.5). The mapmaker, R.M. Chapin, Jr., cleverly oriented the map with Moscow at the lower right and with Europe extending westward toward the top. He symbolized the Iron Curtain as a red, chain-link barricade fronted with a large hammer and sickle and controlled (tethered) in Moscow. However, what Chapin possessed in artistic flair, he lacked in accuracy to both Churchill's concept and to reality. Chapin's Iron Curtain linked Trieste and Stettin in a contrived straight line that ignored actual borders, placing over ninety percent of the Soviet zone of Germany, and a good portion of western Czechoslovakia, outside the Soviet sphere (Fig. 5.6). Moreover, in order to place the city of Berlin behind his stylized Iron Curtain, Chapin relocated Berlin to the border between East Germany and Poland—fifty miles east of its actual location. Aside from the Iron Curtain, no other special map features distinguished the Soviet sphere from the rest of Europe. Polarization of the region had not yet been fully realized on news maps at this date.[24]

Furthermore, Chapin's early 1946 map did not present the Iron Curtain as an entirely impenetrable barrier between East and West. Rather, it depicted Czechoslovakia as a discontinuity, a weak point in the Iron Curtain. Historian Radomir Luža has noted that from 1945 to mid-1947, Czechoslovakia's successful democratic coalition government framed Western hopes that the nation could be a "bridge between East and West."[25] Perhaps Czechoslovakia was shaded lighter than the other nations to reflect this bit of optimism. Chapin imaginatively utilized the nation's

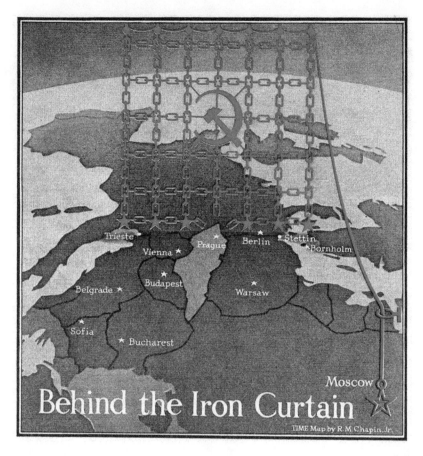

Fig. 5.5 The first American news map known to portray to the Iron Curtain, published in *Time* magazine two weeks after Churchill's 1946 speech, relocated Berlin to the Polish border to put it behind the curtain and preserve the barrier's straight line appearance

east–west orientation to make it appear as the only break in the heavy chain links of the Iron Curtain. This portrayal of Czechoslovakian exceptionalism departed from Churchill's description of a Soviet monolithic empire in Eastern Europe.

Between Churchill's speech in early 1946 and the beginning of the Berlin Crisis in mid-1948, many American news cartographers vacillated between placing the Soviet zone of Germany outside or inside the Soviet

Fig. 5.6 British politician Winston Churchill and American mapmaker Robert M. Chapin, Jr., depicted the "Iron Curtain" in distinctly different ways in 1946. Churchill's "Iron Curtain" progressed circuitously along national political borders from Stettin to Trieste. Chapin's "Iron Curtain," however, comprised a straight line between the two cities. (Map compiled by author)

sphere. Indeed, most news journals mapped the Soviet zone as a neutral region, outside the Soviet sphere. This changed in July 1947 when Stalin rejected Marshall Plan aid for Eastern Europe that included the Soviet zone of Germany. Thereafter, the Soviet zone was almost always shown behind the Iron Curtain on maps. The cartographic migration of the Iron Curtain westward to include the Soviet zone of Germany is best illustrated by news maps printed in the *New York Times*. Unlike weekly news journals which rarely republished the same maps, the *Times* relied on a relatively limited set of standard maps to illustrate foreign news events. These maps varied little through time except for subtle changes that reflected recent news items. In early June 1946, a *New York Times* map entitled "How the Communist Vote Has Varied in Europe's Elections" illustrated the percentage of parliamentary seats won by communist parties in the 1945 general elections (Fig. 5.7).[26] The *Times* symbolized the Iron Curtain as a raised, jagged wall labeled with a prominent text block. The Soviet zone of Germany was in front of the Iron Curtain—outside the Soviet sphere of influence. But the curtain's iconic impermeability was challenged by the mapmaker's method of illustrating the national communist vote data. In general, nations were shaded progressively darker to represent higher

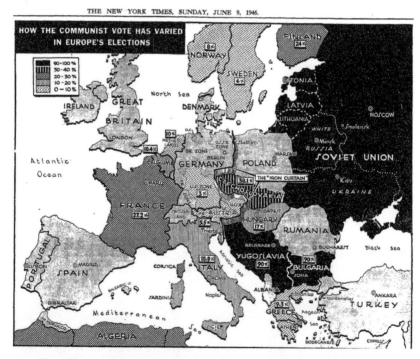

Fig. 5.7   In June 1946, the *New York Times* portrayed post–World War II Europe in multilayered "shades" of communist influence, and the Soviet zones in Germany and Austria were located to the west of the "Iron Curtain"

communist vote percentages, a visual device that introduced an unintended element of ambiguity. Non-democratic nations were shaded light
gray, which made Romania and Poland—nations inside the Soviet sphere
with Soviet-controlled governments—appear as noncommunist as Spain
and Portugal.[27] The numerical criteria of the shading key made France,
with 27.2 percent communist seats, look like a far-flung satellite of the
Soviet Union. Although French-controlled regions of North Africa had
no parliamentary elections, these regions were shaded like France, which
gave the impression that communism had spread there, too.

Stalin's denial of Marshall Plan aid to all areas controlled by the Soviet
Union (excepting the Soviet zone of Austria) in July 1947 compelled the
New York Times mapmakers to tweak their map of Cold War Europe. In
early November 1947, the *New York Times* published a map entitled "The
Split in Europe Between East and West," which placed the Soviet zone of
Germany behind the Iron Curtain (Fig. 5.8).[28] Although the same base
map was used as in the June 1946 map, the Soviet sphere, now defined in
economic rather than purely political terms, appeared much more threatening. Curiously, the July 1947 map placed the Soviet zone of Austria
behind the Iron Curtain even though it appeared to receive Marshall Plan aid.

The Berlin Crisis of 1948–1949 cemented the Soviet zone of Germany
firmly within the Soviet sphere of influence on American maps. The formal
partitioning of Germany in 1949 merely effected a shift in mapmakers'
labels, from the "Soviet zone" to "East Germany." The inclusion of this
region behind the Iron Curtain remained the same throughout the duration of the Cold War. Mapping the Iron Curtain to include East Germany
was a major departure from Churchill's famous oratory. The Polish city of
Stettin was now too far east of the western limit of the Soviet sphere to
serve as the northern endpoint of the Iron Curtain. And although Greek
and Yugoslavian interest in Trieste kept that city popular on news maps
throughout the early Cold War period, Stettin declined in importance
(and in frequency of appearance on maps) after the Iron Curtain migrated
to engulf East Germany. Notably, while the June 1946 map included both
cities, the November 1947 map omitted them.

Churchill's Iron Curtain rhetoric was not generally embraced by the
British Parliament as his party did not control the Parliament at the time of
his speech. Similarly, the British press tended to eschew Churchill's anticommunist worldview. By early 1946, most British news journals, regardless of their political leanings, still rejected the idea that post–World War II
Europe had devolved into a bipolar arena of incompatible ideologies. For

Fig. 5.8   By November 1947, however, the *New York Times* envisioned postwar Europe in Cold War bipolar terms—nations were either "Under Russian Control," "in the Marshall Plan," or neutral. And now the "Iron Curtain" had migrated eastward to claim the Soviet zones in Germany and Austria for the Russians

example, two weeks before Churchill's speech, the *New Statesman and Nation* had criticized "the whole power politics bag of tricks, leaving out all possibilities of a better solution."[29] And only months after Churchill spoke, Conservative journals such as *Truth* recognized the danger of yielding "the soul of Germany as 'danegeld' to communism" but nevertheless promoted friendly relations with the Soviet Union to maintain peace.[30] It follows, then, that British news cartographers, unlike their American counterparts, rarely depicted the dire Iron Curtain on maps of Germany or Europe. From the time of Churchill's speech to the end of 1955, the British national press published eight maps of Europe and three maps of Germany. Only one of those maps—published by the independent "non-party" journal *Time and Tide* in April 1949—utilized Iron Curtain imagery, and in decidedly bland visual terms at that (Fig. 5.9).[31] It is surprising that the Iron Curtain map was not published by a Conservative news journal, such as *Spectator* or *Truth*. Equally noteworthy, the map was published while the liberal Labour Party controlled the Parliament.

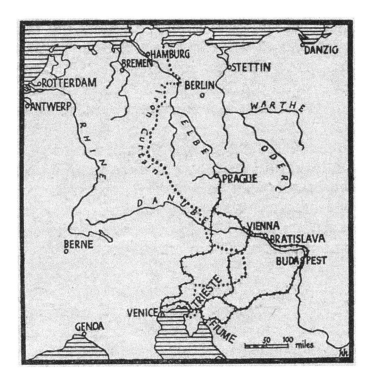

Fig. 5.9 The only British national news map of the Iron Curtain known to exist from 1946 to 1955 was published by *Time and Tide* in April 1949. It was less politically charged than contemporary American news map portrayals of the Iron Curtain. Here the Iron Curtain was merely a dotted line penetrated by rivers, railroads, and, as the accompanying article described, commercial trade

The British press often used provocative anticommunist terminology about Europe, such as "Two Worlds" and the "Iron Curtain," in head-lines and article titles to sell more journals. But these titles usually belied the more politically and economically multilateral world described by arti-cle text and maps. The 1949 *Time and Tide* map, and its accompanying article, described the Iron Curtain in terms of its permeability—not its importance as a European barrier in the Churchillian sense. The article's author, Aldo Cassuto, described Eastern Europe not as a communist monolith, but as a fractured sphere where "a deep rift has divided Tito from the Cominform."[32] On the map, the Iron Curtain was a non-threatening, simple dotted line through which railroads passed unencum-bered between East and West. The map's absence of national boundaries emphasized connectivity by river and rail traffic across Europe and the Iron Curtain. Though the author described how Stalinization had stifled river trade in the northern Danube Valley, Eastern European nations near Yugoslavia benefited from the Tito–Stalin rift, through trade with the West via the Mediterranean port cities of Trieste and Fiume. This was yet another example of how the British press viewed the Cold War in eco-nomically multilateral terms rather than the politically bipolar terms popu-lar in Churchill's speech and in the American press.

A contemporary conservative American (or British) reader could be forgiven for believing that the April 1949 *Time and Tide* Iron Curtain map, apolitical as it was, was misleading. It was in the very same month, after all, that the North Atlantic Treaty Organization (NATO) had been formed and had (at least in the American press), for all intents and purposes, unified capitalist Western Europe with its American and Canadian counterparts. What was the Iron Curtain now if not the great-est icon of the East–West Cold War split? Perhaps some of the accusations raised in the 1944 Royal Commission on the Press were true. Perhaps Socialist-leaning newspaper tycoons had quashed the freedoms of Fleet Street. Perhaps this map's whitewashing of the growing Cold War bipo-larity in Europe was another example of the "Left Can Speak to Left" soft Communism ideology alleged to dominate the editorial desk of *Time and Tide*. Certainly the journal had only a year prior felt the need to refute accusations that advocates "of the doctrinaire Socialist [were] effectively strangling free expression." Such accusations, however, ignored the jour-nal's anti-Stalinist stance evident throughout the mid-1940s.[33] And any similar accusations directed at the 1949 Iron Curtain map would have mistaken its lack of anticommunist imagery for communist sympathy.

The Iron Curtain itself was, after all, an anticommunist concept, and as mentioned, *Time and Tide* was the only British weekly to portray it on maps in the early Cold War period. Moreover, the unknown mapmaker had been careful to indicate the then recent and ominous migration of the Iron Curtain westward to include East Germany after the Berlin crisis.

Although the Iron Curtain was not depicted as an impenetrable barrier on British news maps, the ultimate fate of Czechoslovakia in the Soviet bloc garnered special attention. In the first American map of the Iron Curtain discussed earlier, the mapmaker capitalized on the east–west orientation of the nation. Czechoslovakia was portrayed as an island of democracy in Eastern Europe that pierced the Iron Curtain at a head-on perpendicular angle. After the Soviet invasion of Czechoslovakia in 1948, however, the nation's same east–west orientation, and the protrusion of its western borders into the FRG, made the nation a symbol of Soviet aggression in the British press. In March 1948, *Time and Tide* published a political cartoon, with the image of Stalin superimposed over Eastern Europe (Fig. 5.10).[34] Czechoslovakia was seen as Stalin's machine gun with a sign hanging from it that read "To The West." The only other nations labeled on the map were the USSR and Poland—to emphasize the "fall" of Czechoslovakia and Poland. Ironically, earlier mapmakers in Nazi Germany had also used Czechoslovakia's east–west orientation on maps of Europe to cast the nation as a "Slavic fist" that challenged German land claims.[35] In 1936, a map was published in Berlin entitled "The Eastern Front of German Cities outside the German State Territory," with a caption that read "This drawing is done in anger" (Fig. 5.11).[36] The image of a Czechoslovakian "Slavic fist" was part of the larger Nazi conception of a "beleaguered eastern front," visualized by a bold black line on the map. Though similar in directional orientation to the Iron Curtain, the Slavic "eastern front" was a conceived *ethnic* line of eastern European cities heavily populated by Germans, but outside Germany.

The cartographically inclined cartoons of *Time and Tide*'s "Ghilchik" not only afforded the journal a rare medium that departed from the traditional text over imagery preference of the Fleet Street but also married the political with the geopolitical. In the case of 1948 Czechoslovakia, probably few readers believed the accounts that Foreign Minister, Jan Masaryk, had "jumped" from his bathroom window only days before. Rather, as Ghilchik's imagery hinted, Masaryk's untimely and suspicious death was proof that the so-called bloodless communist takeover of the Czech government in February was not so innocent after all. Thus ended the

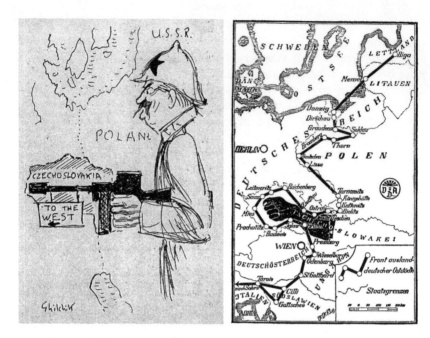

Figs. 5.10 and 5.11   *Time and Tide*'s portrayal of the "fall" of Czechoslovakia to the Soviets in a 1948 cartoon map (left) was similar to Nazi map portrayals of the nation as the keystone of a Slavic front in Eastern Europe before World War II (right). Both maps capitalized on the nation's east–west orientation as a challenge to a perceived north–south-oriented barrier

Western hopes that the heretofore moderate coalition Czech government would continue as the exception to Stalinist oppression. And as one historian later noted, the natural death of the nation's moderate President Edvard Beneš the following September only confirmed that "the last glimmer of democracy [had] flickered out of East Central Europe."[37] More specifically, Ghilchik's anti-Stalinist cartoons throughout the late 1940s challenged contemporary charges of communist sympathy among editorial staff at *Time and Tide*. As such, his renderings may be viewed as a sort of contemporary visual companion to Churchill's Iron Curtain rhetoric. Stalinist meddling in Czechoslovakia and Yugoslavia, the Berlin crisis, Stalin's denial of Marshall Plan aid to Eastern Europe, the victory of Chinese communists, and the Soviet acquisition of the atom bomb convinced Ghilchik that the Churchillian view was "the realist school."[38]

LINKING COMMUNISM WITH NAZISM

American news cartographers began conflating Nazism and communism during World War II with retrospective map sets that linked the recent Soviet occupation of Eastern Europe with past Prussian and Russian territorial gains in the same area. In this exercise, Poland was a favorite subject. Although Poland garnered no special attention in news articles early in the war, the Soviet occupation in 1942 made the nation "a touchstone for the ominous Soviet threat."[39] Other news maps criticized the Nazi–Soviet Nonaggression Pact of 1939 that divided Poland between Germany and the Soviet Union. These American maps identified encroachments on Polish territory dating back to the late eighteenth century to show a tradition of German and Soviet (Russian) aggression. In January 1944, *Newsweek* published two maps that showed "How the eighteenth century and the Nazi-Soviet Partitions sliced up Poland."[40] Late eighteenth-century claims on Poland by Austria, Prussia, and Russia were linked to the twentieth-century Nazi–Soviet Pact. By using similar shading patterns for Russia and the Soviet Union, and for Prussia and Germany, the maps presented a cogent history of German–Russian cooperation to oppress Poland. A similar set of six maps that conveyed the first three partitions of Poland (in 1772, 1793, and 1795), the Polish Republic (1921–1939), the 1939 Nazi–Soviet Pact, and post–World War II Poland were published in *U.S. News and World Report* in March of the following year.[41] In this map set, Prussian, German, Russian, and Austrian encroachments on Polish soil were colored or shaded to link them symbolically.

Despite a short-lived Red Scare among British Conservatives in 1942, which prompted many national cartoonists to portray Stalin and Hitler as "virtually the same person," wartime British news maps generally did not strongly link Nazism with Soviet communism in Europe.[42] Rather, in retrospective map sets published at the war's end, Soviet expansion in Eastern Europe was often seen as simply the latest example of power politics that dated back to the Versailles Treaty of World War I. Again, this speaks to a general British pattern of viewing Cold War politics in more multilateral (and less anticommunistic) terms than did the Americans. In a three-map set published in the *London Tribune* in mid-August 1945, cartographer J.F. Horrabin summarized the "European Chess-Board: 1925–1945" with maps entitled "the 1920's," "the 1930's," and "1945."[43] The "1920's" map of Europe showed "domination of the continent from the West" by France's "cordon sanitaire" of Eastern European nations against the Bolshevik threat. The "1930's" map featured "domination from the center" of Europe by way of the Berlin–Rome Axis, with no mention of the Nazi–Soviet Pact featured on contemporary American maps. Horrabin's "1945" map, as discussed earlier in Chap. 4, did not envision Eastern Europe as a part of a Soviet monolith. Although the map's caption described Soviet influence as "dominant in all the Balkan countries except Greece," the map clearly distinguished the Soviet Union from Eastern Europe with prominent borders and varied unique shading patterns.

Unlike their American counterparts, British mapmakers saw the unfolding of European politics as a history of domination from eastern *and* western nations; capitalist *and* communist, fascist *and* democratic. The British view was much less rigidly ideological than the American and broader, more multilateral in its considerations. Nonetheless, after 1945, growing Cold War tensions ultimately brought British foreign policy and public opinion closer to the American point of view, drawing more ties between Nazism and Soviet communism over time.

The progressive conflating of Nazism and communism that occurred in the United States as the Cold War developed seemed an easier leap for Americans. Although President Franklin Delano Roosevelt had earlier made a sharp distinction between the two systems while courting a Soviet alliance during World War II, President Harry S. Truman readily linked Nazi Germany and Soviet Russia in American foreign policy after American–Soviet relations began to deteriorate in 1946.[44] Truman blamed the Greek Civil War on a perceived "Hitler-like fifth-column intrusion by the Russians."[45] In 1947, he stated that "[t]here isn't any difference in totalitarian states ... Nazi, communist, or fascist."[46] The American ambassador to the Soviet Union, George Kennan, was of a like mind.[47]

Numerous American news articles were published, highlighting similarities between Nazism and Soviet communism in the late 1940s and early 1950s. In February 1948, *Look* magazine labeled Soviet communism as the "heir to fascism" by noting that the Soviets and the Nazis both believed in the infallibility of their leaders, promoted a single ruling party, had a militarist history, and even saluted the same way.[48] *Look* recalled the Nazi threat with a photo of Hitler *and* Mussolini. This amalgamation of former Axis powers as a Nazi threat oversimplified recent European history for American readers and offered a clear, if inaccurate, portrayal of Nazi–Soviet expansion.

In 1950, *Time* magazine cartographer, R.M. Chapin, Jr., played off these simplifications in a map entitled "Three Faces of Europe."[49] As with the World War II–era map retrospectives on Poland, Chapin's map sought to put European history into context, dating back to World War I. His "Three Faces of Europe" map summarized World War I, World War II, and the Cold War in three maps that blamed European instability on the Central powers, Axis powers, and the Soviet Union, respectively. Separate flags distinguished World War I–era Germany from Austria–Hungary, and World War II Germany from Italy. Nonetheless, monochromatic coloring of the regions conquered by these countries blurred national boundaries. The singular red landmass occupied by the Soviet Union on the third map appeared as merely the latest manifestation of a legacy of Central (World War I) and Axis (World War II) power aggression.

In the dearth of British news maps that characterized the early Cold War period, cartographic links between Nazism and Soviet communism were rare. British politicians, and the press, generally viewed early Cold War politics in more multilateral and complex terms than did the Americans. British international concerns were dominated by economic matters rather than political ideology for the first ten years after World War II.

The British Conservative Party, however, was a unique voice in England and regularly linked German fascism to Soviet communism throughout the early Cold War period. Beginning with Winston Churchill's Iron Curtain speech in March 1946, which compared any appeasement of Stalin to the disastrous 1938 Munich Agreement with Hitler, Churchill became iconic in the British press for his staunch anticommunist stance— even as most British national news journals reacted negatively to the Iron Curtain speech. Indeed, the only news imagery that linked Nazism to Soviet communism was in the form of political cartoons. And most of these cartoons were humorous jabs at Churchill's rhetoric, not indictments against Stalin or East Germany.[50] Yet, a handful of British cartoons did manage to link Stalin to Hitler with geographic or cartographic imagery. Although *Time and Tide* cartoonist "Ghilchik" had often lampooned Churchill's parallels between Stalin and Hitler, the tenth anniversary of the beginning of World War II finally compelled the artist to portray Stalin and Hitler in a peculiarly sinister light. In early September 1949, *Time and Tide* published a cartoon showing a giant Stalin, fist raised, stomping toward the hills of Yugoslavia.[51] With the smiling ghost of Hitler lurking over his shoulder, a pocketful of Soviet files on Finland, and a speech balloon reading "My patience is exhausted," Stalin's approach went unnoticed by the sleeping rooster labeled "Tito." A distant sign pointing toward the Mediterranean rounded out the British concern that the Stalin–Tito rift could spur Stalin to invade Yugoslavia, as he did Finland ten years earlier, and then, perhaps, the Mediterranean Basin. The real fear was that of a modern Soviet blitzkrieg.

Astonishingly, the British press often used political cartoons with cartographic imagery to compare the Nazi menace to American economic and foreign policy in the early Cold War period. In late 1945, for example, the *Serial Map Service* lamented the American no-fly zone for international commercial flights over the United States. It stated "even Nazi Germany, before the war, agreed to the passage of international air traffic along approved routes."[52] Similarly, amid American-led political talks over the rearmament of West Germany in early 1951, the *London Tribune* published a cartoon that predicted the Krupp family of industrialists, who had supplied arms to Germany in World War I and World War II, would be back in business.[53] As several Nazi officers looked on, Krupp hovered over a map of Europe and gestured to portraits of German leaders William I, Otto von Bismarck, and Adolf Hitler. The cartoon caption read "Krupp: Business as usual, gentlemen!"

One of the most compelling connections made between Nazi Germany and Soviet communism in the American press was the portrayal of Soviet "slave labor" camps as continuations of Nazi concentration camps. Historians Les K. Adler and Thomas G. Paterson have argued that, although Americans were aware of Soviet labor and exile camps before World War II, the publicized horrors of Nazi concentration camps after the war "stamped the image of the concentration camp … on the Russian camps."[54] As a result, Clare Boothe Luce, Congresswoman and wife of *Time* magazine owner and editor Henry Luce, spoke out in 1946 against Soviet labor camps.[55] Other influential American politicians, such as United Nations representative Willard Thorp, Senator J. Howard McGrath, and American Ambassador to Poland, Arthur Bliss Lane, also publicly associated Nazi and Soviet labor camps in the early Cold War period.[56] By the late 1940s, the Central Intelligence Agency (CIA) began associating communism with slavery in its various propaganda campaigns. Through its international Radio Free Europe and Radio Liberty programs, as well as its domestic "Crusade for Freedom" initiative, the Cold War came to embody a struggle between the "free world" of the West and communist "enslaved peoples" of the East.[57]

American news journals made the Nazi–Soviet connection as well. In early 1948, Conservative *Look* magazine described ten links between fascism and communism—number seven was the "widespread use of slave labor."⁵⁸ *Look* also made this point with maps. In October 1947, it published "The Truth About Russia's 12,000,000 Slave Laborers."⁵⁹ The map described a "network of slave camps" throughout the Soviet Union.⁶⁰ To put the large number of slaves into perspective, an inset map of the United States was included with fourteen western states colored black. These had a combined population of approximately twelve million people. But only states with very low population-to-area ratios were used (Texas and California were omitted) to generate an alarmingly large bloc of states that covered roughly half the United States. The mapmaker could have chosen a single state—New York, with a 1947 population of twelve million—to make the same point, but this would not have created such an effective cartographic comparison.

Several news maps singled out East Germany as a communist slave state in the late 1940s and early 1950s. And the most common way to visually denote areas of slavery, industrial or political, was to enclose them with barbed wire. The Berlin crisis prompted many news journal maps to visualize the divided city as a captive slave isolated with a wall of barbed wire. A map on the cover of *Time* magazine, in July 1953, included a portrait of GDR General Secretary Walter Ulbricht.⁶¹ All of East Germany (except West Berlin) was painted red, contrasted against the pale gray surrounding areas of Europe. Barbed wire imprisoned the GDR, and Ulbricht looked on indifferently while East Berlin erupted in flames. Other maps indicted rural locations in the GDR as slave labor camps. In November 1954, *Newsweek* published a map entitled "Communism's Atomic Slave State" that singled out a region on the border of East Germany and Czechoslovakia where slave labor was allegedly being used to mine uranium.⁶² As with the 1953 *Time* cover map, aside from the large text block, the only symbol denoting the area as a slave labor camp was a ring of communist-red barbed wire enclosing several mining locations. An inset map reminded American news readers just how close the slave camps were to West Germany.

At least one contemporary Latin American newspaper employed cartographic imagery that portrayed American military operations in South America as postwar Nazism. In a heated response to an alleged buildup of American military air forces in Santiago (Chile), Rio de Janeiro (Brazil), and Buenos Aires (Argentina), an anonymous journalist stated, "Thousands of Nazi agents living in the United States endanger the security of the Americas. The Nazi technique coincides with the old imperialist dreams of Uncle Sam." Published in March 1946 in *La Epoca de Buenos Aires*—an Argentinean news journal sympathetic to the recently elected populist

President Juan Domingo Peron—the article included a map of the Americas, with the United States colored bright red with a large white swastika covering its center (Fig. 5.12). Red arrows traversed a curved line from "Washington" south to the three South American cities. The map caught the eye of *Newsweek* editors, who reprinted it in the "Pan America Week" section along with the aforementioned quote in early April of the same year. To put a communist spin on the Brazilian criticism, *Newsweek* also included an account of Brazilian Communist Party leader Luiz Carlos Prestes who, in a recent public plea to keep his party from being banned by national law, vowed that Brazilian communists would not support any future "imperialist war against Russia."[63]

Fig. 5.12 While American news journals maps were portraying Eastern European communists as Nazis, an Argentinean journal map presented US military expansion in South America as Hitleresque. This map appeared in *La Epoca de Buenos Aires* in March 1946 and was reprinted in *Newsweek* the following month

La Epoca. Buenos Aires
An Argentine shudder over the Yankee "Nazi" threat

By the time the *Newsweek* article was published, relations between the United States and Argentina were strained. Peron had already shown his willingness to play the Soviets against the Americans, and vice versa. As US–Soviet animosity heated up over Iran, Peron aroused American suspicion by opening diplomatic relations with the Russians. At the same time, he publicly supported the proposed United Nation's Act of Chapultepec—a legal forerunner to the 1947 Inter-American Treaty of Reciprocal Assistance, also known as the Rio Pact—which envisioned an American-led mutual defense pact of Western Hemisphere nations. To make matters worse, the American government had only recently wrapped up an official investigation into Argentina's possible past collusion with the Axis powers. The resulting 1946 State Department Blue Book had accused former president Ramón Castillo (1942–1943) of accepting Nazi election contributions in exchange for publicly supporting Hitler's cause. More menacing were the allegations that de facto president and Major General Pedro Ramirez (1943–1944) had negotiated a deal to buy six submarines and several military aircraft from the Germans. Nor did it help that Ramirez had spent time studying Mussolini's military tactics while in Rome in 1932. Perhaps equally threatening were American-reported statistics documenting an explosion in Argentinean defense spending which rose over 470 percent from 1941 to 1945—a suspicious fact considering the nation's neutrality until the last days of the war.[64]

So it was amidst American Cold War anxiety over hemispherical unity that accusations of Nazism were hurled at South American critics, and the critics returned the favor. One recalls that the three nations where American military buildup was criticized by the map—Argentina, Brazil, and Chile—were the eponymous cofounders of the "ABC Alliance" that had opposed US-led Pan Americanism proposals in the early 1900s (see Chap. 4). Their governments had a history of interpreting "Pan Americanism" as "American imperialism." But by the time the map reappeared in *Newsweek*, the Argentinean's had seen writing on the wall. *Newsweek* reported on the same page that Argentinean government had recently replied to the Blue Book allegations. Although the 50-page official reply characterized the Blue Book investigation as a "lamentable intervention in internal political affairs," it was also careful to reassure the more powerful Americans (in a somewhat accusatory tone) that "Argentina does not aspire to any American hegemony." And the same document's proclamation that Argentina would not support "the formation of regional blocs of nations of any kind" was reversed the following year when the nation, along with Brazil, Chile, and twenty other Western Hemisperic nations, signed the Rio Pact for mutual defense.

GERMANY: THE LINE BETWEEN EAST AND WEST

By the end of World War II, concerns over Europe and a divided Germany dominated the peace talks at Yalta and Potsdam. However, the breakdown of Allied cooperation in the rebuilding of Europe by early 1946, as mirrored in Churchill's portentous Iron Curtain speech, ultimately led many British and American politicians to lament the development of a monolithic Soviet bloc in Eastern Europe. Also in that year the Greek Civil War and Soviet interests in Iran and Turkey drew Anglo-American attention away from Germany. From a Western perspective, the communist menace formed in Eastern Europe had expanded into Asia. As early as 1944, Western leaders acknowledged that the Soviets had a legitimate security concerns in Europe and the Far East. So it was not surprising that Stalin's post–World War II foreign policy was dominated by fear of invasion by Germany and Japan.[65] Nonetheless, the breakdown between Anglo-American and Soviet camps after World War II fomented new Western suspicions of Stalin's motives. It was Churchill's Iron Curtain speech that first labeled the Soviet Union a "ruthless, totalitarian power ... seeking domination in both Europe and Asia."[66] The British and American presses quickly employed provocative Churchillian catch phrases and concepts of global bipolarity. The Western conception of the Soviet sphere of influence grew from an Eastern European communist bloc to include a Eurasian landmass that stretched from the Soviet zone of Germany to the Sakhalin Islands of Northern Japan.

The American press avidly embraced Churchill's warning of the Russian communist threat in Europe, with news maps that painted Eastern Europe as a singular, red bloc dominated from Moscow. By mid-1946, news cartographers applied the same generalizations about Soviet communism in Eastern Europe to areas under communist control in the Far East. For example, the 1946 "Two Worlds" map (Chap. 4), published by *U.S. News and World Report*, linked events in Europe, via the Soviet landmass, to the Far East, and this map was discussed as an early charting of Cold War spheres of influence.[67] But in another sense, the map represented the linking of East and West in the American mind. Eastern Europe, "Russia," and Mongolia constituted the Soviet sphere and appeared on the map as a deep red juggernaut. This map's Mercator projection exaggerated the size of the Asian landmass, causing the Soviet sphere to appear even more impressive. The 1946 reader's attention was drawn to areas of recent Soviet expansion in Manchuria and North Korea with the use of pink shading.[68] The Soviet sphere, already firmly established in Eastern Europe, was doubtlessly expanding to the Far East. (The inclusion of Finland—a noncommunist nation with a history of war against the Soviet Union—in the Soviet sphere was problematic.)

By mid-1946, the British press, too, was keenly aware that events in Europe were tied to Soviet interests in Asia and the Far East. For Great Britain, linking East and West was nothing new. As discussed in Chap. 4, one of the chief postwar concerns of the British Foreign Office was reasserting control over its crumbling empire in the Far East and elsewhere. British economic interests in China and the predicted independence of India kept British news readers familiar with Eurasian affairs.[69] Moreover, the British press was generally sympathetic to Soviet interests in the Far East by the end of World War II. The new American military presence in the Pacific Ocean was seen by the press not only as a legitimate British concern, but also a challenge to Soviet dominion over eastern Asia.

The idea that the Iron Curtain symbolized the division not just between Eastern and Western Europe, but also between Europe and Asia, gained prominence in British journals shortly after Churchill's speech. British concerns over the Soviet Asiatic threat raised the stakes for an occupied Germany. In August 1946, a journalist for *Truth* commented on the uncertain fate of postwar Germany. He stated that "[t]he choice lies between accepting Germany back into the comity of Europe or driving her to … the Asiatic press-gang."[70] The Asiatic Soviet menace was not expressed in map form in the British press immediately after World War II. As discussed in Chap. 2, postwar British news maps generally did not portray areas large enough to describe the entire Soviet Union, let alone a Eurasian Soviet threat. The only press maps that portrayed larger sections of the Eastern Hemisphere were featured in air travel ads. While ad maps reinforced British commercial ties with the Far East, they were usually devoid of national boundaries and overt political commentary.[71] However, the absence of national boundaries itself was a tacit political statement—commerce was more important than Cold War politics for British travel companies immediately after World War II.

American news maps began to visualize a Eurasian Soviet menace shortly after Churchill's Iron Curtain speech in the late 1940s and early 1950s. Communist revolts in China and Korea also fueled American fears that Stalin intended to destabilize Western influence in the East. The 1949 "fall of China" to communism was by far the most important issue for American cartographers. Since before World War II, under the leadership of the American-backed Chiang Kai-shek, China's enormous population and square mileage served as a buffer between the Soviet Union and the political instability of French Indochina. By 1943 Chiang's Nationalist Party government was identified as the "fourth policeman" of the antici- pated new postwar world.[72] Aside from the American presence in Japan, all of the Far East was in China's sphere of influence. The Soviet Union's sphere was confined to Eastern Europe during World War II.[73] China's value to the United States in the Far East was similar to Czechoslovakia in Eastern Europe; it was a showpiece of positive East–West relations. The communist revolt in China, though slow and intermittent since the 1920s, erupted again in 1947 and coincided with the development of the Containment policy in the American State Department.[74]

After 1949, American news maps often portrayed Eastern Europe and the new People's Republic of China as Soviet satellites. The onset of the Korean War in June 1950 only propelled this trend even further. American capitalist control of Japan was now more important as a bulwark against Asiatic communism, and as a sort of counterweight to the West German bulwark against European communism.[75] Subsequently, mapmakers employed many innovative techniques to cultivate a Soviet–Eurasian communist world in the minds of American news readers. For example, recall the "Two Worlds" map noted in the Introduction. Also, as noted in Chap. 4, a July 1950 *Newsweek* map entitled "What We're Up Against" cleverly conceived a "red-inked Eurasian landmass."[76] The familiar Eastern European communist bloc was fragmented because Yugoslavia was recog- nized as outside the Soviet sphere (so was Finland). The nations of China, Mongolia, and North Korea were colored the same as Eastern Europe. Dark-red arrows indicating "threatened areas" in Eastern Europe were identical to arrows that emanated from China and North Korea into non- communist areas of Southeast Asia and Indonesia. Also, the uniform gray coloring of all other nations outside the Soviet-controlled landmass sup- ported the idea of a bipolar world. The *Newsweek* mapmaker dramatically emphasized the Soviet Union's dominance over its satellite regions, with a large and bold script rendering of the "U.S.S.R." The manipulation of place names on maps was not only used to portray a Soviet–Eurasian threat; it was also used to politically differentiate the FRG from the GDR. Following the formal partitioning of Germany in 1949, the FRG was often referred to as the democratic "German Federal Republic," "West's Germany," or the "Republic of Germany."[77] On the other hand, East Germany was portrayed as a puppet state of Moscow, with terms such as "The Soviet Zone," "Stalin's Germany," or "Russia's Germany."[78]

The cartographic devices used to link the Soviet sphere in East Europe to China and the Far East remained popular in the American press throughout the early Cold War period. They complemented a general American political and public assumption that Chinese communism was simply an extension of Soviet power.[79] The anticommunist Chiang Kai-shek drew upon his own troubled history with the Soviets in reaching the same conclusion.[80] But these ideological assumptions overlooked the many factors recognized by the British press that actually separated Chinese and Soviet communism.

The American perception of a powerful Chinese–Soviet link was in part illusory. Joseph Stalin and Chinese communist leader Mao Tse-tung were not the best of friends. On the verge of the communist rebel victory in 1948, Mao had been refused a personal meeting with Stalin on the border of China and the Soviet Union.[81] In January of the following year, and although Chinese Communist Party (CCP) forces dominated most of China, Stalin sent a representative to arbitrate a truce for fear of future American military involvement on Chiang Kai-shek's behalf.[82] Mao's victory, however, rallied Chinese nationalism and reinforced his declaration made in the early 1940s that the CCP would be independent of the Soviet Union.[83] The CCP generally followed the Soviet model of socialism, but only as long as it accommodated traditional Chinese culture and society.[84]

Even after the Korean War began, British politicians generally rejected American notions of a Soviet-controlled CCP, and the American press took due notice. In September 1950, an anonymous *Newsweek* journalist lamented that "British officials are now very dubious of reported good relations between Mao Tse-tung and the Soviets … [they believe that] Mao is not the bad fellow he is purported to be."[85] The absence of news maps depicting a Eurasian communist threat reflected the general opinion of the British press that communist China was an independent threat and not part of a Eurasian–Soviet empire. For the Chinese, even the CCP, the Russians were hardly an ally. They had long represented a threat across the Asian land bridge. As a journalist for *Time and Tide* noted in December 1950, "the belief that the Chinese will … become a vassal of … Russia seems hardly tenable … [because] the Russians represent the ancient danger from the steppe."[86] Conversely, many British journalists found direct links between Germany and the Far East. Contemporary British author Douglas Jerrold similarly saw Germany as an Eastern nation, as it squared off in both World Wars against a perceived bloc of Western nations represented by England, the United States, and France. His views echoed those

of Thomas Mann a generation earlier, who saw World War I as the culmi-
nation of much older struggle between Germany and a French-centered
Western realm.[87]

For the British press, issues concerning the division of Germany were
metaphorically and practically tied to the Korean War. In mid-1952, a
journalist for the *New Statesman and Nation* feared that Anglo-American
talks on rearming West Germany could effect "a new and more dangerous
Korean parallel in the middle of Europe."[88] Stalin's death in March 1953
caused widespread unrest in East Berlin in June—one month before the
Korean War ended—and prompted the same journal to state that "[a]
resumption of normal trade across the Iron Curtain would be the best way
of creating a favorable ... political conference on Korea."[89] However, news
maps illustrating a German–Korean connection did not exist in the British
national press from 1945 to 1955.

A CASE STUDY IN AMERICAN ANTICOMMUNISM: *TIME*
MAGAZINE'S "WEST'S GERMANY" MAP

On the momentous occasion of the formal partitioning of Germany into
two states in late 1949, *Time* magazine published a large multicolor map
entitled "West's Germany" (Fig. 5.13).[90] The map accompanied an article
in the magazine's Foreign News section, and both sought to summarize
the state of affairs in West Germany and its future in Cold War Europe.
Though the map was labeled "West's Germany," in fact it depicted both
West and East Germany. The inclusion of nearby East Germany was critical as it allowed the mapmaker, the aforementioned Robert M. Chapin,
Jr., to visually compare the two states in both subtle and obvious ways.
Chapin's cartographic comparison aptly characterized *Time* magazine's
strong anticommunist position in the early Cold War period while also
playing upon American preconceptions of Cold War Germany.

The title of the map was very clever, very anticommunistic, and very
American. It was not labeled "West Germany," as virtually all later American
and European maps would be. Nor was it labeled the "Federal Republic of
Germany" (FRG), its formal designation. Rather, the title "West's Germany"
was appropriated to relate that this new state, separate and superior to communist East Germany, belonged to the Western capitalist world. Certainly,
no maps produced in West Germany have ever used this possessive title. On
the contrary, the West German government has had a history of rejecting
Cold War partitioning on maps, actually lamenting the lost "Three

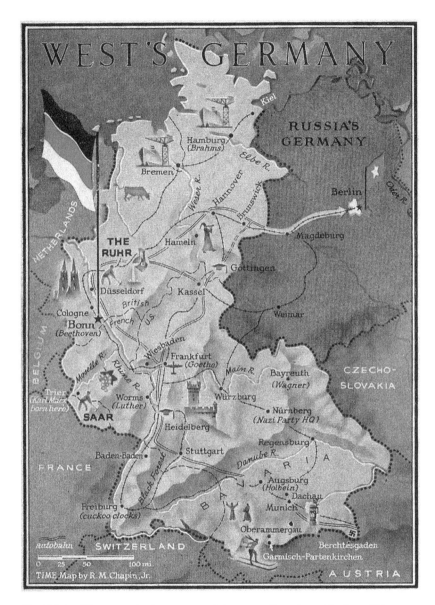

Fig. 5.13 *Time* magazine's coverage of the recent formal partitioning of Germany in late 1949 included this map which utilized numerous cartographic manipulations to glorify capitalist West Germany and vilify communist East Germany

Germanys" as noted earlier. Beyond this, the "West's Germany" title would have been offensive to the West German people at the time as it devalued the new state's sovereignty and trivialized it to pawn status in the Cold War struggle between the United States and the Soviet Union superpowers.

Similarly, Chapin's labeling of East Germany, or the German Democratic Republic (GDR), on the map as "Russia's Germany" demoted that new state to little more than a puppet of the Soviet Union. This negative bias toward the GDR was repeated throughout the early Cold War period in many American news journals. During the same period, the FRG was more commonly labeled simply "West Germany," avoiding any hint of a puppet government. The American press sought to frame the FRG as a more legitimate, free, and democratic state than its eastern counterpart as the Cold War heated up. The inventive naming on Chapin's map may seem a superficial and obvious propaganda tactic. But the power of toponyms, accurate or manufactured, to relate notions of nationality and empire is of no small significance, especially when these labels are dispersed in the national media through imagery. Media historian Michael Kahan has noted the unique role the media has played in validating the creation of new nation-states in the twentieth century. This has been especially relevant when new nations were cognizant of "threats (real or perceived) from outside the polity" where "patriotism, forged and reinforced by the media of the day, was the obvious vehicle."[91] Although Kahan was referring to nation building throughout the twentieth century, his point grew in pertinence during the early Cold War period as communist and capitalist nations squared off for domination of Europe. *Time*'s subtextual cartographic labeling of a divided Germany, along with the other tactics discussed later in the chapter, is a high example of a biased process whereby the FRG was championed while the GDR was vilified.

The deliberate and differential coloring of the "West's Germany" map easily conveyed the idea of a divided and polarized Germany, with the communist half portrayed as a dense, almost featureless menace. It is interesting to note that although the map focused on West Germany, that state had virtually no coloring save the large flag. The reader's eye is immediately captured by the ominous red "Russia's Germany." Visual media expert Edward Tufte has described the exceptionally heightened attention the color red commands within the human visual spectrum, giving it a higher priority to map readers. To the Western mind, the color red has a generally agitating effect that tends to evoke feelings of "fire, warning, heat, blood, anger … and communism."[92] To this end, the selective red coloring of East Germany catches the readers' attention as a dangerous, communist place.

Of course to communist readers, the color red is the universal color of the revered communist state representing the blood of the proletariat. Every communist nation in history has relied heavily upon the color red for their national flags, ceremonial accoutrements, posters, official stamps, postage stamps, and so forth. However, *Time* magazine and most other American national news journals regularly played on the more negative American associations with the color red to vilify communist nations on maps and in text. To read about the "red sweep" in Europe, "red China," "reds in the Reich," and so forth was a call to arms against the communist threat.

Chapin's selective use of flags to represent the two German states was purposefully misleading and sought to denigrate the GDR. On the map, the West German flag was largely correct in design—that is, a flag consisting of three horizontal bars, colored, from top to bottom, black, red, and yellow. Chapin's FRG flag, nevertheless, had the lowest bar colored white, not yellow. This was a forgivable minor error as yellow ink was not available for use in newsprint in the 1940s, although the glossy magazine covers could use yellow. Indeed, the cover of this particular *Time* issue did display the FRG flag with the correct yellow lowest bar. The flag used to represent the GDR, however, was purposefully misrepresented as a red flag with a white star in the center. The actual GDR flag, like the FRG flag, comprised black, red, and yellow horizontal bars. But the GDR flag also displayed a circular seal of yellow wheat enclosing a yellow hammer and compass—symbols of GDR agriculture and industry. Aside from the circular seal, the GDR flag was absolutely identical to the contemporary FRG flag. This degree of flag parity simply would not do. Rather than suggest even the most tangential similarity of East and West Germany, Chapin employed the same generic red flag for the GDR that he regularly used to represent many communist regimes on *Time* maps of Europe and Asia. This had the dual effect of devaluing communist nations and linking them to a conceived international communist threat controlled by Moscow.

Similarly, the relative sizes and orientations of the two German state flags on the map served to validate the FRG and invalidate the GDR. The FRG flag was over three times larger than the GDR flag and symbolized a more important West German state. Of course, the flags were shown flying in opposite directions to denote opposed political orientations. The FRG flag was caught in a westerly wind, while the GDR flag lapped toward Moscow in the east.

Of all the features of the "West's Germany" map, the use of German cultural and industrial icons is most striking. To be sure, the map accompanied an article on West Germany, and it is no surprise that these icons centered on that state. But the comparatively barren East German state was not totally devoid of symbolism. Rather, the GDR was selectively decorated to make several Cold War propagandistic points. The map's portrayal of German transportation routes promoted the notion that the capitalist FRG was industrially developed and the communist GDR was not. The double solid line that spanned the FRG represented, as noted in the map legend, the vast Autobahn roadway built by the Nazi regime. The map had the roadway ending at the GDR border, even though, in reality, it spanned both German states. Were American map readers to believe the Autobahn did not exist in the GDR? Apparently so. Superior roads meant a superior quality of life to Americans in the late 1940s when the car culture was just beginning to explode. A lack of national roads in the GDR was a serious indictment of the communist state. Similarly, Chapin crisscrossed the FRG with railroads, but the single rail line shown in "Russia's Germany" was drawn merely as an extension loop of the FRG rail network. The omission of GDR transportation routes on Chapin's map is even more suspicious when compared to a similar map that appeared in *Time* magazine in August of the following year. This map, entitled "Reds in the Reich," portrayed the GDR replete with highways, the Autobahn, and railroads. Geared for an entirely different "message," this map was meant to illustrate the military threat of the GDR. In a predictable reversal of icon artistry, the FRG was suddenly devoid of the same transportation modes.[93]

The "West's Germany" map's treatment of German culture and history was shamelessly biased toward the FRG. A cursory look at the map implies that virtually all German culture originated in the FRG, while the communist GDR remained a vast uncivilized, unrefined wasteland. West Germany's Gothic cathedral at Cologne, Hamelin's Pied Piper, and the universities at Göttingen and Heidelberg were all valid claims. The West German city of Bonn displayed composer Beethoven's name in parentheses to indicate the site of his birth—a fact also mentioned in the accompanying article. Trier was noted to be the birthplace of Karl Marx (ironically); Hamburg claimed the composer Johannes Brahms; Augsburg correctly claimed painter Hans Holbein (the elder); and Frankfurt claimed author Johann Goethe. From the map, one would assume the other Western German cities with celebrity names in parentheses indicated their respective birthplaces as well. Worms claimed religious reformer (Martin) Luther, and Bayreuth claimed composer (Wilhelm) Wagner. However, Luther was not born in Worms—that city was merely the site of his ill-fated trial. Similarly, Wagner was not born in Bayreuth—that city was (and is) merely the site of an annual festival in his honor. Actually, Luther was born in Eisleben, and Wagner was born in the great publishing center of Leipzig—two cities nestled firmly in the GDR by 1949. Yet neither of these two cities even appeared on the map.

The only cities depicted in the GDR were Berlin, Magdeburg, and Weimar. Berlin's importance is obvious as the capitol of unified Germany and as the site of the then recent Berlin crisis (1948–1949). West Berlin also contained a sizeable population of Western capitalist citizens. One could argue that Magdeburg (pop. $293,959$) should be shown because it was a major city on the route to Berlin. But why was Weimar (pop. $45,957$) shown, while much larger East German cities such as Leipzig (pop. $679,159$) and Dresden (pop. $619,157$) were not? As with the inclusion of smaller FRG cities of Dachau and Berchtesgaden, GDR's Weimar was probably included to remind readers of Germany's troubled Nazi past. Weimar, as the seat of the Weimar Republic that ruled Germany before Hitler seized power, recalled the old German order when Germans were ruled by democracy rather than by fascism, and later, communism. Showing Weimar deeply entombed within the communist bloc was a reminder that democracy was dead in the GDR.[94]

In general, the selective inclusion of German cities on both sides of the map's Cold War border worked to emphasize certain overlapping points from the accompanying article. First, both the map and the article went to great lengths to remind American readers of Germany's Nazi past. The article began, "It was 16 years since Adolf Hitler had seized power," and continued to label the then West German Chancellor Konrad Adenauer as "without a doubt the most important German since Hitler." The map illustrated this point with selective and sometimes dubious Nazi sites that would normally not be included on a map of this small scale. Strangely, FRG's Nürnberg was labeled as "Nazi Party HQ" when, in fact, Nazi Party headquarters were always in Berlin. Second, both the article and map explicitly reinforced the long-held notion of the duality of German history, as the article states, a history of "both monster and genius." But in Chapin's Cold War slant, "West's Germany" embodied both, while East Germany embodied only the monster. Lastly, the map portrayed the FRG as having tremendous industrial potential and cultural legacy, a beacon dimmed only by its Nazi past. The GDR was hopelessly devoid of industry and culture in both the map and article treatments. Its legacy was the horror of Nazi fascism, yet alive in the guise of communism.

Chapin's "West's Germany" map compared West and East Germany on many levels. The comparison relied heavily on the arbitrary inclusion and exclusion of roads, cities, railroads, and cultural symbols across the Iron Curtain. Such a comparison neatly illustrates J.B. Harley's point that maps exert just as much influence by what they omit as by what they display.[95] But Harley was examining singular maps, each made by a different mapmaker, and maps sourced from different eras to show commonality through diverse cultures and genres. The multiple maps of Cold War Germany drawn by Chapin for *Time* magazine, however, offer an opportunity to consider Harley's inclusion–exclusion principles in a series of maps made by the same person describing the same region over time. One map shows the FRG to be replete with roads and the GDR absent from them to portray the FRG as superior. A later map reverses this portrayal to brand the GDR as a mobile military threat to the FRG. It is apparent, then, that comparisons of these two serial news maps illustrate a higher degree of subjectivity and political bias than either single map can, because the same mapmaker drastically alters his portrayal of the same region to convey different political messages.

The "West's Germany" news map is noteworthy for its extensive iconography, symbolism, and rhetoric. Indeed, this map ranks as one of Chapin's most stylistic creations. No contemporary British news map exists with such artistic flair, and in fact, British-made news maps of postwar-occupied Germany are relatively rare. No such maps exist in any British weekly news journals from 1945 to 1955. However, the *Serial Map Service* (*SMS*) did publish two maps dealing with postwar Germany. Predictably, British cartographic portrayals of Cold War-divided Germany were much less anticommunistic and more even-handed in their comparisons of West and East Germany than contemporary American maps of the region.

The first *SMS* map depicting postwar German lands, entitled "Soviet Zone of Germany," was published in December 1946.[96] Though it appeared over eight months after Churchill's "Iron Curtain" speech, the map contained no indication of that conceived anticommunistic barrier. And unlike Chapin's "West's Germany" map, or for that matter any of his other maps of Cold War German lands, the *SMS* map aptly reflected that the Autobahn and German railroads indeed covered both capitalist and communist areas. Chapin's earlier gross underrepresentation of GDR Autobahn roads and railroads in his "West's Germany" map becomes all the more suspect when one views the more realistic presentment of GDR transportation in the *SMS* map. Here, Berlin was correctly shown to be a major transportation hub linking all of Central Europe. Similarly, Chapin's selective omission of GDR resources alongside a bountiful FRG is a patent contrast to the *SMS* map's depiction of a GDR replete with industrial and agricultural zones. Aside from the map's title, the *SMS* "Soviet Zone of Germany" map did not seek to tie the GDR to Soviet communism, or to the communist bloc of Eastern Europe in any regard. Nor did it make any political distinction between capitalist Western Europe and communist Eastern Europe. Rather, the GDR appeared to be an independent European state blessed with a plethora of resources, scenic mountains, and an extensive transportation network that linked East and West. Such a positive, apolitical cartographic portrayal of the GDR never appeared in the contemporary American press.

Although no British ad maps focusing primarily on postwar Germany have been found in this study, many smaller-scale ad maps of Western Europe and Eurasia were published which included German lands. Ad maps for British airlines, international banks, and Fleet Street political periodicals—companies all promoting British interest and trade to German lands on both sides of the Iron Curtain—were published frequently after World War II. But these ad maps usually "commented" on postwar Germany by leaving German lands blank—the opposite of Chapin's approach. For example, in mid-1950, Barclay's Bank published an ad promoting British travel to Europe for the holiday season (Fig. 5.14).[97] The artwork-heavy ad included a map of Western Europe visualizing all the places poetic Mary might go with her lamb. Of the ten nations depicted on the map, six of them were accompanied by merry cartoon figures welcoming Mary—Denmark, Holland, France, Switzerland, Austria, and Italy. The areas of Belgium and Sweden were too small to garner such embellishments. The nation of Spain was virtually cut off from the map and boasted no cartoon Spaniard waving to Mary. The exclusion of Spain as a friendly travel destination is understandable. By 1950 the nation was still not a member of the United Nations (not until 1955), nor was it a member of NATO (not until 1982). Curiously, a feverish cartoon Russian Cossack loomed over the unnamed communist areas of East Germany and Poland. Even more curious is that the central, large area of Germany had no anthropomorphic national cartoon figure.

Fig. 5.14 This 1950 ad map for Barclay's Bank promoted British travel to Western Europe. Though most nations were accompanied by cartoon figures, the central nation of Germany was not. British ad maps often left German lands blank as the Fleet Street press was unsure of the nation's political future in the early Cold War period

Why was Mary not welcomed by a cartoon German in the British press ad map? Why was Germany left blank save for a text label? It was probably because the British press, much like the contemporary American press, was still uncertain about Germany's future in 1950. The nation had been formally divided into two states less than a year prior. The ad map did not acknowledge this recent Cold War partition—political turmoil would hurt travel sales. Many Brits were wondering what kind of Germany would emerge from the ashes of the old. Would it be barbaric as in the Middle Ages? Would it seek a new imperialism as before World War I? Would it be a new Nazi nation? Or as a contemporary ad for the British journal *Current Affairs* commented concerning West Germany, "how much has changed since 1945? Or 1939? Has Western Germany taken ... the spirit of ... Western Democracy? Shall we arm the Germans?" In the ad a West German man peruses three helmets on the wall—that of a barbarian, an imperial

German officer, and a Nazi stormtrooper. Better to leave German lands blank on British ad maps until these questions could be answered. Yet Barclay's 1950 ad map was not completely devoid of Cold War political rhetoric. Superficially, *Time and Tide*'s employment of "Mary Had a Little Lamb" symbolism was itself a reaffirmation of Anglo-American capitalist culture. The poem, after all, was a product of early American Industrial Revolution society—a society that itself had originated in Manchester. The British Isles, however, were omitted from the map. In their place was "Mary" who embodied all things British, especially those perspective British tourists considering Cold War Western Europe as a holiday destination. (Or, to paraphrase that old poem, the ad map contemplated anywhere that the British "Mary" *might* go.) And that destination was a playground virtually free from Cold War strife. The horrors of Stalinization were also omitted from the map as only the western fringe of Communist Eastern Europe could be seen, but only as a hint of territory emerging from a dark, hatch-marked land that looked for all the world like an unknown Eurasian sea. And for any traveler longing to visit, as Churchill had termed them in his seminal "Sinews of Peace" speech, "all the capitals of the ancient states of Central and Eastern Europe" now behind the Iron Curtain, a solitary and dour Russian Cossack offered an inhospitable glare.

NOTES

1. *U.S. News and World Report*, v. 18, n. 6 (Feb. 9, 1945): 20–21.
2. Ibid., see article "Tightening Noose on Berlin: Nazi Fight Against Panic," 19.
3. Mary Fulbrook, *The Divided Nation: a History of Germany, 1918–1990* (New York and Oxford: Oxford University Press, 1992), 94. See map set entitled "Territorial annexation, 1935–9."
4. *Facts In Review*, v. 2, n. 5 (February 1940): 33. See Mark Monmonier, *How to Lie with Maps* (Chicago and London: University of Chicago Press, 1996), 102–103.
5. For a summary of these changes, see J. Robert Wegs and Robert Ladrech, *Europe Since 1945: a Concise History* (4th ed.) (New York: St. Martin's Press, 1996), 8–10.
6. Louis Liebovich, *The Press and the Origins of the Cold War, 1944–1947* (New York: Praeger, 1988), 43.
7. See maps entitled "How Germany Will Be Occupied" in *U.S. News and World Report*, v. 18, n. 12 (Mar. 23, 1945): 23; "Trouble Spots" in *Time*, v. 45, n. 22 (May 28, 1945): 21; "Three Worlds and Their Problem Spots" in *Newsweek*, v. 27, n. 5 (Feb. 4, 1946): 35; "Behind the Iron Curtain" in

Time, v. 47, n. 11 (Mar. 18, 1946): 24; and "How the Communist Vote has Varied in Europe's Elections" in New York Times v. 95, n. 32,278 (Jun. 9, 1946): E5.

8. F.S. Northedge and Audrey Wells, Britain and Soviet Communism: the Impact of a Revolution (London: Macmillan, 1982), 112–113.

9. D.F. Fleming, The Cold War and its Origins, 1917–1960 (vol. 1) (Garden City, NY: Doubleday, 1961), 506.

10. Wegs and Ladrech, 9–11.

11. GDR officials traditionally have not voiced concerns over losing "Polish Germany" since doing so would have conflicted with Soviet state policy.

12. Time magazine, v. 62, n. 9 (Aug. 31, 1953): 19.

13. See Christiane Lemke's essay "Citizenship Law in Germany: Traditional Concepts and Pressures to Modernize in the Context of European Integration," published in the proceedings of Harvard Focus: Europe, Spring 2001, p. 6. Online text: http://www.gps.uni-hannover.de/europe/citizenlaw01.pdf.

14. (no author), Statistisches Jahrbuch für die Bundesrepublik Deutschland (Stutgartt and Köln: W. Kohlhammer, 1955).

15. Time magazine, v. 62, n. 9 (Aug. 31, 1953): 19.

16. See Serial Map Service, v. 9, n. 1 (Oct. 1947): 1.

17. See Denis Wood, The Power of Maps (New York and London: The Guilford Press, 1992), 85–87; Mark Monmonier, How to Lie with Maps (2nd ed.) (Chicago and London: The University of Chicago Press, 1996), 118–122; and J.B. Harley, The New Nature of Maps: Essays in the History of Cartography (Baltimore and London: The John Hopkins University Press, 2001), 83–108.

18. Julius W. Pratt, A History of United States Foreign Policy (2nd ed.) (Englewood Cliffs, NJ: Prentice-Hall, Inc., 1965), 460.

19. For a full text of Churchill's speech, see http://www.historyguide.org/europe/churchill.html

20. Peter G. Boyle, "The British Foreign Office View of Soviet-American Relations, 1945–46" in Diplomatic History, v. 3, n. 3 (Summer 1979): 314.

21. Fraser J. Harbutt, The Iron Curtain: Churchill, America, and the Origins of the Cold War (New York and Oxford: Oxford University Press, 1986), 199.

22. Ibid.

23. Harbutt, 198–199.

24. Time magazine, v. 47, n. 11 (Mar. 18, 1946): 24.

25. Radomir Luža, "Czechoslovakia between Democracy and Communism" in Charles S. Maier's The Cold War in Europe: Era of a Divided Continent (Princeton: Markus Wiener, 1996), 94. Stalin's intention to solidify his control over Eastern Europe became known in the summer of 1947 and ended any Western ideas of East–West cooperation through Czechoslovakia.

26. The *New York Times*, v. 95, n. 32,278 (Jun. 9, 1946): E5.

27. By this time, the Polish and Romanian democratic governments were not freely elected under Soviet direction, since such elections would surely have ousted the dominant Communist parties in both nations. See Wegs and Ladrech, pp. 30–33.

28. The *New York Times*, v. 97, n. 32,796 (Nov. 9, 1947): E1.

29. Quote was taken from an anonymous journalist reacting to Walter Lippmann's promotion of balance-of-power treaties between the Soviet Union, Britain, and the United States. See article "Mr. Lippmann at the Ringside" in *New Statesman and Nation*, v. 31, n. 783 (Feb. 23, 1946): 131.

30. Godfrey Turton, "The Comity of Europe" in *Truth*, v. 140, n. 3648 (Aug. 9, 1946): 128. A "danegeld" describes a medieval European tribute paid to avoid conquest by marauding Vikings.

31. Aldo Cassuto, "Ports and Politics" in *Time and Tide*, v. 30, n. 15 (Apr. 9, 1949): 345.

32. Ibid.

33. See "Government, Press and Newsprint," in *Time and Tide*, v. 29, n. 21 (May 22, 1948): 1.

34. *Time and Tide*, v. 29, n. 12 (Mar. 20, 1948): 301.

35. Guntram Henrik Herb, *Under the Map of Germany: Nationalism and Propaganda, 1918–1945* (London and New York: Routledge, 1997), 173.

36. Martin Ira Glassner, *Political Geography* (New York: John Wiley and Sons, 1993), 228–289.

37. James Wilkinson, *Contemporary Europe: a History*, 9th ed. (Upper Saddle River, NJ: Prentice Hall, 1998), 374.

38. See "Ghilchik" cartoons in *Time and Tide*: v. 27, n. 11 (Mar. 16, 1946): 249; v. 28, n. 21 (Jun. 6, 1947): 593; v. 29, n. 3 (Jan. 17, 1947): 65; v. 29, n. 9 (Feb. 28, 1948): 217; v. 29, n. 15 (Apr. 10, 1948): 373; v. 29, n. 28 (Jul. 10, 1948): 717; v. 30, n. 36 (Sep. 3, 1949): 883.

39. Liebovich, 46.

40. *Newsweek*, v. 23, n. 3 (Jan. 17, 1944): 29.

41. *U.S. News and World Report*, v. 18, n. 10 (Mar. 9, 1945): 22–23.

42. Northedge and Wells, 76. For information on the 1942 Red Scare, see James Curran's and Jean Seaton's book *Power without Responsibility: the Press, Broadcasting and the New Media in Britain* (London and New York: Routledge, 2003), p. 55.

43. See Horrabin's map entitled "The European Chess-Board: 1925–1945" in the *London Tribune*, n. 450 (Aug. 10, 1945): 7.

44. John Lewis Gaddis, *Strategies of Containment: a Critical Appraisal of Postwar American National Security Policy* (New York: Oxford University Press, 1982), 9–10.

45. Les K. Adler and Thomas G. Paterson, "Red Fascism: The Merger of Nazi Germany and Soviet Russia in the American Image of Totalitarianism, 1930's–1950's" in *The American Historical Review*, v. 75, n. 4 (April 1970): 1055.
46. Ibid., 1046.
47. Ibid., 1047.
48. (no author), "Communism: Heir to Fascism" in *Look*, v. 12, n. 3 (Feb. 3, 1948): 28–29.
49. *Time*, v. 55, n. 1 (Jan. 2, 1950): 36.
50. *Time and Tide*, v. 29, n. 20 (May 15, 1948): 509; *New Statesman and Nation*, v. 48, n. 1239 (Dec. 4, 1954): 729.
51. *Time and Tide*, v. 30 n. 36 (Sept. 9, 1949): 883.
52. E. Colston Shepherd, "America's Place in the Air—New York: Port of Exchange" in *Serial Map Service*, v. 7, n. 1 (October 1945): 2.
53. *London Tribune*, v. 15, n. 725 (Feb. 9, 1951): 4.
54. Adler and Patterson, 1053.
55. Ibid.
56. Ibid., 1053–1054.
57. Kenneth Osgood. *Total Cold War: Eisenhower's Secret Propaganda Battle at Home and Abroad* (Lawrence, KS: University Press of Kansas, 2006), 40–41.
58. *Look*, v. 12, n. 3 (Feb. 3, 1948): 28–29.
59. Ibid., v. 11, n. 16 (Oct. 28, 1947): 35–36.
60. Ibid., v. 11, n. 16 (Oct. 28, 1947): 35–36.
61. See cover of *Time*, v. 62, n. 2 (Jul. 13, 1953).
62. *Newsweek*, v. 44, n. 19 (Nov. 8, 1954): 46.
63. Ibid., v. 27, n. 14 (Apr. 8, 1946): 53.
64. Wilfrid Hardy Callcott, *The Western Hemisphere: Its Influence on United States Policies to the End of World War II* (Austin, TX and London: University of Texas Press, 1968), 412–414.
65. Gaddis, 8–9.
66. Adler and Paterson, 1056.
67. *U.S. News and World Report*, v. 20, n. 22 (May 24, 1946): 21.
68. The Yalta Conference of February 1945 gave the Soviet Union the Kurile Islands, lower Sakhalin, and control of railroads in South Manchuria. The United Nations mandated North Korea to the Soviet Union and South Korea to the United States. See Gaddis's *The United States and the Origins of the Cold War, 1941–1947* (New York and London: Columbia University Press, 1972), pp. 78–79.
69. C.J. Bartlett, *British Foreign Policy in the Twentieth Century* (New York: St. Martin's Press, 1989), 71.
70. Godfrey Turton, "The Comity of Europe" in *Truth*, v. 140, n. 3648 (Aug. 9, 1946): 128.

71. See British Overseas Airways Ads in *Time and Tide*, v. 27, n. 29 (Jul. 20, 1946): 691; *Spectator*, v. 177, n. 6161 (Jul. 26, 1946): 99; and *Truth*, v. 141, n. 3670 (Jan. 10, 1947): 45.

72. Gaddis, 10.

73. Thomas G. Paterson, *On Every Front: the Making and Unmaking of the Cold War* (New York and London: W.W. Norton, 1992), 41–42.

74. Rhoads Murphey, *A History of Asia* (4th ed.) (New York and London: Longman, 2003), 386.

75. Pratt, 494.

76. *Newsweek*, v. 36, n. 3 (Jul. 17, 1950): 14.

77. See maps in *U.S. News and World Report*, v. 33, n. 2 (Jul. 11, 1952): 22; *Time*, v. 54, n. 23 (Dec. 5, 1949): 30; *The American*, v. 149, n. 3 (March 1950): 25.

78. See maps in *Time*, v. 54, n. 23 (Dec. 5, 1949): 30, and v. 55, n. 19 (May 8, 1950): 22; *The American*, v. 149, n. 3 (March 1950): 25; *U.S. News and World Report*, v. 33, n. 2 (Jul. 11, 1952): 22.

79. D.F. Fleming, *The Cold War and its Origins, 1917–1960* (Garden City, New York: Doubleday, 1961), vol. 2, 584.

80. Ibid.

81. See Shuguang Zhang's essay "Threat Perception and Chinese Communist Foreign Policy" in Melvyn P. Leffler's and David S. Painter's (eds) *Origins of the Cold War: an International History* (2nd ed.) (London and New York: Routledge, 1995), 279.

82. Ibid.

83. Roderick Mcfarquhar and John K. Fairbank (eds), *The Cambridge History of China* (Cambridge: Cambridge University Press, 1989), vol. 14, 64.

84. Ibid., 64–65.

85. (no author), "Key to Conflict and its Significance" in *Newsweek*, v. 36, n. 11 (Sept. 11, 1950): 25.

86. Marice Collins, "The Mind of China" in *Time and Tide*, v. 31, n. 49 (Dec. 9, 1950): 1249–1250.

87. See Douglas Jerrold, *The Lie About the West: A Response to Professor Toynbee's Challenge* (London: J.M. Dent and Sons, 1954); Martin W. Lewis and Karen E. Wigen. *The Myth of Continents: A Critique of Metageography* (Berkeley: University of California Press, 1997), 59.

88. *New Statesman and Nation*, v. 43, n. 1107 (May 24, 1952): 600.

89. Ibid., v. 45, n. 1162 (Jun. 6, 1953): 688.

90. *Time*, v. 54, n. 23 (Dec. 5, 1949): 30.

91. Michael Kahan, *Media as Politics: Theory, Behavior and Change in America* (Upper Saddle River, NJ: Prentice-Hall, 1999), 2–3.

92. Edward Tufte, *The Visual Display of Quantitative Information* (Cheshire, CT: Graphics Press, 2001), 154.

93. *Time*, v. 56, no. 6 (Aug. 1950): 26–27
94. East German city populations were taken from *Statistisches Jahrbuch für die Deutsche Reich* (Berlin: von Reimar Hobbing, 1949).
95. Harley, 67.
96. See *Serial Map Service*, v. 8, n. 3 (Dec. 1946): map 385.
97. Barclay's Bank ad, *Time and Tide*, v31, n23 (Jun. 10, 1950): 590

CHAPTER 6

Conclusions

In his 1856 speech before the Smithsonian Institution arguing for the creation of an American national map archive, German geographer Johann Georg Kohl lamented the popular practice of discarding older maps in favor of more accurate modern ones. Quoting Kohl in her book entitled *Mapping the Nation*, Susan Schulten agreed that "Such practices meant that many old maps were simply gone forever ... Maps had yet to be 'raised to the dignity of historical documents.'"[1] Generally speaking, historic maps have since garnered proper academic attention with the conspicuous exception of historic news journal maps. They have yet to be granted their historic dignity. No doubt this is partly due to the ephemeral nature of news cartography. As cartographic historian Dennis Reinhartz pointed out, the term "ephemeral maps" describes maps not made for long-term use, but for "transient use," and includes maps in news maps, travel brochures, political cartoons, and advertisements. However, Reinhartz rightly argues that the temporary status of ephemeral maps belies their potential to shape public perception of foreign places over long periods of time.[2] This study has endeavored to show the power and legitimacy of news journal maps, both in the form of news maps and cartographic ads, as primary historical documents. Hopefully it has been shown that these maps provide a unique medium—a body of combined imagery and text that at a glance conveys contemporary ideas of geography, politics, war, and culture—that urgently deserves greater attention from modern historical

© The Author(s) 2019
J. P. Stone, *British and American News Maps in the Early Cold War Period, 1945–1955*, Palgrave Studies in the History of the Media,
https://doi.org/10.1007/978-3-030-15468-4_6

scholarship. In the same ways and for the same reasons that historians study, and have long studied, exclusively textual documents including private and public correspondence, government publications, diaries, and books, they should also be studying cartographic imagery published in news journals in order to better understand the past. But until very recently, the handful of cartographic studies by Walter Ristow, Mark Monmonier, Patricia Gilmartin, and others discussed here notwithstanding, even cartographic historians have largely ignored this valuable primary resource. Historians' neglect of news journal cartography is more egregious given the discipline's long reliance on news journals as primary sources. One could argue that this scholarly oversight is a result of the historian's traditional preference for text over imagery. Yet numerous fine cultural histories have in recent decades focused on imagery—paintings, propaganda posters, advertisements, movies, and, yes, even cartography—but news journal cartographic imagery has somehow gone largely unnoticed.

This study has also endeavored to show the many ways that the study of news journal maps and cartographic ad imagery can benefit the historian. A consideration of a nation's news journal maps can reveal a wealth of knowledge about how that nation's news readers were informed about, and sometimes convinced to see, the unfolding and changing realm of geography, geopolitics, war, travel, the cultural "other," and numerous other societal and cultural constructs. Moreover, given the serial nature of news journal publications, news cartography offers a *chronology of development* of these constructs. These scholarly benefits are all shared with strictly textual documents. But news cartography offers more—it offers what textual documents can never offer—a constructed *visual* record that reveals literally how historical agents have envisioned their changing world over time. And given the widespread circulation of news journals, especially before the advent of television, studying a nation's news cartography grants the historian a unique survey of popular conceptions of the political world.

This has certainly been true of British and American news journal maps from the early Cold War period. News maps were arguably the most influential cartographic medium for shaping public attitudes about foreign places in the pivotal period between the end of World War II and 1955. These maps comprised a powerful visual medium for relating foreign news, national fears of communism, and the dynamic geopolitics of the early Cold War period. Although Britain and the United States were the closest of allies in the fight against communism after World War II, they nevertheless held significantly different worldviews. Anglo-American differences in this regard were shaped as much by political ideology as by the geographic location of the two nations. This study has traced these differing worldviews through their many expressions in news maps appearing in the British and American weekly presses.

Long before World War II began, British and American news journals had developed very different styles of journalism as related to national political parties. American journals all claimed political neutrality, while each journal was nevertheless owned by politically biased individuals. By the 1940s, most American journals were dominated by moderate to conservative political interests. No major liberal news journals existed. The British press, however, featured journals whose owners and editors publicly acknowledged their differing political biases. The range of political partisanship ranged from far-left to far-right. However, by the end of World War II, most British journals, conservative or liberal, held the same economic concerns of the failing empire.

By 1945, American and British news journal maps portrayed the war effort and the world very differently. Most of these differences were imposed by the contrasting economic factors in each country, but differing cartographic traditions were also evident. American news maps with their flashy colors and dramatic icons may have been grudgingly envied in Britain, but more staid British journalistic traditions downplayed such seemingly garish imagery. Also, World War II rationing in England affected the Fleet Street ability to reproduce colorful newsprint at high speeds. Moreover, American news mapmakers had developed as a distinct professional group, with their own organizational departments and, in some cases, individual renown. British news mapmakers, however, remained relatively unprofessional, informal, and without specialized departments. As a result, American news maps were generally more vibrant, colorful, politically rhetorical, and exclusive than their British counterparts. British news maps tended to be black and white, informally drawn, repetitive, and comparatively unimpressive.

Dependence on flat projection maps, though, united both nations' cartographic trends as did a phenomenal upsurge in the use of maps during the war. When the war was over, American-made Mercator maps readjusted their positioning of the world's continents to favor the postwar public mood of isolationism, while British maps retained their worldview—a view that de-emphasized the Western Hemisphere while centering on the British Empire in the Eastern Hemisphere. All of the features of American news maps were products of staff cartographers, while many of the distinguishing British map features resulted from copying previously published, privately made maps. American news maps usually detailed land areas while leaving water bodies unremarkable, whereas the British tradition of maritime trade was evident in their maps' textured portrayals of seas and oceans. British news maps and ad maps were occasionally oriented with true North away from the top of the map, continuing a long maritime tradition of favoring coastal positioning—a trend American news and ad maps would not embrace until after World War II.

News maps in the American press were colorful, were plentiful, and were created using latest technology. They were products of a national press that was revitalized by World War II, and they catered to a public with a penchant for images with their news. National news journals, regardless of their political bias, tended to portray foreign and domestic concerns with a reliable deference to conservative values of nationalism, anti-fascism, and anti-communism. Although all American news journals had direct ties to national politics, they nevertheless presented their news under the guise of political objectivity. Cooperative American news cartographers intently embellished the Cold War narrative, taking great care in preparing their weekly journal maps. These maps, born of considerable effort and skill, were seldom reprinted or recycled for later use in altered form.

Certainly, the American press controlled superior resources and more professionally trained staff cartographers relative to the British press. However, these factors cannot alone account for the striking visual appeal of American news maps. Innovative projections, bold use of color, evocative text labeling and icons, and a strong reliance on geostrategic themes were cultivated by a new generation of mapmakers with unconventional training. Two of the most influential mapmakers, Richard Edes Harrison and Robert M. Chapin, Jr., borrowed from their training in architectural design to develop visually powerful news maps that captured the reader's attention and brought vitality to foreign news items. American national news journal editors, often participants active in politics, granted their staff cartographers a large degree of artistic license to produce maps designed to cultivate public support for World War II and Cold War foreign policies. Beginning in the late 1930s, the most popular news journals, including *Time*, *Fortune*, and *Newsweek*, developed strong traditions of in-house map design that informed the development of news cartography throughout the early Cold War period.

The rise of the Air Age played its own part in shaping American news maps. Although this study has shown that the first modern age recommendations for abandoning Mercator projection maps and their inherent distortions of the higher latitudes began in the terrestrial railroad and maritime industries, man's conquest of the air and the concomitant rise of the "Airman's View" dominated the demand for map projections that more accurately portrayed the roundness of the globe. The return of polar projection maps followed a renewed interest in Arctic regions that had recently been made accessible through advances in powered flight. These persuasively oriented maps relayed a sense of physical connectivity between nations in the higher latitudes. While the evident proximity of the Soviet Union to the United States on polar projection maps was reassuring during World War II, the very same closeness cast a pall of alarm in the early Cold War period. Unlike the Mercator projection which displayed all the world's landforms at a glance, Air Age projections "peered down upon" selected sections of the globe, by necessity obscuring up to half the earth over the "horizon." It is an irony, then, that while Air Age technology advanced a mapping of the earth with greater precision than ever before, Air Age news maps (with their new focus on the sphericity of the earth) actually obscured more of the earth than did Mercator maps.

American news cartographers capitalized on the new availability of an Air Age "horizon line" on maps to theorize about what friend or foe might lie waiting beyond. Most often, the horizon line was portrayed as the extent of American power and security, beyond which loomed the omnipresent Soviet communist menace. Occasionally, however, the horizon was conveniently used to exclude the Soviet Union, or other undesirable communist regions, from maps appearing in travel advertisements. Omitting the Soviet Union was an especially daunting task on maps advertising air travel across the Arctic Circle, but it was nevertheless a prominent practice. Ad maps, especially those relating to air travel, frequently used polar projections to portray an interconnected and accessible world for tourists contemplating routes across the Arctic. Travel ad maps had an obvious interest in portraying the world as borderless and peaceful even during World War II and into the mid-1950s. And yet, none of this is to deny that Mercator projection maps during this period remained popular for analyzing foreign relations, as well.

The North Pole received far more attention in American news and ads maps than did the South Pole. This reflected the reality that most of the earth's landmasses are located above the equator. However, American and

204 J. P. STONE

Soviet animosity across the Arctic Circle was a prime factor, too. American-made polar projection maps of the South Pole usually portrayed the region as a scientific frontier rather than a geopolitical arena. The few political maps of the region showing Antarctic territorial claims usually gave equal legitimacy to all nations involved, reflecting a general American strategic disinterest in the area.

Much of American foreign policy had been codified within the 1823 Monroe Doctrine, dividing the world into large, unilateral "spheres of influence." The American sphere, or Western Hemisphere, was envisioned as a safe harbor from European colonial instability despite frequent American intervention in European colonial affairs and Latin American nations. Gaining new importance in the Allied struggle of World War II, the Monroe Doctrine delineation was eventually eclipsed by the developing capitalist "Anglo-American sphere," and later the "free world" in early Cold War news maps. Though the Monroe Doctrine itself lost importance in the wake of international programs such as the Marshall Plan and the Truman Doctrine, spheres of influence were still valuable concepts for visualizing the competition between capitalist and communist realms. The postwar Stalinization of Eastern Europe, the Chinese communist revolution of 1949, and the Korean War convinced most Americans that all communist forces in Eurasia were mere puppet regimes controlled by the Soviet Union. Even during World War II, American news maps had begun to view the Soviet sphere as a dangerous extension of Stalin's hunger for power. By the late 1940s, Cold War bipolarity rhetoric was part of the American worldview lexicon, and US news maps melded all communist nations together as a threatening monolithic "communist world." In the following decade, President Eisenhower's "New Look" national security policy raised the specter of massive nuclear destruction, even as US propaganda stretched to assuage the nightmarish implications with a cartographic "Atoms for Peace" postal stamp. Meanwhile, the American press never acknowledged an American empire in the Western Hemisphere, although Britain and the Soviet Union did.

Germany dominated American concerns in Europe during and after World War II. The mapped image of Nazi Germany was often an alarming symbol used to rally American support for the Allied war effort. After 1945, the occupied zones of Germany were portrayed in terms of Cold War polarization. The capitalist zones under American, British, and French control were viewed together as "free Germany" even before the formal portioning of East and West Germany in late 1949. The Soviet zone of

Germany, and later the German Democratic Republic (GDR), was de-legitimized as a puppet state of the Soviet Union on maps. Meanwhile, Winston Churchill's Iron Curtain rhetoric reinforced the idea that Cold War Germany represented the boundary between the free West and the communist East. And considerable efforts were made to link the GDR to communist advances in China and Korea on world maps in the late 1940s and early 1950s.

News maps in the early Cold War era constituted a vital medium for legitimizing or de-legitimizing sections of occupied Germany. This study has illustrated that although Britain and the United States led the coalition to unify and reform West Germany in the face of a common communist enemy, their respective politicians and national presses envisioned Germany in very different ways. Gone were the World War II–era size-equals-strength comparisons in the American press of a mapped image of Germany superimposed over the United States. The much smaller GDR did not lend itself to that. Instead, American news maps sought other ways to vilify the new communist German state.

American news maps all but ignored the idea of "Three Germanys" championed by West German culture. And when such maps did find their way into American journals, they highlighted sharp distinctions between the Federal Republic of Germany (FRG) and the GDR. Contemporary British maps of the "Three Germanys," however, tended to treat all three realms equally, with no vilification of the GDR. As the American press embraced Iron Curtain symbolism on news maps, British maps all but ignored Churchill's iconic barrier. For the British press, Cold War Europe was complex and multilateral, not obviously bipolar, and the Americans were often seen as suspicious as the communists.

The maps discussed here, and the worldviews they connote, offer valuable insight into American and British perceptions of Germany's place in world affairs in the early Cold War period. These map portrayals of Cold War Germany are excellent examples of Edward Herman's and Noam Chomsky's much argued "capitalist model of propaganda," presented in their seminal 1988 work, *Manufacturing Consent*. The authors (not without considerable controversy) outline a number of formidable interlocking "filters" through which the "inequality of wealth and power [have] multi-level effects on mass media interests" and "routes [of] money and power are able to filter out the news … and get their messages to the public." One of the model's media-shaping "filters" has been *fear of communism*. Likened to a national religion, the authors view epidemic fear of this sort as a potent control mechanism to fracture and silence dissent. Among American news journals, *Time* magazine proved an apt conduit for this national obsession, given owner Henry Luce's personal campaign against communism and his personal relationship with the Republican Party.[3]

Although Herman and Chomsky, and many others, have refined and expanded the notion of capitalist propaganda since the late 1980s, there have been no serious attempts to examine the role news maps have played in media propaganda. Cartographic historian Patricia Gilmartin, for example, has noted the absence of any published works by geographers on this topic since A.K. Henrickson's 1975 study of propaganda maps used in World War II. Given news maps' unique power of visual and political persuasion, and their potential for use in propaganda, clearly more studies in this field are necessary.[4]

Britain's war-ravaged economy severely restricted the national press's ability to design and print news maps in large quantities during and after World War II. Government rationing of paper and colored inks lasted well into the early Cold War period. No national weekly news journals printed in color except on special occasions such as Christmas or New Year's Day. As a result, news maps in most national journals were relatively simplistic, black and white, hand-drawn portrayals with a distinctively non-professional appearance. The monthly *Serial Map Service* (*SMS*) provided the only exception to these generalizations as its maps easily rivaled American news maps in terms of color usage and refined artistry.

Most national news journals were admitted organs of the British political system, and they presented the news with unabashed bias. But these journals did not generally employ professional staff cartographers, reflecting the traditional British preference for text over graphics. Professional cartographers from private map publishers were occasionally contracted to design more complex maps requiring greater skill, but prohibitive costs discouraged this practice. Most maps appearing in the British press were rendered in large scale and, as such, were not suitable for experimenting with projections or Air Age perspectives. Moreover, these simpler "locator maps," as they were called, were commonly recycled in altered form, for multiple use, especially during World War II. For readers who craved news cartography, some news journals promoted separately sold superior maps.

British news maps, however, were not completely without artistic appeal. Surrounding the stark white landforms and unadorned political borders were richly depicted waterways that revealed a British affinity for all things maritime. Even the most simplistic locator maps often portrayed waterways with artistic line-shading reminiscent of maps in professional British atlases produced centuries earlier. The British reliance on the oceans and waterways as avenues of sovereignly partially explains their affinity for maps with artfully detailed waterways. But more than this, for people who had never known an open terrestrial frontier in the American sense, the seas were their frontier. The world's waterways were not an incubator for frontier democracy in the Turnerian sense. Rather, they were frontiers of commerce and empire. On maps from the Age of Exploration to the Cold War era, the rich treatment of waterways reflected the richness of empire conveyed by maritime trade. Stylized waves hinted at beckoning frontiers that lay beyond the lands rendered in locator maps. Did the advent of the Air Age, and later the Space Age, ultimately lead British mapmakers to abandon their attention to waterways? Future studies could answer these questions.

A partial answer to this quandary may be found in the examination of British air travel ad maps that saw Air Age transport as a continuation of maritime concerns. A common theme was a "world without coastlines," subtly recalling the British naval tradition while promoting travel to the British Empire. However, Air Age map projections, which became popular after World War II, generally were not concerned with waterways. As the Cold War heated up after 1946, British news maps increasingly focused on the land-based superpowers. The *Serial Map Service* published several polar projection maps predicting postwar air routes over the Arctic Circle until the United States denied access to American air space for British commercial flights in 1946. The British press generally mapped the North Pole as an arena of economic competition, for example, the fishing and air travel industries. Long-standing British territorial claims in the Antarctic, however, compelled cartographers to portray that region as a geopolitical arena in the early Cold War era. This trend was reinforced by rival claims from Argentina, Chile, and the Falkland Islands.

In global geopolitics, Britain preferred its own geopolitical divisions of the globe, "zones of influence." These were generally smaller in area, more politically multilateral, and less blatantly anticommunist and alarmist than America's "spheres." Despite Churchill's impassioned "Iron Curtain" speech, early postwar British foreign policy was more dominated by multilateral economic concerns than fear of totalitarian Russia and communism. The British press rendered a more balanced treatment of economic and communist interests in its news maps. Eastern communistic countries were distinguished by degrees of communism and were usually portrayed in British news maps as separate from Russia. While American news maps portrayed Germany, China, and Korea as epic battlegrounds between East and West, larger-scale British maps addressed these hotspots as more regional in character. British officials ultimately moved forward to take a more American stance against the communist threat, partly driven by dire British economics and defense logistics. And Fleet Street news map imagery did not always keep up with press narrative in reflecting this foreign policy shift.

British political and cartographic moderation also found expression in Fleet Street's treatment of Cold War Germany. The mapped image of Nazi Germany was never an alarmist symbol in the weekly British press. After 1945, occupied Germany was simply portrayed as a multilateral, four-power state and not as a barometer of polarized Cold War tensions. Throughout the early Cold War period, divided Germany was seen in economic rather than political terms. The mapped states of Germany were seldom visually linked to a larger divided Cold War world, often simply a result of British large-scale map rendering. Also, British mapmakers disinclined to link the GDR to communist movements in the Far East.

Both the British and American national presses occasionally linked postwar communism with World War II–era Nazism. The Americans made the connection with text, cartoons, and news maps. The British did so less frequently, primarily with text and occasionally with political cartoons. But the American map trend of linking Nazi slave labor camps to Soviet slave labor was never embraced by the British press which preferred a broader, less simplistic view of Russian affairs. For example, the *Serial Map Service* openly reported that American claims of a Soviet slave state in East Germany were countered by Soviet accusations of British and American "economic enslavement" of Italy in mid-1946.[5] British news maps were inclined to portray Soviet control in Eastern Europe as a continuation of western capitalist imperialism dating back to the 1920s. Again, when the Brits did address Cold War Europe on maps, it was usually in multilateral economic terms, not bipolar political terms as in the American media.

Communist advances in Greece, China, and North Korea in the late 1940s led American news mapmakers to link the GDR and Moscow to the Far East in a perceived unified Euro-Asiatic communist bloc. Predictably, the British press regularly lampooned this American generalization and made sharp contrasts between Soviet, Chinese, and Korean communism. (Most of the British news maps were too large scale to encompass the geographic scope of Eurasian affairs.) For the British, as many of their ad maps illustrated, the Far East was still an open sphere of air travel and trade. There were a number of British ad maps that rivaled the artistic flair of America's Robert M. Chapin, Jr., but they were much less anticommunistic in their treatment of German lands. The Iron Curtain was usually not portrayed, nor was the separate state of communist East Germany. As late as 1951, ads for the British magazine subscription company *Collett's* linked the Iron Curtain to Nazi Joseph Goebbels, not Winston Churchill, and asked, "Is there really a curtain between us and the Soviet people?"[6] Nevertheless, British uncertainty about Germany's future kept ad maps wholly noncommittal where German lands were concerned.

ADDITIONAL CONSIDERATIONS AND SUGGESTIONS FOR FUTURE STUDIES

This study has compared Cold War–era news journal maps from two pivotal world powers and examined important differences and similarities. Future exercises might include comparing examples of British and American news maps with those of the third party in the "Big Three"— the Soviet Union. Unfortunately, the Soviet press did not print maps with the news in the manner that the Western press did. Moreover, official Soviet state maps were classified until the collapse of the Soviet Union in the early 1990s. Such secrecy surrounding state maps is nothing new. J.B. Harley, for example, has noted the development of map secrecy in Spain and Portugal during the 1700s—that is, in Western Europe. During the Cold War, map secrecy relocated to an *Eastern* Europe under the grip of communist command. To date, no academic surveys of these Soviet state maps have been published. The only cartographic imagery currently available from the Soviet press consists of political cartoons in journals such as *Pravada* and *Krokodil*. (Two such map-containing cartoons from the latter journal are included in this study.) The fall of the Iron Curtain has allowed at least one promising analysis of East German maps. In 2006, Lit Verlag edited a book entitled *State Security and Mapping in the German Democratic Republic*. This volume contributes studied insight into why and how GDR mapmakers falsified official state maps from the early 1950s to the 1980s.[7] A companion examination of political cartoons from the GDR would prove useful in this context as well.

A recurrent theme in the present study has been the framing of a polarized world between communism and capitalism, a concept which dominated Cold War period headlines in the United States and Britain. It would be interesting to examine how ideas of polarization were affected by the rise of Third World nations as a challenge to American and Soviet dominance *after* 1955. When, if ever, did the American press recognize that Third World communist movements were not simply extensions of Soviet power? Did British news maps continue to discern between various national communist movements throughout the Cold War?

Arguably, the year 1955 signified the end of what might be called a unified Anglo-American foreign policy in the Cold War. The Suez Crisis of 1956 marked the first publicly acknowledged divergence of British and American goals in the Middle East. The British Foreign Office recognized the legitimacy of communist China long before the American State Department did, fomenting considerable animosity on the American side. Did these and other Anglo-American differences affect how each nation portrayed the world with maps?

The British maps discussed in this study, not including those published by the *Serial Map Service*, were greatly affected by government rationing that began in World War II and lasted well into the 1950s. How did the end of such rationing affect British maps in the remaining years of the Cold War? Did British maps become as colorful and professional in appearance as those in the American press? Or did the British preference for text over imagery stymie a revitalization of news cartography as the Cold War progressed?

Future studies might also address the effect that maps have had on international relations. Do the maps that one country prepares to propagandize its perceptions actually affect the policies and deliberations of other nations? Historian Neil Smith argued that geographers (and presumably mapmakers) have collaborated with government intelligence organizations from the era of the Roman Empire to the present.[8] Negotiations at the Paris Peace Accords after World War I were greatly affected by the "astute understanding of the power of maps" which the American delegation employed to gain support for Wilson's Fourteen Points.[9] A study of the role of news maps in shaping Cold War diplomacy could further mine the historical morass of government–press entanglement. For example, in 1948, the United States House of Representatives cited a 1947 *New York Times* map of communist party membership as its source for communist activity in the world.[10] Surely political orientation of the press was at work here as well, and future studies can shed light on this.

The prevalence of advertising maps in both the British and American presses has only briefly been discussed in this study. Considerably more so in the United States, advertisement mapmakers accustomed to applying visually engrossing icons, colors, and text created news maps with similar attributes. Occasionally, news maps were rendered almost identically to ad maps describing the same mapped areas. For example, in a May 1950 issue of *Newsweek*, two maps were published—one news map and one ad map—both portraying the rubber trade of Southeast Asia in very similar ways.[11] The news map, entitled "Red Threat to the World's Rubber Supply," accompanied interviews with executives from American rubber manufacturers B.F. Goodrich and Dunlop, who warned that communist movements in the region could stifle the American rubber trade. The ad map was placed by the Natural Rubber Bureau, a Washington, D.C.-based lobby group that promoted "more natural rubber … [for] millions of people in Southeast Asia … [and] people living outside the Iron Curtain...."[12] Both maps appeared in the same issue of *Newsweek* and demonstrate how ad maps and news maps might consort to reinforce each other's Cold War alarmist themes. They were both timely reactions to warnings from national rubber manufacturers about the danger of communism in Southeast Asia after the "fall of China" in 1949. The geography was almost identical on both maps, although the news map included more of China to underscore the proximity of the communist threat. Red ink dominated both maps and played upon long established American associations of that color with danger and communism. Both maps creatively augmented their cartographic imagery with vivid artwork to better convey what was at stake. The news map included a graph of dramatically scaled tires indicating relative levels of national rubber exports; the ad map included an icon of an intent Southeast Asian native working a rubber tree.

An important factor that influenced American ad map portrayals of the Cold War world was the perception that the western frontier extended beyond the West Coast and into the Far East. Beginning with the writings of Frederick Jackson Turner in the early 1890s, historians have acknowledged, albeit to differing measures, the significance of the frontier in the American imagination and experience.[13] Though the American frontier was officially closed in 1890, frontier-style rhetoric survived into the Cold War. As historian Martin Ridge has observed, American and foreign presses have portrayed Cold War presidents with strong foreign policies as "either western bad men or steely-eyed sheriffs."[14]

During and after World War II, America-based international businesses frequently portrayed Far Eastern markets as extensions of the American frontier on ad maps. This was especially true of businesses operating in China and the Pacific Rim. A case in point appeared in May 1945 when *U.S. News and World Report* published an ad for Shell Industrial Lubricants which described American air shipments of oil to China as the new Pony Express.[15] Just as Turner envisioned the American frontier as the promoter of democracy at home and in Europe, the Shell ad map saw the new Air Age Pony Express as the guarantor of freedom against Japanese imperialism in China. Ad maps for Northwest Airlines invoked similar frontier allusions by linking post–World War II air travel to the Orient with older American dreams of the Northwest Passage. The following year, an ad map was published in *Time* magazine which saw private passenger air service to China as the fulfillment of the American search for the Eastern markets that began in the early nineteenth century.[16]

Visions of the Far East as the new American frontier during and after World War II accompanied the American military effort to secure the Pacific Ocean—first to thwart the Japanese, and later to contain communism. Although news maps suggesting an actual American empire in the Pacific were rare, ad maps clearly portrayed the region clearly as the commercial domain of the United States. As such, early Cold War–era ad maps of the Far East deserve academic scrutiny because they offered a stark contrast to contemporary news maps that carved the world up into geopolitical spheres of influence. To date, Richard Francaviglia has been the only notable historian to discuss the linking of the American frontier and the Far East in the American mind. Historian and geographer Richard Francaviglia has described a fascinating link between the American frontier and the Middle and Far East in his 2011 book, *"Go East Young Man—Imagining the American West as the Orient."*[17] He presents not the dynamic of an advancing American frontier of influence into Asia, but rather a kind of reverse. Exhaustively, he documents the considerable overlay of Eastern motifs and imagery through which Americans have come to know and internalize their western frontier. The landscape itself, the western culture and lore, regional art, and even commerce are at once a rich experience often related with Eastern references, themes, and names. More pertinent to our study, the "Orientalizing" influence even found its way into ad maps from the American West. Francaviglia's research represents a new direction for analyzing America's important eras. What is it about the American West that has invoked this displacement of Eastern identity upon America's Frontier?

How has this East–West transference affected the advancement of US interests, especially during the Cold War period? And how has this transference been affected in the early twenty-first century with a burgeoning China? This subject is in want of further attention.

As noted in Chap. 3, British press travel ad maps were generally far more innovative and prevalent than were news maps. British Overseas Airway Corporation (BOAC) and British Bristol Aeroplane defied the British news preference for text over imagery with ad maps that were as visually appealing as those made by their American competitors, including Pan American and American Airlines. As a result, British travel ad maps—although far fewer in number than those in the American press—were probably far more influential in the British press. To date, no known studies have examined air travel ad maps in any nation.

Lastly, several important originators of maps referenced in this study deserve more comprehensive coverage. While Susan Schulten has examined the maps of Richard Edes Harrison as a "challenge to American cartography," no large published studies have exclusively focused on maps by Edes' greatest student, Robert M. Chapin, Jr.[18] In 2007, in an online article in the German journal *Comparativ*, I discussed an exceptionally detailed and embellished Chapin map of Germany published in *Time* magazine on the occasion of the formal partitioning of the nation in 1949.[19] Astonishingly, Chapin's body of work remains largely ignored. On the British side, many compelling maps published by the *SMS* are skillful works of propagandistic art that so far have not been examined. Moreover, the arrangement whereby private map publishers were contracted to produce maps for weekly British news journals was temporary—it lasted only as long as government rationing existed. However, this arrangement seems to have been exclusive to the British press and, as such, warrants further study.

NOTES

1. Susan Schulten, *Mapping the Nation: History and Cartography in Nineteenth-Century America* (Chicago and London: University of Chicago Press, 2013), 50.
2. Dennis Reinhartz, "Ephemeral Maps?" in the *Journal of the International Map Collectors' Society*, n. 108 (Spring 2007): 5–15.
3. Edward S. Herman and Noam Chomsky. *Manufacturing Consent: the Political Economy of the Mass Media* (New York: Pantheon Books, 1988), 2–30.
4. Patricia Gilmartin, "The Design of Journalistic Maps/Purposes, Parameters and Prospects" in *Cartographica*, v. 22, n. 4 (1985): 4.

5. *Serial Map Service*, v. 8, n. 10 (August 1946): 151.
6. Collett's Subscription Department ad, *New Statesman and Nation*, v. 42, n. 1079 (Nov. 10, 1951): 543.
7. Dagmar Unverhau, *State Security and Mapping in the German Democratic Republic: Map Falsification as a Consequence of Excessive Secrecy?* (Berlin: Lit Verlag, 2006).
8. Neil Smith, *American Empire: Roosevelt's Geographer and the Prelude to Globalization* (Berkeley: University of California Press, 2003), 89.
9. Ibid., 147–148.
10. US Congress, House, Committee on Foreign Relations, *The Strategy and Tactics of World Communism*, 80th Congress, 2d Sess., 1948, H. Doc. 619, pt. 1D.
11. *Newsweek*, v. 35, n. 22 (May 29, 1950): 62.
12. Ibid., 75.
13. Frederick Jackson Turner, "The Significance of the Frontier in American History," in the *Annual Report of the American Historical Association for the Year 1893* (Washington, DC: GPO and American Historical Association, 1894), 199–227.
14. Martin Ridge, "The Life of an Idea: The Significance of Frederick Jackson Turner's Frontier Thesis" in Richard Etulain's (ed.) *Does the Frontier Experience Make America Exceptional?* (Boston and New York: Bedford/ St. Martin's Press, 1999), 83–84.
15. *U.S. News and World Report*, v. 18, n. 18 (May 4, 1945): 69.
16. *Time*, v. 48, n. 19 (Nov. 4, 1946): 51.
17. Richard Francaviglia, *"Go East Young Man"—Imagining the American West as the Orient* (Logan, UT: Utah State University Press, 2011).
18. Schulten, "Richard Edes Harrison and the Challenge to American Cartography" in *Imago Mundi*, v. 50 (1998): 174–188.
19. Jeffrey P. Stone, "Visualizing Dynamic American Foreign Policy with News Maps in the early Cold War Period" in *Comparativ*, v. 7 (2007). This article is available at the following website: http://geschichte-transnational.clio-online.net/forum/type=artikel.

BIBLIOGRAPHY

INTERVIEWS WITH THE AUTHOR

Paul Pugliese, July 12, 2006.

SELECTED ATLASES

Bartholomew, John. *The Advanced Atlas of Modern Geography*. London: Meiklejohn and Son, Ltd., 1950.

Bartholomew, John. *The Columbus Atlas or Regional Atlas of the World*. Edinburgh: John Bartholomew and Son, Ltd., 1954.

Goodall, George (Ed.). *Cartocraft Geography School Atlas*. London: George Philip and Son, 1947.

MacFadden, Clifford H., Henry Madison Kendall and George Dewey. *Atlas of World Affairs*. New York: Thomas Y. Crowell Co., 1946.

Philip, George. *Philip's Record Atlas*. London: London Geographical Institute, 1934.

Raisz, Erwin. *Atlas of Geography*. New York: Global Press Corporation, 1944.

Statistisches Jahrbuch für die Bundesrepublik Deutschland. Stuttgart and Köln: W. Kohlhammer, 1955.

© The Author(s) 2019   215
J. P. Stone, *British and American News Maps in the Early Cold War Period, 1945–1955*, Palgrave Studies in the History of the Media,
https://doi.org/10.1007/978-3-030-15468-4

SELECTED JOURNAL MAPS AND IMAGERY

AMERICAN

(untitled). *American* 149, no. 3 (March 1950): 25.
"Marshall Plan Giveaway To Europe." *American* 148, no. 2 (August 1949): 24–25.
"Voice Of America." *American* 150, no. 1 (July 1950): 26–27.

FACTS IN REVIEW

(untitled). *Facts In Review* 3, no. 13 (April 1941): 182.
"A Study In Empires." *Facts In Review* 2, no. 5 (February 1940): 33.

FORTUNE

(untitled). *Fortune* 49, no. 5 (May 1954): 105.
"The Massive Retaliatory Power." *Fortune* 49, no. 5 (May 1954): 105.
"Three Approaches to the United States." *Fortune* 22, no. 3 (September 1940): 58.

THE GEOGRAPHIC JOURNAL

"The Geography of Post-War Air Routes: Discussion." *The Geographic Journal* 103, no. 3 (March 1944): 94.
Gregory, J.W. "Recent Literature on the Plan of the Earth." *The Geographic Journal* 32, no. 2 (August 1908): 151.

KROKODIL (REPRINTED IN THE NEW YORK TIMES)

"U.S. 'Imperialism'." *New York Times* 97, no. 32,761 (Oct. 5, 1947): 9.

LIFE

"History Makes New Maps." *Life* 13. No. 5 (Aug. 3, 1942): 58.
"Lend-Lease Map." *Life* 14, no. 13 (Mar. 29, 1943): 13.
"One-Sixth Of The Earth." *Life* 14, no. 13 (Mar. 29, 1943): 61.

LONDON DAILY EXPRESS (LDE)

"The Shadow Cabinet meets, and solves the crisis in the twinkling of an eye." *LDE* no. 15,390 (Oct. 12, 1949): 4.
Wighton, Charles. "Buses Pass Blockade: German Railwaymen Get Order, 'Be at the Ready'." *LDE* no. 15,248 (Apr. 29, 1949): 1.

LONDON TRIBUNE (LT)

"European Chessboard." *LT* no. 450 (Aug. 10, 1945): 7.

LOOK

"The Truth About Russia's 12,000,000 Slave Laborers." *Look* 11, no. 16 (Oct. 28, 1947): 35–36.

NEWSWEEK (NW)

(untitled). *NW* 24, no. 17 (Oct. 23, 1944): 68.
American Airlines ad. *NW* 23, no. 3 (Jan. 17, 1944a): 50.
B.F. Goodrich and Dunlop ad. *NW* 35, no. 22 (May 29, 1950): 75.
"The Beaver's own newspaper kids him about the way he lays down policies...." *NW* 34, no. 17 (Oct. 24, 1949): 36.
"Communism's Atomic Slave State." *NW* 44, no. 19 (Nov. 8, 1954): 46.
Garrett Corporation ad. *NW* 24, no. 14 (Oct. 2, 1944): 10.
"How the eighteenth century and the Nazi-Soviet Partitions sliced up Poland." *NW* 23, no. 3 (Jan. 17, 1944): 29.
"In the Shadow of the Sickle." *NW* 36, no. 14 (Aug. 14, 1950): 25.
"Master Strokes: Overlord, Anvil." *NW* 26, no. 16 (Oct. 15, 1945): 56.
"Over The Top." *NW* 27, no. 11 (Mar. 3, 1946): 40.
Pan American Airlines ad. *NW* 23, no. 8 (Feb. 2, 1944): 44–45.
"Playing With Fire?" *NW* 32, no. 4 (Jul. 26, 1948): 30.
"Red Threat to the World's Rubber Supply." *NW* 35, no. 22 (May 29, 1950): 62.
"Steps to Berlin." *NW* 24, no. 3 (Jul. 17, 1944): 19.
"This is how Walter Lippmann roughs out the division of the world into orbits for peace with power." *NW* 24, no. 2 (Jul. 10, 1944): 96.
"Three Worlds and their problem spots." *NW* 27, no. 5 (Feb. 4, 1946): 35.
"War of Two Worlds: Results of the Summer Campaigns." *NW* 34, no. 18 (Oct. 31, 1949): 24.
"Watch on the Rhine." *NW* 34, no. 24 (Dec. 12, 1949): 34.
"What We're Up Against." *NW* 36, no. 3 (Jul. 17, 1950): 14.

NEW STATESMAN AND NATION (NSN)

George Philips and Son, Ltd. ad. *NSN* 29, no. 745 (Jun. 6, 1945): 360.
Hutchinson Publishers ad. *NSN* 31, no. 781 (Feb. 9, 1946): 95.

NEW YORK TIMES (NYT)

"How The Communist Vote Has Varied In Europe's Elections." *NYT* 95,
    no. 32,278 (Jun. 6, 1946): E5.
"International Rivalry In The Antarctic." *NYT* 97, no. 32,901 (Feb. 22, 1948): E4.
"Location of Byrd's Groups." *NYT* 96, no. 32,509 (Jan. 26, 1947): E10.
"The Split In Europe Between East And West." *NYT* 97, no. 32,796 (Nov. 9,
    1947): E1.
"United Nations General Assembly Opened By President Truman." *NYT* 96,
    no. 32,415 (Oct. 24, 1946): 1.

SATURDAY EVENING POST (SEP)

American Airlines ad. *SEP* 217, no. 19 (Nov. 11, 1944b): 80.
"Stalin's Secret War Plans." *SEP* 225, no. 12 (Sept. 20, 1952): 37.
"Who Owns Antarctica?" *SEP* 220, no. 19 (Nov. 8, 1947): 29.

SCIENCE

"An 'Air Age' Map of the World." *Science* 101, no. 2626 (Apr. 17, 1945): 425.

SERIAL MAP SERVICE (SMS)

(untitled). *SMS* 2, no. 2 (October 1941a): map 105.
(untitled). *SMS* 9, no. 1 (Oct. 1947a): 1.
"Air Junctions Map No. 2." *SMS* 7, no. 1 (October 1945): map 323–324.
"Air Junctions Map No. 3." *SMS* 7, no. 2 (November 1945): map 331–332.
"Australia." *SMS* 2, no. 5 (February, 1941): map 67.
"B.O.A.C. Routes." *SMS* 7, no. 6 (March 1946): map 63–64.
"The British Empire." *SMS* 7, no. 7 (April 1946): 8.
"British Trade Routes." *SMS* 1, no. 2 (October 1939): 5–6.
Economist ad. *SMS* 3, no. 2 (November 1941): 135.
"European Passenger Transport." *SMS* 7, n. 12 (September, 1946): map 370–371.
"The French Empire." *SMS* 7, no. 8 (May 1946): maps 356 and 357.
"Germany." *SMS* 8, no. 3 (Dec. 1946): map 385.

"Middle East Oil Map." *SMS* 7, no. 9 (June, 1946): map 360.
"Proximity to War of America." *SMS* 2, no. 4 (January 1941): map 64.
"Spitzbergen Bases." *SMS* 8, no. 5 (February 1947): 76.
"Services In Operations By The British Overseas Airways." *SMS* 7, no. 6 (Mar. 6, 1946): 63–64.

SPECTATOR

(untitled). *Spectator* 163, no. 5,796 (Jul. 28, 1939a): 164.
(untitled). *Spectator* 163, no. 5,799 (Aug. 18, 1939b): iii.
(untitled). *Spectator* 163, no. 5,800 (Aug. 25, 1939c): 284.
(untitled). *Spectator* 163, no. 5,801 (Sept. 1, 1939d): 323.
(untitled). *Spectator* 163, no. 5,806 (Oct. 6, 1939e): 463.
(untitled). *Spectator* 163, no. 5,807 (Oct. 13, 1939f): 495.
(untitled). *Spectator* 167, no. 5,907 (Sept. 12, 1941b): 253.
"Asia." *Spectator* 163, no. 5,801 (Sept. 9, 1939): 340.
Barclay's Bank of London ad. *Spectator* 183, no. 6,331 (Oct. 28, 1949): 569.
British Overseas Airways ad. *Spectator* 177, no. 6161 (Jul. 26, 1946a): 99.
British Overseas Airways ad. *Spectator* 177, no. 6,171 (Oct. 4, 1946b): 348.
Canadian Pacific Lines ad. *Spectator* 162, no. 5,781 (Apr. 14, 1939): 78.
Horrabin's Atlas History of the Second Great War, Vol. II ad. *Spectator* 165, no. 5,858 (Oct. 10, 1940): 343.
"War Map No. 5" in *Daily Telegraph* ad. *Spectator* 165, no. 5851 (Aug. 16, 1940): 173.

SUNDAY TIMES (LONDON)

(untitled). *Sunday Times*, no. 6072 (Aug. 27, 1939): 12.

TIME

(front cover). *Time* 62, no. 2 (Jul. 13, 1953).
"America's Front Door." *Time* 44, no. 7 (Aug. 14, 1944): 24.
"Behind The Iron Curtain." *Time* 47, no. 11 (Mar. 18, 1946): 24.
"Berlin: Allied Zones of Occupation." *Time* 46, no. 2 (Jul. 16, 1945): 29.
"Bomber's Reach." *Time* 56, no. 10 (Oct. 4, 1950): 16.
"Chart of U.S. Zone." *Time* 47, no. 25 (Jun. 24, 1946): 26.
"Cold War Crystallized: Western Union v. Russian Satellites," in *Time*, v. 51, n. 5 (Feb. 2, 1948): 16.
"Cracks In The Fortress." *Time* 44, no. 4 (Jul. 24, 1944): 23.
"Lost Horizon?" *Time* 52, no. 23 (Dec. 6, 1948): 28.

"Marking Time." *Time* 48, no. 16 (Oct. 14, 1946): 31.
Northwest Airlines ad. *Time* 48, no. 19 (Nov. 4, 1946): 51.
"Piece by Piece." *Time* 51, no. 10 (Mar. 10, 1948): 26.
"Reds In The Reich." *Time* 56, no. 6 (Aug. 1950): 26–27.
"Reshuffle." *Time* 47, no. 4 (Jan. 28, 1946): 26.
"Russian Travel Barrier in the Berlin Area." *Time* 51, no. 15 (Apr. 12, 1951): 35.
"Three Faces of Europe." *Time* 55, no. 1 (Jan. 2, 1950): 36.
"Three Germanys." *Time* 62, no. 9 (Aug. 31, 1953): 19.
"Trouble Spots." *Time* 45, no. 22 (May 28, 1945): 21.
"Two Worlds." *Time* 55, no. 1 (Jan. 2, 1950): 34–35.
"West's Germany." *Time* 54, no. 23 (Dec. 5, 1949): 30.

TIME AND TIDE (TT)

(untitled). *TT* 26, no. 9 (Mar. 3, 1945a): 180.
(untitled). *TT* 26, no. 10 (Mar. 10, 1945b): 200.
(untitled). *TT* 26, no. 48 (Dec. 1, 1945c): 1006.
(untitled). *TT* 29, no. 3 (Jan. 17, 1948a): 65.
Barclay's Bank ad *TT* 31, no. 23 (Jun. 10, 1950): 590.
Cassuto, Aldo. "Ports and Politics." *TT* 30, no. 15 (Apr. 9, 1949): 345.
Gilchik cartoon. *TT* 29, no. 12 (Mar. 20, 1948): 301.
Pan American Airlines ad. *TT* 27, no. 42 (Oct. 19, 1946): 1005.

TRUTH

Bristol Aeroplane ad. *Truth* 138, no. 3591 (Jul. 6, 1945): 9.
British Overseas Airways ad. *Truth* 141, no. 3,670 (Jan. 10, 1947): 45.

U.S. NEWS AND WORLD REPORT (USNWR)

(untitled). *USNWR* 11, no. 3 (July 18, 1941c): 11.
(untitled). *USNWR* 18, no. 21 (May 5, 1945d): 13.
(untitled). *USNWR* 18, no. 10 (Mar. 9, 1945e): 22–23.
(untitled). *USNWR* 39, no. 11 (Sept. 9, 1955): 23.
"Forecast: Weather and War." *USNWR* 11, no. 17 (Oct. 24, 1941): 12–13.
"Greenland: A Warning to Axis—What Occupation of Danish Colony Means to Hemisphere Defense." *USNWR* 10, no. 16 (April 14, 1941): 16–17.
"How Germany Will Be Occupied." *USNWR* 18, no. 12 (Mar. 23, 1945): 23.
"New Approach To Convoy." *USNWR* 10, no. 18 (May 5, 1941): 9.
"The Occupation of Germany." *USNWR* 18, no. 24 (Jun. 15, 1945): 23.
"Secret Cruise of a Russian Submarine." *USNWR* 39, no. 11 (Sept. 9, 1955): 21.

Shell Industrial Lubricants ad. *USNWR* 18, no. 18 (May 4, 1945): 69.
"Suppose Pittsburgh Were Berlin." *USNWR* 18, no. 6 (Feb. 9, 1945): 20–21.
"Two Worlds." *USNWR* 20, no. 22 (May 24, 1946): 21.

GOVERNMENT DOCUMENTS

Audit Bureau of Circulations (U.K.). North Sydney, Australia: N.S.W. Press, biannual. 1940–1955.
Statistiches Jahrbuch für die Deutsche Reich. Berlin: von Reimar Hobbing, 1949.
Turner, Frederick Jackson. "The Significance of the Frontier in American History" in *Annual Report of the American Historical Association for the Year 1893.* Washington, D.C.: GPO and American Historical Association (1894): 199–227.
U.S. Congress. House Committee on Foreign Relations. *The Strategy and Tactics of World Communism.* 80th Congress, 2d Sess., 1948. H. Doc. 619, pt. 1D.

ONLINE IMAGERY

The Granger Collection. http://www.authentichistory.com/images/1900s.

BOOKS AND JOURNALS

(untitled). *Look* 12, no. 3 (Feb. 3, 1948b): 28–29.
(untitled). *New Statesman and Nation* 43, no. 1,107 (May 24, 1952): 600.
(untitled). *New Statesman and Nation* 45, no. 1,162 (Jun. 6, 1953): 688.
(untitled). *Serial Map Service* 8, no. 10 (August 1946): 151.
(untitled). *Time and Tide* 28, no. 35 (Sept. 13, 1947b): 976.
"6 Flights A Week To Lisbon Planned." *New York Times* 89, no. 29,902 (Dec. 7, 1939): 1.
"17 Airlines Fight M'Carran's Bill." *New York Times* 93, 31,474 (Mar. 26, 1944): 36.
Adler, Les K. and Thomas G. Paterson. "Red Fascism: The Merger of Nazi Germany and Soviet Russia in the American Image of Totalitarianism, 1930's–1950's." *American Historical Review* 75, no. 4 (April 1970): 1055.
"Airplanes and Maps." *New York Times* 42, no. 31,074 (Feb. 21, 1943): E8.
Allen, H.C. *Great Britain and the United States: a History of Anglo-American Relations (1783–1952).* London: Odhams Press, 1954.
"Army, Navy Oppose One Ocean Air Monopoly." *New York Times* 94, no. 31,847 (Apr. 5, 1945): 25.
Barnhisel, Greg and Catherine Turner (Eds.). *Pressing the Fight: Print, Propaganda, and the Cold War.* Amherst and Boston, MA: University of Massachusetts Press, 2010.

Bartlett, C.J. *British Foreign Policy in the Twentieth Century.* New York: St. Martin's Press, 1989.

Bartlett, K.S. "More Antarctic Surprises Due?" *Boston Globe* 151, n. 82 (Mar. 23, 1947): A5.

Beale, Howard K. *Theodore Roosevelt and the Rise of America.* Baltimore: Johns Hopkins University Press, 1956.

Bertrand, Kenneth. *Americans in Antarctica, 1775–1948.* New York: American Geographical Society, 1971.

Bowman, Gerald. *Men of Antarctica.* New York: Fleet Publishing, 1958.

Boyd, Julian P. and Charles T. Cullen, et al (Eds.). *The Papers of Thomas Jefferson.* Princeton: Princeton University Press, 1950.

Boyle, Peter G. "The British Foreign Office View of Soviet-American Relations, 1945–46." *Diplomatic History* 3, no. 3 (Summer 1979): 307–320.

Brewer, Susan A. *To Win the Peace: British Propaganda in the United States during World War II.* Ithaca and London: Cornell University Press, 1997.

"British to Open New Air Service." *Los Angeles Times* 59 (Mar. 31, 1940): 2.

"British Wings." *New York Times* 88, no. 29,744 (Jul. 2, 1939a): E8.

"British Wings." *New York Times* 88, no. 29,781 (Aug. 8, 1939b): E6.

Brzezinski, Zbigniew. *Game Plan: a Geostrategic Framework for the Conduct of the U.S.-Soviet Contest.* Boston: Atlantic Monthly Press, 1986.

Burnett, D. Graham. *Master's of All They Surveyed: Exploration, Geography, and a British El Dorado.* Chicago and London: University of Chicago Press, 2000.

Butler, David and Gareth Butler. *British Political Facts, 1900–1985.* New York: St. Martin's Press, 1986.

Byrd, Richard E. "Why We're Sailing South." *Los Angeles Times* 66 (Jan. 12, 1947): E4.

"Byrd Suggests Polar Defenses." *Los Angeles Times* 60 (May 2, 1941): A11.

Callcott, Wilfrid Hardy. *The Western Hemisphere: Its Influence on United States Policies to the End of World War II.* Austin and London: University of Texas Press, 1968.

Camrose, William Ewert Berry (First Viscount). *British Newspapers and their Controllers.* London: Casswell Press, 1950.

Childs, David. *Britain since 1945: a Political History.* New York: St, Martin's Press, 1979.

Cohen, Bernard. *The Press and Foreign Policy.* Princeton: Princeton University Press, 1963.

Collett's Subscription Department ad. *New Statesman and Nation* 42, no. 1,079 (Nov. 10, 1951): 543.

Collins, Marice. "The Mind of China." *Time and Tide* 31, no. 49 (Dec. 9, 1950): 1249–1250.

"Communism: Heir to Fascism." *Look* 12, no. 3 (Feb. 3, 1948): 28–29.

"Competition In Air Urged By 17 Lines." *New York Times* 94, no. 31,853 (Apr. 10, 1945): 20.

Corn, Joseph J. *The Winged Gospel: America's Romance with Aviation, 1900–1950*. London and New York: Oxford University Press, 1983.

Cosgrove, Denis. *Apollo's Eye: a Cartographic Genealogy of the Earth in the Western Imagination*. Baltimore and London: The Johns Hopkins Press, 2001).

Curran, James and Jean Seaton. *Power without Responsibility: the Press, Broadcasting and the New Media in Britain*. London and New York: Routledge, 2003.

Dent, Borden D. *Cartography: Thematic Map Design* (3rd Ed.). Oxford: William C. Brown Publishers, 1990).

Dierkx, Marc L.J. "Shaping World Civil Aviation: Anglo-American Civil Aviation, 1944–1946." *The Journal of Air Law and Commerce* 57 (Spring 1992): 795–840.

Dodds, Klaus. *Geopolitics in Antarctica: Views from the Southern Oceanic Rim*. Chichester, West Sussex, England: Wiley, 1997.

Doenecke, Justus D. *Not to the Swift: The Old Isolationists in the Cold War Era*. London: Associated University Presses, 1979.

Edmonds, Robin. *The Big Three: Churchill, Roosevelt and Stalin in Peace and War*. New York and London: W.W. Norton, 1991.

Elkins, Caroline. *Britain's Gulag: The Brutal End of Empire in Kenya*. London: Pimlico Press, 2005.

"Empire Airlines Get U.S. Motors." *Boston Globe* 137, no. 92 (Apr. 1, 1940): 8.

"Entire Western Hemisphere Put in New Security Zone." *Boston Globe* 152, no. 58 (Aug. 27, 1947): 1.

Epstein, Leon D. *Britain—Uneasy Ally*. Chicago: University of Chicago Press, 1954.

"Explorer Pays Britons Honor." *Los Angeles Times* 48 (Apr. 17, 1929): 13.

"Facts Behind the Witch-Hunts." *New Statesman and Nation* 45, no. 1150 (Mar. 21, 1953): 345.

Farquhar, Roderick and John K. Fairbank. "The People's Republic, Part I: the Emergence of Revolutionary China, 1949–1965," *The Cambridge History of China (vol. 14)*. Cambridge: Cambridge University Press, 1989.

"Farthest South." *Los Angeles Times* 48 (Apr, 28, 1929): B4.

"First Billion Plan For World Airline." *New York Times* 93, no. 31,468 (Mar. 21, 1944): 10.

Fisher, Irving. "A World Map on a Regular Icosahedron by Gnomonic Projection." *Geographical Review* 33, no. 4 (October 1943): 605–619.

Fite, Gilbert C. and Jim E. Reese. *An Economic History of the United States*. Boston: Houghton Mifflin, 1973.

Fleming, D.F. *The Cold War and its Origins, 1917–1960* (Garden City, NY: Doubleday and Co., Inc., 1961).

"Formation of Ice Bergs and their Passage from North." *Boston Globe* 97, no. 141 (May 23, 1920): 55.

Fox, Matthew. *Religion, USA: Religion and Culture by way of* Time *Magazine.* Dubuque, IA: Listening Press, 1971.

Francaviglia, Richard. *Go East, Young Man: Imagining the American West as the Orient.* Logan, UT: Utah State University Press, 2011.

Fulbrook, Mary. *The Divided Nation: a History of Germany, 1918–1990.* New York and Oxford: Oxford University Press, 1992.

Gaddis, John Lewis. *Strategies of Containment: a Critical Appraisal of American National Security Policy during the Cold War.* New York: Oxford University Press, 2005.

"Germans in Antarctic, Byrd Party Reports." *Los Angeles Times* 60 (May 6, 1941): 2.

Gilmartin, Patricia. "The Design of Journalistic Maps/Purposes, Parameters and Prospects." *Cartographica* 22, no. 4 (1985): 1–18.

Glassner, Martin Ira. *Political Geography.* New York: John Wiley and Sons, 1993.

Goode, J. Paul. "The Homolosine Projection: a New Device for Portraying the Earth's Surface Entire." *Annals of the Association of American Geographers* 15, no. 3 (September 1925): 119–125.

Greenwood, Sean. "Frank Roberts and the 'Other' Long Telegram: the View from the British Embassy in Moscow, March 1946." *Journal of Contemporary History* 25, no. 1 (January 1990): 103–122.

H.M.F. "The Battle of Antarctica." *Los Angeles Times* 60 (Feb. 19, 1941): A4.

Haffner, Sebastian. "The Communist Curtain: 'Russian Sphere of Influence in Europe'." *Serial Map Service* 8, no. 10 (July 1947): 162–163.

Harbutt, Fraser J. *The Iron Curtain: Churchill, America, and the Origins of the Cold War.* New York and Oxford: Oxford University Press, 1986.

Harley, J.B. "Deconstructing the Map" in John Agnew's *Human Geography.* New York: Blackwell, 1996.

Harley, J.B. *The New Nature of Maps: Essays in the History of Cartography.* Baltimore and London: Johns Hopkins Press, 2001).

Harrison, Richard Edes. Letter entitled "Maps Have Their Limitations" in *New York Times* 42, no. 31,079 (Feb. 26, 1943): 18.

Hathaway, Robert M. *Great Britain and the United States: Special Relations since WWII.* Boston: Twayne Publishers, 1990).

"Hearings Planned On Air Monopoly." *New York Times* 94, no. 31,785 (Feb. 1, 1945): 18.

Herb, Guntram Henrik. *Under the Map of Germany: Nationalism and Propaganda, 1918–1945.* London and New York: Routledge, 1997.

Heren, Louis. "The Postwar Press in Britain" in Dennis Griffith's (Ed.) *The Encyclopedia of the British Press, 1422–1992.* New York: St. Martin's Press, 1992.

Henrikson, Alan K. "Mental Maps" in Frank Costigliola's and Michael Hogan's (Eds.) *Explaining the History of American Foreign Relations.* Cambridge and New York: Cambridge University Press, 1991.

Herman, Edward S. and Noam Chomsky. *Manufacturing Consent: the Political Economy of the Mass Media.* New York: Pantheon Books, 1988.

Hoffman, Ross. "Europe and the Atlantic Community." *Thought* 20 (1945): 21–36.

"Ike Won't Claim Any Portion of Antarctica." *Boston Sunday Globe* (Aug. 22, 1954): C14.

"International Interest in the Antarctic." *Los Angeles Times* 65 (Nov. 24, 1946): A4.

"Japanese In The Aleutians." *Hartford Courant* 106 (Jun. 17, 1942): 10.

Jerrold, Douglas. *The Lie About the West: A Response to Professor Toynbee's Challenge.* London: J.M. Dent and Sons, 1954.

Jones, Aled. "The British Press" in Dennis Griffith's (Ed.) *The Encyclopedia of the British Press, 1422–1992.* New York: St. Martin's Press, 1992.

Kahan, Michael. *Media as Politics: Theory, Behavior and Change in America.* Upper Saddle River, NJ: Prentice-Hall, 1999.

Kaufman, Edy. *The Superpowers and their Spheres of Influence: The United States and the Soviet Union in Eastern Europe and Latin America.* London: Croom Helm, 1976.

"Key to Conflict and its Significance." *Newsweek* 36, no. 11 (Sept. 11, 1950): 25.

Kimball, Warren F. *Forged in War: Roosevelt, Churchill, and the Second World War.* New York: William Morrow and Co., 1997.

La Feber, Walter (Ed.). *John Quincy Adams and American Continental Empire.* Chicago: Quadrangle Books, 1965.

Langley, Lester D. *America and the Americas: the United States in the Western Hemisphere.* Athens, Georgia and London: University of Georgia Press, 1989.

Leffler, Melvyn P. *A Preponderance of Power: National Security, the Truman Administration, and the Cold War.* Stanford: Stanford University Press, 1992.

Lemke, Christiane. "Citizenship Law in Germany: Traditional Concepts and Pressures to Modernize in the Context of European Integration," in *Harvard Focus: Europe* (Spring 2006): 1–6.

Lewis, Martin W. and Karen E. Wigen. *The Myth of Continents: A Critique of Metageography.* Berkeley: University of California Press, 1997.

Liebovich, Louis. *The Press and the Origins of the Cold War, 1944–1947.* New York: Praeger, 1988.

Lippmann, Walter. *U.S. War Aims.* Boston: Little, Brown and Company, 1944.

"Longest Way Over Shortest Sea Path." *Washington Post*, no. 13,107 (Apr. 28, 1912): SM4.

Luža, Radomir. "Czechoslovakia between Democracy and Communism" in Charles S. Maier's (Ed.) *The Cold War in Europe: Era of a Divided Continent.* Princeton: Markus Wiener, 1996.

Lyons, Louis M. "Shortest Way from Boston to Calcutta Is by Way of North Pole." *Boston Globe* (Nov. 29, 1942): B5 (Sunday editions do not have volume or issue numbers)

Mcfarquhar, Roderick and John K. Fairbank (eds.). *The Cambridge History of China* (vol. 14). Cambridge: Cambridge University Press, 1989.

Mahan, Alfred T. *The Influence of Sea Power upon History, 1660–1783*. Boston: Little, Brown and Co., 1890.

"Map Problems." *New York Times* 93, no. 31,298 (Oct. 3, 1943): E9.

"Maps Are Made More Accurate." *New York Times* 77, no. 25,474 (Oct. 23, 1927): X18.

Mitchell, Nancy. *The Dangers of Dreams: German and American Imperialism in Latin America*. Chapel Hill: University of North Carolina Press, 1999.

Monmonier, Mark. *How to Lie with Maps* (2nd ed.). Chicago and London: University of Chicago Press, 1996.

Monmonier, Mark. *Maps with the News: the Development of American Journalistic Cartography*. Chicago: University of Chicago Press, 1989.

Monmonier, Mark. "The Rise of Map Use by Elite Newspapers in England, Canada, and the United States." *Imago Mundi* 38 (1986): 56.

"The Monthly Record." *The Geographic Journal* 90, no. 4 (April 1940): 324.

Morrel, Sydney. *Spheres of Influence*. New York: Duell, Sloan and Pearce, 1946.

"Mr. Lippmann at the Ringside." *New Statesman and Nation* 31, no. 783 (Feb. 23, 1946): 131.

Mulvaney, Kieran. *At the Ends of the Earth: a History of Polar Regions*. Washington, D.C. and London: Island Press, 2001.

Murphey, Rhoads. *A History of Asia* (4th ed.). New York and London: Longman, 2003.

"Navy Sends Data To Guide Byrd." *New York Times* 78, no. 25, 896 (Dec. 18, 1928): 15.

"New Outlet for West." *Los Angeles Times*, no. 12,070 (Jun. 26, 1909): 6.

"New Zealand Fears U.S. Force Intends to Stay in Antarctic." *Los Angeles Times* 66 (Dec. 12, 1946): 7.

News Chronicle ad. *New Statesman and Nation* 50, no. 1,287 (Nov. 5, 1955): 578.

Northedge, F.S. and Audrey Wells. *Britain and Soviet Communism: Impact of a Revolution*. London: Macmillan Press, 1982.

"Notes from Manywhere." *Chicago Tribune* 53, no. 12 (Mar. 20, 1904): 18.

Osgood, Kenneth. *Total Cold War: Eisenhower's Secret Propaganda Battle at Home and Abroad*. Lawrence, KS: University Press of Kansas, 2006.

Osgood, Kenneth and Andrew K. Frank. *Selling War in a Media Age: The Presidency and Public Opinion in the American Century*. Gainesville: University Press of Florida, 2010.

"Over the Editor's Desk." *Christian Science Monitor* 36, no. 76 (Feb. 26, 1944): WM15.

Paterson, Thomas G. *On Every Front: the Making and Unmaking of the Cold War* (2nd ed.). New York and London: W.W. Norton and Company, 1992.

Perkins, Dexter. *The Monroe Doctrine: 1826–1867*. Baltimore: Johns Hopkins Press, 1933.

Pett, Saul. "Byrd Greets Reds in Antarctica, Says U.S. Has Covered Their Area." *Boston Globe* 169, no. 18 (Jan 18, 1956): 32.

Polyzoides. "Spitzbergen Demand Reveals Red Ambition." *Los Angeles Times* 66 (Jan. 11, 1947): 5.

Pratt, Julius W. *A History of United States Foreign Policy* (2nd ed.). Englewood Cliffs, N.J.: Prentice-Hall, Inc., 1965.

Reinhartz, Dennis. "Ephemeral Maps?" *Journal of the International Map Collectors' Society*, no. 108 (Spring 2007): 5–15.

Reynolds, David. "Rethinking Anglo-American Relations." *Royal Institute of International Affairs* 65, no. 1 (Winter, 1988–1989): 89–112.

Ridge, Martin. "The Life of an Idea: The Significance of Frederick Jackson Turner's Frontier Thesis" in Richard Etulain's (ed.) *Does the Frontier Experience Make America Exceptional?* Boston and New York: Bedford/St. Martin's Press, 1999.

Ristow, Walter. "Journalistic Cartography." *Surveying and Mapping* 17 (October 1957): 369–390.

"Russians Hoist Flag on British Antarctic Area." *Boston Globe* 169, no. 45 (Feb. 14, 1956): 7.

"Says Britain Tried To Curb Our Flying." *New York Times* 95, no. 32,177 (Feb. 28, 1946): 10.

Sexton, Jay. *The Monroe Doctrine: Empire and Nation in Nineteenth-Century America.* New York: Hill and Wang, 2011.

Schulten, Susan. *The Geographical Imagination in America, 1880–1950.* Chicago: University of Chicago Press, 2001.

Schulten, Susan. *Mapping the Nation: History and Cartography in Nineteenth-Century America.* Chicago and London: University of Chicago Press, 2013.

Schulten, Susan. "Richard Edes Harrison and the Challenge to American Cartography." *Imago Mundi* 50 (1998): 174–188.

"Scientific Study Links 9 Nations Over Antarctic." *Boston Sunday Globe* (Nov. 21, 1954): C19.

Shand, James. "English Printing—I." *Time and Tide* 28, no. 30 (August 9, 1947a): 858.

Shand, James. "English Printing—III." *Time and Tide* 28, no. 32 (August 23, 1947b): 906.

Slater, David. "Space, Democracy and Difference: For a Post-colonial Perspective" in David Featherstone's and Joe Painter's (Eds.) *Spatial Politics: Essays for Doreen Massey.* West Sussex, U.K.: John Wiley and Sons, Ltd., 2013.

Smith, Neil. *American Empire: Roosevelt's Geographer and the Prelude to Globalization.* Berkeley: University of California Press, 2003.

Spalding, Elizabeth. *The First Cold Warrior: Harry Truman, Containment, and the Remaking of Liberal Internationalism.* Lexington, KY: University Kentucky Press, 2006.

Stone, Jeffrey P. "Visualizing Dynamic American Foreign Policy with News Maps in the early Cold War Period." *Comparative* 7 (Jul. 13, 2007): 1–23.

Thrower, Norman. *Maps and Civilization: Cartography in Culture and Society.* Chicago and London: University of Chicago Press, 2001).

Tufte, Edward R. *The Visual Display of Quantitative Information.* Cheshire, CT: Graphics Press, 2001.

Turton, Godfrey. "The Comity of Europe." *Truth* 140, no. 3,648 (Aug. 9, 1946): 128.

"U.S. Plans Claim to Huge Slice of Antarctic Sector." *Los Angeles Times* 66 (Jan. 6, 1947): 1–2.

"U.S. Reserves Its Claims in Antarctic." *Los Angeles Times* 66 (Dec. 28, 1946): 4.

Ullman, Richard H. "America, Britain, and the Soviet Threat in Historical and Present Perspective" in William Roger Louis's and Hedley Bull's (Eds.) *The "Special Relationship": Anglo-American Relations since 1945.* Oxford: Clarendon Press, 1986.

Uncle Dudley. "Khrushchev's Program." *Boston Globe* 169, no. 49 (Feb. 18, 1956): 6.

United Nations charter, Article 21, Chapter VIII, Section C.

Unverhau, Dagmar. *State Security and Mapping in the German Democratic Republic: Map Falsification as a Consequence of Excessive Secrecy?* Berlin: Lit Verlag, 2006.

Weathersby, Kathryn P. "Should We Fear This?: Stalin and the Danger of War with America." Cold War International History Project: Working Paper No. 9. Washington, D.C.: Woodrow Wilson International Center for Scholars, 2002.

Watry, David M. *Diplomacy at the Brink: Eisenhower, Churchill, and Eden in the Cold War.* Baton Rouge: Louisiana State University Press, 2014.

Wegs, J. Robert and Robert Ladrech. *Europe since 1945: a Concise History* (4th ed.). New York: St. Martin's Press, 1996.

Wilford, John Noble. *The Mapmakers: the Story of the Great Pioneers in Cartography—from Antiquity to the Space Age.* New York: Alfred A. Knopf, 2000.

Wood, Denis. *The Power of Maps.* New York and London: The Guilford Press, 1992.

Woods, Randall Bennett. *A Changing of the Guard: Anglo-American Relations, 1941–1946.* Chapel Hill and London: University of North Carolina Press, 1990.

Worswik, G.D.N. and P.H. Ady. *The British Economy, 1945–1950.* Oxford: Clarendon Press, 1952.

"Would Curb Survey." *Washington Post,* no. 12, 468 (Jun. 29, 1940): 4.

Yergin, Daniel. *Shattered Peace: the Origins of the Cold War and the National Security State.* Boston: Houghton Mifflin, 1978.

Zhang, Shuguang. "Threat Perception and Chinese Communist Foreign Policy" in Melvyn P. Leffler's and David S. Painter's (eds.) *Origins of the Cold War: an International History* (2nd ed.). London and New York: Routledge, 1995.

INDEX[1]

© The Author(s) 2019   229
J. P. Stone, *British and American News Maps in the Early Cold
War Period, 1945–1955*, Palgrave Studies in the History of the Media,
https://doi.org/10.1007/978-3-030-15468-4

CPSIA information can be obtained
at www.ICGtesting.com
Printed in the USA
LVHW071430090619

620631LV00016B/864/P

9 783030 154677